MAKING THE NUMBER

BLURBS TK

Press Contact:
Will Weisser
Portfolio
212-366-2613
Will.Weisser@us.penguingroup.com
Publication date: October 2008

MAKING THE NUMBER

HOW TO USE SALES BENCHMARKING TO DRIVE PERFORMANCE

GREG ALEXANDER, AARON BARTELS, and MIKE DRAPEAU

Portfolio

To my fabulous wife, Brooke, an "A" player in every way. **GA**

To my entrepreneurial parents, Robert and Diana Bartels,
and my brothers, Doug and Ross—I owe it all to you. **AB**

To my Mary, my all, and our seven children. **MD**

CONTENTS

FOREWORD

Making the Number: How to Use Sales Benchmarking to Drive Performance is a tour de force, a masterful guide that connects all the important dots, showing exactly how almost every sales organization can improve dramatically.

As a management psychologist, I have assessed and coached more than sixty-five hundred top executives, including more than a thousand sales executives from leading companies throughout the world. Greg Alexander impressed me as the best of the best. In one year, he took one of the worst-performing sales regions of high-tech EMC and catapulted it to the #1 spot . . . annihilating the competition. I have said in four books on talent assessment: Always look at the numbers—the actual performance first and foremost. Alexander not only did it, but fine-tuned the Sales Benchmark Index methodology so that others can do it, too.

If you were to thumb through *Making the Number* at random, you might hit on one page and think, "Alexander must be a Ph.D., a professor," but on another page you might think he must be an IT professional, an HR executive, a corporate strategist, a CEO . . . and all those conclusions would be correct in this sense: Alexander not only grasps all those points of view but incorporates the essence of each in his sales-benchmarking methodology. Any sales executive *not* taking such a broad and deep view is apt to become a dinosaur.

I know Greg Alexander to be a dynamic sales executive, but he is also a "quant." He says there is no "silver bullet," but he comes close to offering one with a proven benchmarking methodology that sorts through a zillion numbers and helps companies focus like a laser on the few that truly make the difference. Most sales executives I have assessed crunch numbers that do not mean much. They have complex ways of monitoring and measuring their sales force, but when they say their sales force did not generate great numbers, it is obvious there was an inefficient and ineffective focus on the wrong things. Alexander's method isolates the right metrics and partners with IT for the right analyses . . . and partners with finance to drive shareholder value . . . and partners with HR to be sure talented salespeople are hired and compensated to drive the right metrics . . . and partners with the CEO to be sure the whole system drives strategic goals.

Bottom line, no sales executive I have assessed does a better job of taking a sophisticated, holistic view of sales and using it in the most practical way imaginable, with superb results. *Making the Number* is sure to become a best practice. When I assess future vice presidents of sales and coach them, I will measure them against the skills and competencies spelled out in *Making the Number,* and advise them to fill in their knowledge gaps and embrace this best practice. I have a short list of books I recommend to all aspiring general managers, presidents, and CEOs, and *Making the Number: How to Use Sales Benchmarking to Drive Performance* is the newest addition to that list.

> Bradford D. Smart, Ph.D.
> —Cofounder of "Topgrading" with son Geoff Smart
> —Author of *Topgrading: How Companies Win by Hiring, Coaching, and Keeping the Best People*

TIPS FOR READING THIS BOOK

Y ou are time starved, overworked, underresourced, and under lots of pressure. Needless to say, finding time to read is more than difficult. Not to worry. This book has been created not only so you can reach your sales and career goals, but also so you can maximize your time. Each of the four sections in this book has been written to meet specific needs. Let us help you get the most out of this book and sales benchmarking. Here is how it is organized:

SECTION I

If you want to answer the question, "why benchmarking for sales and why now?" start right at the beginning. Section I makes the case for benchmarking as a sales function and explains the power of the management technique. This section also provides examples of successful implementations of benchmarking in other professions and makes the connection to sales. It nets out what is in it for you and helps you understand how your sales force can benefit from this approach. If you are new to the concept, this section will be invaluable.

Section I lays the groundwork for why macroeconomic changes are paving the way for benchmarking. Chapter 1 covers the main means by which companies can acquire a sustainable competitive advantage and how the forces of globalization and commoditization are not-so-gradually eliminating options. Chapter 2 delves into the concept of *Customer Experience* as a means of achieving a competitive advantage, even in the current economic environment, and asserts that the key to establishing a unique customer experience is through the transformation of sales forces. Chapter 3 provides the story of a mythical corporation to show whether the corporate world is ready to embrace sales benchmarking as a technique to achieve sales force transformation. Chapters 4 and 5 discuss sales-benchmarking concepts from a personal level, answering the question "What's in it for the sales leader and the sales rep?" Chapter 6 discusses the overall tradition of corporate benchmarking and provides background on how it applies to other business functions. Chapter 7 introduces the application of benchmarking to the sales profession and what this means to those at all levels in the sales hierarchy. If you already understand the discipline of benchmarking and have determined you want to apply it to your sales force, you may skip this section and move on to the next one.

SECTION II

Section II picks up where Section I left off and takes the reader into a more intimate exploration of the benchmarking discipline, specifically as it applies to the sales profession. Interestingly, Chapter 8 begins with a discussion of what sales benchmarking is not. This approach is meant to establish some lines of demarcation between sales benchmarking and other concepts or ideas that are similar but not actually part of it. Chapters 9 and 10 cover sales benchmarking from a strategic perspective and then from a tactical (i.e., process-based) perspective. Chapter 11 captures the unique interplay between sales benchmarking and the technique of best-practices adoption. Chapter 12 introduces the concept of *World-Class,* a term that describes the best of the best, providing the high-water mark for which organizations shoot when they begin sales benchmarking. The chapter also covers why world-class is important and how it relates to the relevant peer-group comparison. Finally Chapter 13 addresses the need for a sales force to become self-aware and presents an exercise for categorizing a sales force, then determining its maturity level. This is the last point of preparation before embarking on the sales benchmarking journey.

SECTION III

This section is for those who are ready to get started in sales benchmarking. It describes a detailed how-to methodology in five easy steps, providing a blueprint for benchmarking the sales function. Chapter 14 teaches how to select sales metrics, and chapters 15 and 16 explain how to gather, compute, and compare sets of internal and external data points. Chapter 17 addresses the next step, *Focused*

Action, and demonstrates how to solve uncovered problems. Chapter 18 deals with the need to enshrine the sales-benchmarking effort within a larger ongoing corporate continuous-improvement program so that benefits are not lost and future opportunities are exploited.

This section is detailed. We want you to get the biggest bang for your buck, so we packed this section with everything you will need to become an effective sales benchmarker. If you are looking for something to read to kill some time on a plane, you should wait until you land to read this section. Think of it as a bit higher on the educational scale but lower in entertainment value than your typical sales book (a textbook as opposed to a novel). Prepare to be challenged.

For some in the sales profession, especially those used to a career spent "netting issues out," this section may prove a challenge. Some executives may turn this section over to their sales operations staff with the dictate to "read this and tell me what I need to know." For those inclined to use this approach, we suggest that you at least read the summaries at the conclusion of each chapter. Understanding these concepts is critical to being able to transform your sales force with the benchmarking discipline, so skip them at your peril.

SECTION IV

This section presents a range of issues you will need to navigate to enshrine sales benchmarking in your organization. Chapter 19 captures the most common counterarguments you may face when attempting your first sales-benchmarking project and gives you the ammunition you will need to overcome them. Chapter 20 lists some of the implementation obstacles that often arise when contemplating whether sales benchmarking is a valid concept, worthy of application in the corporate environment. Those who have attempted other organizational-change management projects know well how important overcoming resistance to new concepts can be. The section wraps up with a conclusion that includes an action plan for sales leaders to inject the benchmarking discipline into their own organizations.

Last, if you feel you are in the top 10 percent of the profession and want a glimpse into a major new breakthrough, move right to the epilogue, which introduces the most exciting thing to impact the sales-improvement industry in the last twenty-five years—peering networks. This is our attempt to make good on the claim "You heard it here first." What will be the eventual result of this trend? Simply this, the demise of legacy sales-consulting and sales-training companies. Sales consultants have been rewarded for advocation methods that often fail to produce as advertised. We will show you how these antiquated business models are threatened by this new trend and what some likely outcomes will be.

SECTION V

We believe people learn best from their peers. This section profiles sales benchmarking in action at some of the world's leading companies. Learn how Dean Mansfield, vice president of worldwide operations at NetSuite, sells millions of dollars of enterprise software with no outside sales force and has a productivity rate fifteen times the enterprise-software industry. Learn how Gerry Wagner, vice president of sales at Discover Financial Services, plays the role of David to the Goliaths of MasterCard and Visa. If you lead a sales force going up against market leaders with near monopolies, you will gain much from Gerry's wisdom. Be introduced to David M. R. Covey, senior vice president of U.S. sales at Franklin Covey, and witness how he and his staff educate over eighty thousand people each year on the "7 Habits of Highly Effective People." Through David's sales force, each year thousands of people learn how to improve their lives. Get a sneak peek into the nation's largest provider of broadband services—Covad Communications. David McMorrow, executive vice president of worldwide sales at Covad, cut selling expenses by 35 percent and grew top-line revenue by 24 percent. Meet Wayne Eisenberg, vice president of worldwide sales at Smart Modular Technologies, who has kept turnover in his sales department under 10 percent for years by setting realistic quotas each team member can meet. If you agree and want to learn from five of the best, here is proof that sales benchmarking works.

SUMMARY

It has been a pleasure writing this book. We hope that you, our readers, gain us much from reading about sales benchmarking as we have from experiencing it hands-on.

Good selling!

—Greg, Aaron, and Mike

SECTION I

THE TIME HAS COME FOR SALES BENCHMARKING

INTRODUCTION

"I don't like to spend a lot of money confirming old theories."[1]

—T. Boone Pickens, Texas oil tycoon

MONEYBALL

We love sports. We played them endlessly as kids and still spend hours rooting for our favorite teams. Even today, when introduced to new business ideas, we tend to understand them better through the use of sports analogies. So we find it easier to teach others new business ideas in a similar way. To introduce the concept of sales benchmarking, the best sports analogy we can find is the outstanding season experienced by the 1999 Oakland A's baseball team.

> In 1999, Major League Baseball Commissioner Bud Selig called the Oakland A's an "aberration" because of their remarkable success. The A's won more games during the regular season than all but one team in the league, and they did it with the second lowest payroll of any other team. In business, this is called "success with limited resources."[2]

So how did they do it? In his book *Moneyball*, author Michael Lewis introduced one of the great controversial business leaders of our time—Billy Beane, general manager of the Oakland A's. Beane realized he could not beat the big market teams by using the same techniques they did because they could outspend him to victory. He determined that to win, and win consistently, he would have to break from tradition, challenge conventional wisdom, and apply a new methodology when examining players and their talents.[3]

Beane hired a Harvard economist to the front office and together they developed a proprietary statistical analysis to determine which performance statistics had the highest correlation to wins and losses. They looked at thousands of metrics captured on each player and found that the items scouts used in their evaluations had little bearing on the outcome of games. Home runs, runs batted in, and batting average—the standard means for measuring player performance—might determine which players made the All-Star team, but they had a poor correlation to wins or losses for their teams. What really counted, they discovered, was the percentage of a player's plate appearances where the player did not make an out and reached first base. They also realized that when playing defense, the metric that mattered most was getting the opponent's batters out when they hit the ball and preventing them from reaching base, not the more favored statistic of fielding percentage.

With this new benchmarking approach, Beane and his statistician could measure each and every player's relative numbers on these two items. This data drove their decision making in determining which players they drafted and which they acquired through free agency. It is true that many of the best players had high scores in both the legacy means of assessing player performance and the new statistical paradigm adopted by Beane. What was interesting, though, was that many players, especially those on the margin, might have relatively higher scores on the legacy metrics (RBIs, home runs, errors) but low scores on the metrics Beane was tracking. This is the area where Beane found the greatest opportunity. He and his staff were able to value players that other teams were not seriously considering because he knew, and could literally prove, that these players would contribute more to the future success of the A's. In addition, he was able to avoid bidding wars for those players who scored relatively high in the traditional metrics but not as highly in the ones Beane was tracking. Not only did Beane have an advantage over other managers in terms of being able to better identify those players more likely to generate wins, but also he captured an economic advantage in that the players he collected were not as valued by others and so could be obtained for less investment. His success, therefore, was twofold—better players and a lower payroll.

Collection of these players onto a series of A's teams produced more wins than any other team in baseball, and no one but Beane and his staff knew how they did it. This, in a nutshell, was an exercise in benchmarking.

As in baseball, so, too, in sales—the numbers don't lie.

Can benchmarking be deployed in sales with the same level of success that it is deployed in professional baseball? You bet it can.

RUDIMENTARY SALES BENCHMARKING—THE W-2

The scoreboard for sales professionals is and has always been the pay stub. Companies, at least the good ones, only pay salespeople when they sell something. Accordingly, the number one personal benchmarking statistic for sales professionals is their W-2. The pay stub, therefore, represents the crudest form of sales benchmarking. Having been a sales leader, Greg Alexander can attest that using even this most basic form of peer "comparative analysis" can work wonders in terms of impact and motivation. For instance, asking a potential sales representative to bring along a copy of the his last three W-2 forms to an interview is a wonderful technique to separate the wheat from the chaff. Does past personal revenue provide the one and only metric pointing towards future sales performance? No, but like any good metric, it does several things—it helps you check on the veracity of stated performance, it provides an understanding of directional correctness (are things trending up or down), and it helps set future expectations (i.e., how should a potential compensation package be structured).

Using the W-2 in this way works, but this approach is limited to the interaction between a sales manager and a potential employee and so constitutes just the tip of the benchmarking iceberg. The W-2 technique does not address the many and various organizational aspects of the corporate sales world, which are the focus of this book and the reason that sales benchmarking is a tool of great power in helping assess sales force performance.

SALES AS AN ART?

So, if sales benchmarking works in such a rudimentary form, why aren't more organizations developing more elaborate sales-benchmarking techniques and embedding sales-benchmarking disciplines in their day-to-day decision making?

The short answer is that salespeople and sales leaders make their money through talking and dealing. They think of sales as an "art," not a science, and they like to talk about things that cannot be measured—things like their client relationships and their territory knowledge. This reliance on sales artistry represents job security and market worth in their minds, and they closely guard it. This attitude developed and matured throughout the twentieth century and has since hardened into received wisdom to the point where most sales leaders no longer even consider whether it is true or not. We will evaluate the legitimacy of this "wisdom" throughout the book.

This lack of introspection on the key issue of whether sales can be evaluated in a consistent and quantitative fashion has been exacerbated by the persistent memory of times when sales compensation reached extraordinary levels. The market bubble experienced from 1998 to 2001 saw a commensurate explosion in sales-executive compensation plans. The details of these plans and the riches reaped by those who profited from them are a story for another book. What matters about this period with regard to the sales profession is that it established an unprecedented expectation about what was possible, even merited, in terms of sales compensation.

In this day and age, as a sales leader, if you can still convince an employer to hire you, pay you a big salary plus a lofty bonus with a generous expense account, good for you! However, for most of the sales executives the days of extraordinary compensation plans as a commonplace occurrence are at an end. Even the most accomplished, productive, and impactful sales leaders have a difficult time negotiating compensation packages that once were considered mediocre.

Consider these facts:

- The average shelf life of a vice president of sales is nineteen months.
- Turnover in the sales profession (reps and managers) has consistently equaled or exceeded 40 percent.
- The number of salespeople who miss their numbers every year approaches 40 percent (It's not surprising that these two numbers run together, as they are intimately related.)[4]

THE DAWN OF DATA

We live in an information age. Organizations use data to aid in decision making in almost every facet of their work. For example, universities assess potential students based on standardized test scores and compare applicants based on a common set of performance metrics (e.g., SAT or ACT scores). Realtors consult large databases of home-selling activity to develop comps (short for "comparison," naturally) for their customers so as to better determine at what price a house can be purchased or sold. These are just two of a vast number of examples where we encounter benchmarking in our daily lives. We are somewhat aware that we use data more now than in the past. What we have yet to grasp fully, though, is that we are using this data to compare ourselves to others to aid in decision making. That is the essence of benchmarking—using a relevant peer group to serve as the basis for quantitative comparison.

THE IMPACT OF TECHNOLOGY

We also live in a technology era. The pace of change and improvement in this area has transformed not only our jobs, but our lives, too. The use of Internet technologies to enable many-to-many connectivity has been the foundation of scores of new businesses, software applications, and personal productivity tools. The details of this fundamental global trend have been captured in an ongoing stream of books, online articles, magazines, and other media outlets dedicated to explaining and even evangelizing such technology change. What is important to understand with regard to benchmarking is that these information era trends have transformed a variety of corporate functions (e.g., manufacturing, finance, and distribution). For example, a chief financial officer (CFO) today can monitor his or her relative performance by simply clicking on Yahoo Finance. One click and, presto, on the screen are the thirty financial ratios taught in business school—with detailed data that juxtaposes how your organization is performing against similar companies. This host of financial indicators compares current and past organizational performance against a relevant industry group. There is even an ability to compare projected future performance!

What has happened in these other disciplines has finally begun to impact the sales profession. For instance, corporate buying agents are using online reverse auctioning and Dutch auctioning to purchase goods and services, even for large-scale technology needs. This type of activity represents a form of benchmarking (i.e., comparing one vendor's offer against another's) and has thoroughly disrupted the sales cycle and methodology for those whose products and services are now subject to this unique form of purchase comparison. Whereas this form of sales comparison is one driven by the customer toward (some would say against) the suppliers, there is a deeper aspect to benchmarking that has yet to be fully realized or appreciated. That aspect is firmly located in the front office, particularly with the chief executive officer (CEO). CEOs have long been eager to ask their sales leaders to prove that they are executing as well as or better than their peers. This is a conversation the CEO holds regularly with the CFO and other functional heads of the organization, but has yet to conduct with the VP of sales. CEOs are inceasingly satisfied with anecdotal evidence, the standard war story that comes naturally to those sales leaders who continue to believe that sales is artistry. CEOs want hard numbers and they will not stop until they get them.

NOTE TO CHIEF SALES OFFICERS

Forty percent of you miss your sales quota every year. That means four out of ten of you make less money than your compensation plan anticipates as most compensation plans are based on quota attainment.

Ouch!

But the board members, CEOs, shareholders, and customers of your organization actually pay a bigger price when you underperform. As a senior executive, you are (unintentionally) destroying shareholder wealth by letting your sales force continue to perform in a vacuum. Small wonder that the CEO is dissatisfied when you are unable to demonstrate what passes for acceptable performance, not to mention superior performance. How many other departments or functions would accept a 40 percent failure rate?

If you are a VP of sales, this discussion should be meaningful because you will, on average, lose your job every nineteen months—not a pleasant fact. This reality of job turnover does not bode well for your personal career.

The good news is this—sales benchmarking can be your key technique to drive up share price, and this book will show you how.

NOTE TO OTHER SALES PROFESSION

Do you have a sales number to meet but don't know how you're going to do it? Is your boss asking questions about your numbers that you can't answer? Do coworkers always seem to get the best territories, more realistic quota assignments, and the promotions you want? Are you not making the kind of money you want to make? Are you tired of winging it?

If so, this book is for you.

Why? Because the 40 percent turnover problem that dogs the sales leader is none other than your job. If the numbers haven't caught up to you yet, they will. Pundits, consultants, headhunters, and even your spouses would probably give you this advice—don't get too comfortable where you are and keep your resume up to date.

Above all, this book should show even the casual reader how sales benchmarking can transform a sales organization and drive positive operating and financial results in a predictable and quantifiable manner. In our careers, we have trained sales leaders and companies across the globe on how to implement data-driven decision-making to achieve revenue growth—transitioning from the old mentality of *sales as an art* to a new paradigm of *sales as a science*. As part of this transformation effort, we have leveraged a database of sales-related information that represents, in our minds, the first information repository designed to benchmark organizational sales effectiveness. Using this database and its attendant metrics, it is possible to determine which drivers of sales force excellence, if improved, would have the most impact on business outcomes.

FINAL THOUGHT—DEATH OF A SALESMAN

Regis McKenna, a guru before his time, wrote a seminal work in 1993 about relationship marketing. In his work he said the following about the inherent malleability of the sales profession, something which has always stuck with us:

> *Selling is a disparate task, tailored to the times and to the vicissitudes of different types of goods and services. Over the last century, salesman have peddled their wares on foot, by horse-drawn wagon, railway, telegraph, automobile, airplane, telephone, radio, television, and now by computer and satellite. Because sales are so directly linked to profits, new tools and techniques for winning new business are always welcome.*[5]

This is sales—it is always needed and has always conformed, reformed, and transformed itself with the times. This time is no different. We hope to show you that sales benchmarking is another wave of change set to sweep across those sales landscape and the sales professionals most adept at accepting and implementing change will thrive on it. Those that are not, will not.

CHAPTER 1

SOURCES OF COMPETITIVE ADVANTAGE

It has been said that arguing against globalization is like arguing against the laws of gravity.

—Kofi Annan, seventh secretary general of the
United Nations

W hy is a book about sales benchmarking beginning with a discussion on global trends and strategic factors? Shouldn't we just dive right in and start discussing how to do sales benchmarking?' The simple answer is, no. In order to appreciate why sales benchmarking is critical for executives, managers, and even front-line salespeople, it is necessary to take several steps backward. In doing this, we shall consider some macro trends that are shaking up corporate America, and how all this is impacting the sales profession, both now and in the future. Armed with this introductory sense of why, we can all better understand the compelling case to engage in sales benchmarking sooner rather than later.

GLOBALIZATION

In his pathbreaking book, *The World is Flat*, Thomas Freidman made the convincing case that ten forces taken together have permanently "flattened" the world.[1] What he means is that longstanding obstacles to unrestricted commerce—geographic separation, time lag, language barriers, cultural mis-understanding, historical enmity, geopolitical turmoil, prohibitive trade tariffs, and so on—have begun to dissipate due to these ten forces. Although govern-mental reaction to the September 11, 2001, terrorist attacks has counteracted some of this international openness, the trend in business is unmistakable and the pace of globalization relentless. Simply put, Freidman's book prepares us for a world where competition, even for the most elemental of products and ser-vices, could come from anywhere at any time.

What is the nature of this competition?

For those of us in the developed economies, such competition is likely to come from a third world labor force where the average wage for an hourly worker is pennies per day. Essentially, your most viable competitor may be willing to work a long day for the equivalent of a bowl of rice. Is your company prepared to combat a threat of that severity? If so, upon what basis can you compete and win?

There has been an ongoing debate on the significance of globalization, even as its reality is now too well established to deny. Its detractors insist that America is threatened with virtual impoverishment from unfair trading practices by countries that use their low labor costs to win business away from American corporations that are rendered impotent through restrictive regulations and high-priced labor. Its supporters say that economists Adam Smith and David Ricardo had it right—nations have certain comparative advantages, and fric-tionless world trade only allows these differences to be leveraged more effectively to the benefit of all. They point to rising standards of living and economic growth that accrue to those nations that trade most vigorously and freely. Although there may still be ups and downs reflected in the breadth and depth of globaliza-tion, one thing is for certain—it is relentlessly inevitable.

SOURCES OF COMPETITIVE ADVANTAGE

In order to understand how your organization might form a coherent and com-pelling response to the threat of global competition, let us first examine the sources of competitive advantage. Once we understand what these are, you can evaluate each of them. This will enable you to determine which would be most advantageous to your corporate strategy, given changes in the increasingly com-petitive global marketplace.

Michael Porter, probably the world's foremost authority on competitive dy-namics, has published two seminal works on this topic—*Competitive Advantage* and *Competitive Strategy.* Each book represents a profound exploration of the causes and consequences of competitive differentiation, examining the factors that influence it as well as how it has changed over time. Porter outlines three basic approaches organizations can use to establish and maintain competitive advantage in their respective marketplaces. These strategies are overall cost leadership, differentiation, and focus.[2]

> *Overall Cost Leadership* describes how companies can achieve and defend a low-cost provider position, yet still retain enough return to sustain the business model. Cost leadership can be achieved through technology, labor force selectivity, or even process innovation.
>
> *Focus* is built around the ability to orient a product or service towards a specific market segment, buying group, or geographic market. Organizations pursuing a focus strategy must be able to demonstrate convincingly that they can serve the defined market segment more effectively than all other competitors.
>
> *Differentiation* is fixated on establishing and leveraging the uniqueness of a product or service such that customers demand it from the supplier and substitute offerings are insufficient. Differentiation can be achieved through many techniques and can produce significant returns; in fact, these techniques often lead to premium pricing. Some of these approaches, though, rely on leveraging external enforcement by governments (i.e., patent infringement) or on maintaining ongoing expensive internal product development capabilities.

Although Porter identified and described these competitive strategies in the early 1980s, they continue to be relevant. What has changed in the intervening years, and Freidman described this intimately in his book, is that the ten flattening forces have taken a toll on the ability of organizations to sustain these competitive advantages over time. It is, in fact, due to this gradual reduction in sustainability that the need for sales benchmarking arises. Let us first, however, explore how each of Porter's strategic options to establish competitive advantage is faring today.

WINNING ON PRICE

Overall cost leadership, also known as price differentiation, was the rage in the 1990s. Many corporations recognized an opportunity to be the low-cost provider in their industry and took advantage of it by reducing their cost structures as much as possible. Cost was relentlessly removed from all areas of the business, and these savings were passed along to customers and clients. Outsourcing, supply chain optimization, offshoring, and strategic sourcing were some of the successful strategies used during much of this time to achieve overall cost leadership. In fact, many companies (Dell, Wal-Mart, Dollar General, etc.) that reoriented their business model around these principles enjoyed healthy returns.

An unintended side effect of this strategy has been the proliferation of copycat pricing. Moving manufacturing to China, shifting a customer service call center to India, and deploying online reverse auctioning are tactics that were once thought avant-garde, but have now been successfully replicated, both by American as well as foreign companies. The emergence of equally efficient cost-cutting competitors (Costco vs. Wal-Mart, Lenovo vs. Dell, Dollar Tree vs. Dollar General) has demonstrated that this comparative competitive advantage is not long lasting. As future companies contemplate which strategy to adopt to separate themselves from the competition, they would be well advised to consider that differentiating on price (overall cost leadership) is reaching a point of diminishing returns.

WINNING WITH FOCUS

Focus is a viable strategy for those companies that can afford to limit their product or service in such a specific way as to appeal to a defined subset of the marketplace. This targeting of the market can be based on gender, age, geography, profession, or language. It succeeds when you can convince the customer that the higher price is worth the value you deliver as a focused supplier of a particular segment. This higher price is necessary to support the higher costs required to sustain a focus strategy. This can be a long-term profitable approach but is limited by the size of the chosen target market; the larger the market, the more likely it is the twin strategic forces of cost and differentiation will make the focus strategy more difficult to defend.

WINNING THROUGH DIFFERENTIATION

The most common strategy for developing competitive advantage is through differentiation. In a sense, this strategy is something of a grab bag of items that all reflect the same general goal of making a product or service unique. The focus is not so much on the customer or end user, but on the extraordinary usefulness, speed, or attractiveness of the product or service—the overall "betterness" of what is being served up to the customer. Each of the following is a legitimate type of differentiation strategy:

- *Superior Branding*—Usually created through large marketing and advertising investment, this approach is successful when it creates an aura of excellence or hipness about the product in the mind of the target customer. Examples are NIKE for shoes, BMW for cars, REI for outdoor gear, and Coke for soft drinks.
- *Product Quality*—Companies achieve this distinction when they are able to deliver a product or service free of defect. Poor product quality was seen as a major detractor at the end of the twentieth century, and achieving a market position as a premium-quality provider carried with it a competitive edge. By adopting a product-quality-improvement program, companies are able to squeeze costs out of product manufacturing or assembly because they come to understand better the process in order to reduce defects. Almost all companies involved in manufacturing, consumer goods, and heavy industry leverage this aspect of differentiation. As we discuss below, this approach has dwindled in its significance based on widespread adoption.
- *Compelling Product Features*—Countless companies have used product or service features to establish themselves in their respective marketplaces. The feature/function battle is a common one in business-to-business sales campaigns as well as consumer retail sales. What is instructive about this approach to differentiation is that its benefit is fleeting and the ability to sustain feature leadership is a difficult one.
- *Service Uniqueness*—This approach is the companion to compelling product features. Since many businesses are built on delivering a service rather than a product, companies have sought to differentiate by making their service so uniquely attractive that it represents their competitive advantage. Examples of this include a whole new category of business software known as Software as a Service (SaaS) with category providers like SalesForce.com as well as consumer service operations like ServiceMaster.
- *Logistics Superiority*—This approach to differentiation hinges on the deployment of a set of people, process, technology, and hard assets (facilities, transportation, communications, etc.) that creates a unique ability to deliver a solution to a customer. There is no single aspect upon which to base the differentiation strategy; instead, it is all parts working in synchronicity

that establishes the uniqueness. Such approaches are expensive and can be time-consuming to build but, once erected, pose a formidable barrier to effective competition. Examples of this approach include Dow Corning for chemicals, Proctor and Gamble for package goods, and Pfizer for health care.[3]

- *Channel Supremacy*—Many companies eschew direct sales forces in favor of an indirect channel or some pursue both go-to-market sales models. There are some that develop their indirect sales channel so well that it constitutes a comparative competitive advantage. This occurs because its relationship with those companies, dealers, or contractors that resell its product/service is a frictionless, productive, and profitable one. Getting more "feet on the street" using this approach can become the reason to stay in business. Examples of such superior channels include Caterpillar, HP, and IBM as well as franchisee operations such as McDonald's, True Value hardware, and Krispy Kreme.

- *Technological Advance*—This approach typically results from some break-through advancement in the corporate lab that leads to the commercial-ization of an invention. Because of the difficulty in achieving such an event, this form of differentiation strategy is rare (and expensive). Exam-ples include Xerox in copiers (in the 1960s), GE in microwaves (in the 1970s), EMC with cached memory for storage arrays (in the 1980s), 3M with Post-it notes (in the 1990s), and Apple with its new iPhone.

- *Customer Service*—This approach captures the relationship between the company and its customer. It is the only approach to differentiation that innately begins with the customer and works backward: What do custom-ers want? What do they like? How can their needs (both conscious and subconscious) be met? The telling feature of this approach is that all em-ployees of the company understand that their first responsibility is ex-traordinary customer service. This attitude of customer-centric behavior permeates all business functions. Examples of this approach include Southwest for commercial airlines, UPS for parcel shipment, American Express for financial services, and Nordstrom's for retail.

With the exception of—customer service, each of these approaches to dif-ferentiation has become or is becoming less viable in today's marketplace. There are several reasons for the overall diminishment of the differentiation strategy. Globalization is, of course, a major factor in making differentiation a less feasible and profitable strategy, particularly with regard to the speed with which content, product, and service can be copied. Add to that the inability of governments to enforce property rights and patent law infringement internationally, and the bottom line is this: What can be exported to a lower-cost, more efficient provider will be. It may be instructive to examine one of the differentiation approaches, product quality, to see how it evolved over time.

WHAT HAPPENED TO PRODUCT QUALITY?

In the 1970–1990 time period, many businesses focused on improve product quality. Prior to that time, there were often large, noticeable differences in product quality between competing entities. Customers could be won in greater volume (or at least fewer lost) by having an advantage in the area of product quality. Total Quality Management (TQM), based on the work of W. Edwards Deming, became a favored corporate initiative; it was on every manufacturing executive's agenda. As a result, quality management programs were implemented almost universally in an attempt to achieve differentiation through superior quality. Quality-based programs such as ISO 9000, Lean Manufacturing, the Malcolm Baldridge Award, and Six Sigma rose to prominence as well. Each had a different spin, but they all sought to eliminate defect from process. In a sign of success of these efforts, today quality is no longer a topic of boardroom discussion, as its adoption has resulted in a common expectation for high quality. As a result, companies can no longer retain and gain customers based on the virtues of product quality alone. There is no more premium and no more differentiation obtained through this approach.

CUSTOMER EXPERIENCE—TWENTY-FIRST-CENTURY CUSTOMER SERVICE

We chose product quality, but could just have well chosen the other approaches to a differentiation strategy. All have been wholly or partially reduced in their effect by the relentless pace and reach of globalization. All, that is, except for the last one—customer service. There is something quite different about customer service as it was envisioned by Michael Porter. The one aspect elemental to the customer service approach that is only incidental to the other differentiation approaches is simply this—people. An organization that succeeds with a differentiated customer service strategy must have, above all else, an ability to connect with customers, clients, and prospects in a way that sets it apart. Human-to-human interaction is the key. This is one reason why you cannot outsource your favorite hairdresser, masseuse, or dry cleaner—they need to be physically near you and you need to interact with them. We call this intimate interaction the customer experience, and winning with this is the way to establish competitive advantage in the twenty-first century.

Before turning to Chapter 2 to learn more about this customer experience, let us stop and summarize what is significant about globalization and competitive advantage. The bottom line is this—globalization is not so gradually annihilating prior strategies for sustainable comparative advantage, leaving only those that are either highly niche focused or are related to the customer experience.

TO REVIEW

- Globalization is a fact of nature, and its impact on our economy, institutions, and corporate structures will only increase over time.
- There are three basic sources of strategic competitive advantage—overall cost leadership, focus, and differentiation
- Based on copycatting and commoditization, overall cost leadership is a difficult strategy to sustain.
- Focus is a viable, but limited, approach due to its need to target market niches.
- Differentiation is the most varied strategy and has many options, including superior branding, product quality, compelling product features, service uniqueness, logistics superiority, channel supremacy, technological advance, and customer service.
- Customer service is the most sustainable and sure of those options available to twenty-first-century companies. In an expanded view of this approach, we shall call it customer experience.

CHAPTER 2

CUSTOMER EXPERIENCE

"Everything starts with the customer."

—Louis XIV, King of France

I n the last chapter we established that, for organizations wishing to impact a broad market segment, capture new customers, and obtain a long-lasting competitive advantage, the only still-effective strategy is that of differentiation through customer experience. This chapter will explore the details of this customer experience, give some prime examples of its best practitioners, and then connect customer experience to the need to radically transform the sales function.

Buyers are no longer satisfied with standard "dog and pony" pitches or mediocre value propositions. Brand allegiance is virtually nonexistent in today's hypercompetitive market. Having a great product or service no longer earns high margins, or even closes a sale. Instead, such things are now just expected. Commoditization has had a leveling impact for sure, so the seller often tries to better address buyer needs by improving its own expertise and mastery of its presales process. Such approaches, useful as they are to sellers, only incrementally help buyers and they do nothing to create a unique customer experience.

SHIFT OF POWER FROM SELLER TO BUYER

For those who have been members of the sales profession for many years, even decades, the advent of the twenty-first-century has brought some disquieting times. Previously, in the standard business-to-business transaction and even most of the business-to-consumer transactions, the preponderance of advantage lay with the seller. The seller possessed deep knowledge of its own products, the marketplace, the competition, and the buyer's habits and predispositions. The buyer might have had a need or a desire to buy something but with relatively limited information to aid him or her in the process. The occasional *Consumer Report* or corporate purchasing department might have helped with basic product education or in negotiating a lower cost, but these did not fundamentally impact the buyer-seller dynamic, where the seller held all the face cards. What has turned the tables on the buyer-seller relationship is the explosion of information now placed in the buyer's hands courtesy of technology that enables him or her to communicate, even passively, with legions of other buyers to leverage their expertise.

One ramification of this explosion of social media is that the Internet has armed the consumer against ineffective, legacy corporate messaging efforts. Physically disparate but not disinterested outsiders (known as citizen marketers) are increasingly collaborating with each other to form bands of devoted enthusiasts. Such citizen marketers constitute one of the twenty-first century's versions of Alexis de Tocqueville's celebrated decentralized American social communities. The coordination of these individuals is influencing companies' customer relationships, product design, and marketing campaigns. They are democratizing traditional notions of communication and marketing, even entire business models. In a book on this type of citizen marketing, authors Jackie Huba and Ben McConnell noted that "citizen marketers create what could be considered marketing and advertising content on behalf of other brands, products, or organizations. . . . They are on the fringes, driven by passion, creativity, and a sense of duty."[1] The sales profession must understand that marketing departments have already been disintermediated by these citizen marketers. Sales is next. Marketing and sales can no longer operate within the corporate four walls outside the scrutiny of social marketers who have taken an interest in their product or service.

Further, the various Internet-based technologies, blogs, wikis, social networking, and other forms of virtual communication have enabled buyers to meet their needs via some aspect of self-service. In years past, buyers would contact sales staff to obtain product information; no longer. All the basics of product information are now presented through a browser interface. Mediocre salespeople need no longer carry a bag with product brochures that they translate to clueless customers. The explosion of SaaS offerings and open-source software allows customers to use products over an extended period in a self-service model without ever speaking with a salesperson. As a prospect's usage of these "free" products reaches a more mature point of adoption, the prospect may feel the need to acquire help to control complexity or introduce more compelling features. It is at this point that the provider's sales force is engaged. Those sales forces are highly specialized, trained, motivated, and adept at satisfying experienced buyers.

Something similar holds true for the retail market, where businesses meet directly with consumers instead of other businesses. Product or service information can now be obtained prior to the store visit via Internet searches, eBay, and any number of social network sites dedicated to that product or lifestyle area. Therefore, instead of regurgitating this information, retailers must create some sort of emotional bond with the target buying community. This bond must be stronger than the twin lures of better product and better price, which are only fleeting advantages. In fact, this bond, which is in essence the customer experience, will eventually be the reason the consumer goes shopping in the first place, having supplanted the product or service that is being offered within the context of the retail environment. Take the rise of Starbucks (and its imitators like Caribou Coffee), for example.

STARBUCKS AND WHOLE FOODS

How many people start their day with a cup of coffee from Starbucks? Don't you just love when they write your name on the cup and wish you a good day? It makes you feel good. This feeling is part of the unique customer experience they are fostering. How powerful can a positive customer experience be? Consider that coffee is, truly, a commodity—you can trade a coffee futures contract on the Chicago Exchange. Yet on our way to work in the morning we pass by the gas station, offering a warm cup of coffee for 50 cents, and wait in line at a Starbucks and pay $2.50 for the same item. We knowingly pay five times as much for a commodity. Why? Simply, the customer experience. Take another example—grocery stores. Most people have visited a Stop & Shop, Safeway, Food Lion, or A&P. Compare one of those stores to a Whole Foods store. Both sell food—the shelves are largely lined with the same item. What is the difference? It is the customer experience. Whole Foods' track record demonstrates that the buying public, even the more highly informed buying public who is well aware of the price differentials, is willing to pay 20 percent more for a carton of milk from Whole Foods. In a book with the evocative title of *Chocolates on the Pillow Aren't Enough: Reinventing The Customer Experience,* Jonathan Tisch noted that service-based industries have to go beyond the realm of good service to provide an experience that's truly exceptional-and thus, truly memorable.[2] Tisch used examples from many different industries on how to leverage and exploit linguistic, cultural, and other ethnic differences to provide stylized experiences. In each of his examples, the product or the service is largely generic and the successful company is the one that can provide a memorable environment that seems somehow customized to the needs, even the desires, of the customer. This is customer experience at its zenith.

If putting on a good show to win or retain new customers is what is now necessary, where are many going to turn for expertise and advice? To those most known for entertainment—Hollywood and the theater industry in general. In a book by Pine and Gilmore called *The Experience Economy: Work Is Theater & Every Business a State,* the authors focused on how to add pizzazz to a service or create a compelling service around currently lifeless products and services.[3] They believe that, to survive, companies must "learn to stage a rich, compelling experience." Add their voices to the many who now realize customer experience is not just a means to establishing a new competitive advantage, but a necessary survival strategy.

THE LINK BETWEEN CUSTOMER EXPERIENCE AND THE SALES FORCE

What does this have to do with the sales function? Who within the corporation owns the customer experience? It is the sales force. Therefore, being world-class in this area is now more important than ever, which just begs the question, "Can't sales force effectiveness be copied just as easily as adopting a low-price strategy or establishing unique product features?" No, it cannot. Why not? Simply, a corporation cannot clone human beings. In other words, copying a system, a process, or a product is one thing. Reverse engineering a manufacturing effort or cobbling together a duplicate IT system may be difficult but doable. What resists such effort, though, is the attempt to mass produce someone else's customer experience. The complexities of a people-centric differentiation strategy (the unique blend of emotions, ethnicity, attitude, experience, and language) defy a copycatting approach. Therefore, being consistently expert in the sales function is sustainable because it creates a customer experience that cannot be cloned.

In the past, however senior corporate leadership has not been focused on sales force execution. Though sales is viewed as a "must have" function, it has not typically been considered a source of competitive *differentiation*.

Should we be surprised by this? Frankly, we should. As McKenna said in his book on relationship marketing published in the early 1990s:

> *Today, a "salesman" can be anything from a decidedly non-human computer-ized phone connection to a sophisticated purveyor of information whose con-sultation and services can bring added profits to your business. High technology salespeople draw on a broader spectrum of skills than did their predecessors and these new skills boost their image in the business world. They are not seen as peddlers but as knowledge professionals. Armed with higher education, sales training, persuasive persistence, and a constant stream of updated information from computers, high technology sales people have become the Great Differen-tiators for their products and companies.[4]*

So if McKenna recognized this about salespeople that long ago, there is little excuse for executives to suggest they did not realize their sales force is a strategic asset that should be mined for its differentiating qualities.

It is only a matter of time before CEOs start asking their sales leaders to *prove* that they are executing and selling as well as the competition. And, as with other strategies, sales force execution is relative. The space between a company's sales force capability and the aggregate capability of the rest of its industry's sales forces defines the quantifiable opportunity. Leaders of companies will soon want to understand how to measure this differential because it will indicate the size of the improvement opportunity represented by sales force transformation. We believe that once sales force execution is widely recognized by companies and their CEOs as a source of sustained competitive advantage, the method by which a CEO manages his sales force will change substantially.

Consider these statistics:

- The average shelf life of a sales manager is fifteen months.
- Almost four out of ten salespeople will lose their jobs this year.

- An average of 27 percent of salespeople do not produce enough even to cover their loaded employment costs.

Armed with these numbers, CEOs will increasingly demand quantitative evidence that supports whatever the sales leaders are trying to sell to senior management about their ability to hit the number. Why is such a high rate of failure acceptable when it comes to sales organizations? No other function within a company is allowed to underperform this way. This level of failure has thus far been tolerated only because sales executives have not been expected to understand how to apply benchmarking and data-driven decision making to their business. But ignorance of such skills and functions will soon no longer be tolerated.

For sales leaders, the time to get ready is now.

So we have learned how macro changes have eliminated one source of competitive advantage after another, leaving customer experience as the remaining sustainable option. Further, we have determined that sales force execution is the means of obtaining this unique customer experience. The next question logically follows: Are the sales forces of American companies ready for the challenge?

We shall see.

TO REVIEW

- Power and knowledge are shifting from the seller to the buyer as buyers leverage new technologies to work together, inform themselves, and take advantage of user self-service opportunities.
- This shift in power has major implications for sales force effectiveness: Since buyers are sharper, only the better-prepared sales forces will succeed in the new buying environment.
- With commoditization and globalization diminishing other competitive advantage strategies, maximizing customer experience has become the *new normal.*
- Whole Foods and Starbucks represent just two examples of this trend toward providing a unique, compelling, and customized environment in which customers/clients can consume a corporate product or service. The product or service is incidental, even tangential, to the experience. The key is to connect with the buyer emotionally.

- The way in which most companies, especially those in the business-to-business selling model, connect with their customers is through their sales force. The sales force, therefore, represents the means to achieve a notable customer experience.
- Companies will increasingly turn to sales force transformation as a means of establishing sustainable competitive advantage.

CHAPTER 3

ARE OUR SALES FORCES READY?

"All that is necessary to break the spell of inertia and frustration is to—act as if it were impossible to fail."

—DOROTHEA BRANDE, WRITER AND EDITOR

MILLENNIUM PRODUCTS:
A STORY OF SALES STRATEGY WITHOUT SUBSTANCE

Imagine the plight of John Davidson, CEO of Millennium Products, a mythical $5 billion manufacturing firm. That time of year was approaching again—Q4. John had been asked by the board and key investors to set expectations for the following year. He arranged a day of meetings to bring together his cross-functional leadership team. John had given them his strategic guidance and asked each of them to lay out their needs for the upcoming year in an action plan. John indicated these plans would be presented to him at a formal meeting in early October.

As the meeting day approached, John's executive assistant assured him everything was arranged—the meeting room readied, lunches ordered, presentations developed, and golf reservations made. Indeed, it all started out well. Each department gave a strong pitch, demonstrating how they had impacted the bottom line in the previous year, what their recognized deficiencies were, how their plans reflected the company's strategic goals, and how they planned to contribute to the company's expected financial success. One by one, the functional department heads withstood the scrutiny and skepticism of John and the board members. As the day neared its completion, a nervous chatter slowly built up in the boardroom. There was one final presentation to go—the one most board members, and certainly John, had been waiting for throughout the day. Larry Kevlin, the executive vice president of sales, was on deck. John asked him to begin.

Larry was a charismatic guy and knew how to deliver a great presentation. He paused in all the right places. He played on their emotions and fears. He highlighted flashy graphic points in his presentation using a cutting-edge laser pointer that no one else in the boardroom have ever seen. He always had the greatest technology and the latest toys. He was very comfortable talking about sales campaigns, new customers, upselling, account penetration, and other sales-related concepts. Larry promised that his sales team would overdeliver; he did so with confidence, even humility. After all, he had produced outstanding results at his previous company and had done well at Millennium in the short time he had been aboard.

One of the board members, Randall Acworth, had been jiggling the keys in his suit pocket as Larry ran through slide after slide. Eventually, the jiggling reached a crescendo. Randall, usually taciturn by nature, leaned back in his chair and let out an audible sigh. *Enough is enough,* he thought. At this point, Randall cleared his throat and interrupted Larry.

"Tell us how you plan to make these numbers. Nothing you say seems concrete. It is all very, um, conceptual. Where is your proof? Where is your supporting evidence?"

Heads nodded, but no one said a word. The CEO wiped his brow.

Larry shot back, probably a bit too acerbically considering that Randall was an influential board member, "Sir, here is just such an important number for your consideration. I need a 25 percent increase in headcount to meet the aggressive targets John has set for us for next year." With this, Larry turned to the rest of the board, looking for indications of support, of understanding, even of empathy.

The CEO politely interrupted, "Larry, before we go on a hiring binge, let's look at our personnel churn. What was turnover in the sales force last year and what did it cost the company?"

Larry clumsily tap danced. "I'm not sure, John," he said. "I wasn't here last year. I will have to get back to you with those numbers."

Another board member chimed in, "But turnover and its associated costs can be calculated. We do this for the other departments any time they propose increases in personnel. These are important numbers to understand before we go throwing new heads into the mix."

Larry nodded, but ignored the issue, preferring instead to continue with his presentation. Larry wrapped up with a glowing finish about the prospects for the future. His sales team was equipped with the right skills to hit its target, if only they were augmented with a few extra bodies. They had built solid relationships and had gained commitments from key clients. But they'd need the support of the management team to succeed. The goals, he reminded them, were high. An increase in headcount was critical to success.

John sat quietly pondering this final presentation long after Larry had left the room. He thought to himself, *The other department heads use data from measurements that are established and well understood to support their decisions. Larry, on the other hand, emphasizes the art of sales and never seems comfortable with data other than quota attainment and revenue generation per head. What is it about sales executives that make them so gun-shy about measuring their performance?*

THE BATTLE OVER SALES STAFF HEADCOUNT

The above scenario plays out in boardrooms all over America. CEOs and board members groan as charismatic sales leaders try to convince them that the sales team—and the company—cannot succeed without an increase in headcount and resources for the sales department. Yet, despite these cost increases, turnover in sales organizations remains at an average of 38 percent. Further, according to the industry benchmark, an average of 40 percent of the salespeople miss their quota targets each year!

Is it mere coincidence that the turnover rate and quota failure rate are almost identical? The bottom line is that salespeople who miss their numbers cost the company—and don't think upper management doesn't know it. If you are a sales leader or a sales professional, rest assured your CEO is well aware of which sales reps and managers are missing their targets and which ones are hitting the high numbers.

How much do bad hires and the resulting turnover cost companies on an annual basis? If one accounts for severance costs, recruiting costs, on-boarding costs, opportunity costs associated with an unproductive or vacant sales position, and the time required to get a new salesperson productive, the cost is overwhelming. Conservatively calculated, such costs typically exceed five times the annual cost of a sales professional's expected compensation. At such a rate, the cost of bad hires is staggering.

Let's quantify that impact.

Recall that benchmarking data reveals the average sales force turnover rate to be 38 percent per year. For a sales leader with a 100-person sales force, 38 sales professionals will be replaced *every 12 months*. Assuming an annual quota of $1 million per sales rep and a fully loaded cost per sales head of $150,000, the yearly cost of sales force turnover can be determined through the following formula:

(Cost per sales head) × (Turnover multiplier) × (Number of sales heads turned over)

This sales leader faces, therefore, an aggregate cost of sales force turnover of up to $28.5 million ($150,000) × (5) × (38). With numbers like that, executives can't afford to blindly approve headcount increases without understanding more about their sales force.

THE CURSE OF CHARISMA

Behavioral scientists believe that people often become leaders because of the superficial impression they make on others, not necessarily the skills they possess.[1] In laymen's terms we call this ability to influence, *charisma*. People with charisma can rise like meteors in sales organizations, but they can fall just as quickly. In fact, the allure of charisma is so great, its effect so well understood and admired, that there are persuasive books that teach executives how to develop charisma as a key influencing technique.[2] Charisma enables emotion to triumph over reason often to the detriment of sound business decision making.

Many organizations are prevented from achieving their revenue goals or improving market penetration because they embrace a mind-set that there is an intangible "golden secret" to the sales profession—something that simply cannot be quantified. Such organizations chase this fairy dust in a variety of ways— through seminars on sales psychology, attempts to foster esoteric management skills, and an emphasis in distributing nonmonetary awards to top performers. They perceive that *salespeople* and *numbers people* represent different and mostly antithetical personality traits. This leads to the conclusion that sales is an art and therefore the only business function not really amenable to scientific analysis.

Recall the professional baseball teams that were continually surprised by the success of the Oakland A's in the era of Moneyball and who, even as Oakland continued their winning ways using more accurate and relevant performance values, continued to recruit new players based on flawed legacy metrics and the promise of future performance. So, too, do the vast majority of sales organizations still operate with a model that overvalues salespeople with charisma and relationship skills. But does charisma affect overall sales results?

DOES BAD BREATH BEAT NO BREATH?

In many fields, from sales to medicine, performance is judged not merely by results but also by the cost of the alternative. Sometimes the alternative to not hiring someone new is not hiring someone at all. *Bad breath beats no breath,* thinks the typical sales manager. Nothing could be further from the truth. And since sales results at a macro level are seldom subjected to quantitative and comparative scrutiny, it is even more difficult to analyze accurately an individual sales professional's performance—either while inside the company or when switching jobs.

Unfortunately, this mind-set that sales is an art sustains a flawed set of habits and behaviors that inform talent management. Sales reps are hired and fired based on their ability to conform to a set of intangible traits and qualities. In addition, staff members who specialize in the analysis of sales-related productivity and financial data are usually relegated to insignificant roles, rarely influential, and largely isolated from executive sales decision making. The result is a perpetual cycle of mistakes, each of which compounds its predecessors, and none of which leads to an awareness that the fundamental assumption underlying these thought processes—namely that sales is an art—should be challenged.

Intangibles like charisma and a strong work ethic often rise to the forefront. But are charisma and a strong work ethic enough? No. A strong work ethic is often just another intangible that salespeople use to elevate their careers—without having to focus on actual results or measurable performance. In fact, there can be a downside to a salesperson having as a key strength a strong work ethic, especially when it is not tempered by other traits that bring it into performance balance. These types of salespeople can work long hours but eventually lose their focus and intellectual energy because they are overworked!

THE SALES CAMPAIGN AS A CHESS MATCH

Sales campaigns are like chess matches. Being armed with the right strategy is important, and the ability to think trumps the ability to work hard. Hard workers tend to focus on "noise"—pieces of information that do not have critical meaning or that bear little on the eventual outcome.[3] Though hard work and discipline are important, they do not necessarily lead to success. To succeed, you have to *work hard and work smart*. So, then, how does one find the "smart" part?

EMPTY SUITS

Have you ever been in the presence of an "empty suit" salesperson? An empty suit is someone who looks good on paper, has command of all the buzzwords, and makes a great first impression. But when it comes to getting the job done, he (or she) cannot produce. This type of salesperson is not willing to do the staff work, lacks intellectual curiosity, and is not usually able to accept critique or comparison. Such salespeople can be sophisticated, charming, and typically more comfortable telling you about their wine collections or latest auto acquisition. Sales leaders are well advised to stay clear of these affable but unproductive "sales artists." Though at one time their good nature and relationship-building skills may have enabled success as a sales professional, their lack of desire to support a culture of measurement will become the death knell to sustained improvement.

Instead, sales managers should look for measurable individual-performance traits and set hiring standards accordingly. One tool to use in determining who these candidates are, how to find and nurture them, and later incorporate them into your organization is called topgrading for sales.[4] You will learn later how sales benchmarkers combine old-fashioned hard work with market-based intelligence and scientific analysis to produce outstanding results. Not only outstanding, but also sustainable.

Another mistaken perception that exists within many corporations is that the sales leader must be doing a good job if he or she is never in the office. Many salespeople are expected to "live on the road," their absence from the office implies they are out with customers selling. When the CEO spends time with customers, he often witnesses an amiable, buddy-buddy relationship between the sales team and the client. This seems to bolster the sales executive's claim that sales is an art and that relationship building cannot be captured in any meaningful analytic sense.

The CEO sees the occasional transaction slip from one quarter to the next, but ultimately forgives this, especially after a particularly emotional sales call with a happy customer. These CEOs need a wake-up call! How many other functions or departments within their company would they allow to persist with a 40 percent defect rate? What would be the consequences if the CFO miscalculated the valuation numbers by 40 percent on the latest acquisition? What would happen if the chief information officer had a downtime rate of 40 percent? The consequences for such failures would be severe. The negative impact on a company's top and bottom line can be just as devastating when the sales leader has a similar percentage of the sales staff unable to meet their performance metric (usually quota attainment).

TIME FOR A CHANGE?

Senior executives are beginning to recognize, even in their own organizations, that sales force execution is their last remaining arrow in a quiver. However, knowing there is opportunity and understanding how to exploit it are two very different skills. Many executives are unsure as to how exactly to transform their sales organizations to attain the breakthrough results they believe possible. One reason is that CEOs do not typically rise through the sales ranks and, therefore, sales organizations largely remain a mystery to them. But there are better reasons than that for their reluctance, namely:

- Expensive rollouts of customer relationship management (CRM) or sales force automation (SFA) software that founder due to sales rep resistance, incompetence of internal information technology (IT) staff, or unreasonable expectations
- Unsuccessful large-scale sales training programs that are not connected to a business justification or do not generate demonstrable returns
- Premium third-party services engagements that do not produce savings or improve efficiency to offset the cost of the consultancy
- Past proposals to generate return through incremental improvement that have not presented sufficient opportunity to warrant a strategic focus

This is enough of a poor track record to discourage even the most steadfast executive. It is not surprising, therefore, that many CEOs have been cautious in demanding accountability of the sales leader in the same way as the other functional heads. The pass that sales executives have received from their CEOs is coming to an end.

Sales benchmarking can dramatically increase revenue growth and decrease the cost of sales. The combined benefit results in a measurable increase in earnings, which translates into an increase in shareholder value. Sales force execution is the next source of sustained competitive advantage and the process needed to realize that benefit is sales benchmarking.

NUMBERS DON'T LIE (OR DO THEY?)

Most of you are familiar with Mark Twain's saying, "There are lies, damn lies, and then statistics."

An article in the *Wall Street Journal* recently illustrated the erroneousness of a conventional wisdom that has led to the waste of millions of dollars by professional football teams. "Why the NFL Is Drafting Benchwarmers,"[5] the author noted that only 30 percent of all draft picks become starters in the league. Because each player drafted receives a contract, many with huge signing bonuses, most NFL teams, when selecting talent, most feel that a failure rate of 70 percent is acceptable. There have been instances where the number one draft pick—usually described as the world's best rookie—was a "bad hire." How can this happen?

The explanation of how this has come to be is an exercise in benchmarking gone wrong.

Pro football scouts draft players based on their performance at what is called the NFL Combine. This is an event where players who have made themselves eligible for the draft come to a stadium filled with talent evaluators from each team. The players are put through a series of exercises aimed at measuring their strength, speed, intelligence, and other attributes thought to be leading indicators of future star potential. Though this is a form of benchmarking, it is also an example of how it can be used incorrectly.

For instance, how much does it matter how fast a running back can run in a straight line for forty yards, without pads and with no one trying to tackle him? Is this an accurate measure of how many touchdowns a running back will score in the future? If a wide receiver can beat all other wide receivers in the vertical jump at the combine, does this mean he will catch more passes once in the league? As it turns out, it isn't.

Hall of Fame players such as Jerry Rice, Tom Brady, and Emmitt Smith were passed over by teams that had the opportunity to draft them because they scored poorly in a statistical category at the combine. In fact, these physical-performance categories have never been proven to be related to past performance in football and more importantly have no predictive ability to future success. In each instance, in NFL draft war rooms across the country, decision makers had video footage of each player performing in live competition in both high school and college, but they gave less weight to actual "production" results and made their decisions based largely on less relevant NFL Combine statistics.

Sales teams do something very similar.

Sales leaders find themselves frequently drafting "players" and making key decisions based on qualitative information such as unverified accomplishments touted on a résumé, an alleged Rolodex of contacts, personal charisma, the firmness of a handshake, and any number of other intangible factors. So how should the talent search process change if it is to transform an organization? First, sales leaders should begin making decisions based on prior production numbers. The equivalent of viewing a sales player's "videotape" is to assess their last several W-2 pay stubs. Since no one inflates their income to pay more taxes, a prospect's W-2 can be a very reliable piece of information, as already discussed in this book's Introduction. If a sales leader wants to evaluate objectively a prospective employee, this is a good way to start. There is much more that can and should be done to bring the discipline of sales benchmarking from an organizational to an individual level. Suffice to say for the moment that the act of enabling data-driven decision making in the pursuit of sales force execution will prevent a sales leader from making decisions based on guesswork or intuition.

THE TRICKLE-DOWN EFFECT

In most organizations, problems in perception start at the top and trickle down to the field sales force, causing a destructive ripple effect. CEOs try to figure out why sales growth isn't where they think it should be, but for the most part, they do not understand the root causes of sales success or failure. One source of their failure is that they compare current poor sales results to post ones. All of the focus on internal performance. Another mistake occurs when they try to learn about the challenges faced by the sales department requesting volumes of data, without really understanding their strategic relevance or the difficulty in obtaining them. Sometimes, they meet with a consultant, glean some ideas, besiege the vice president of sales with questions that a series of reporting mandates to the sales force. Such mandates require salespeople to provide information that largely and solely make senior leadership feel good. Following this flurry of unproductive activity, the sales executive implements a mandatory weekly status call and issues a meeting report.

GARBAGE DATA

This frenzied and nonsystematic approach actually undermines the purpose of collecting information in the first place; i.e., to aid in making informed decisions. For instance, how does a Friday afternoon call report detailing who salespeople met with, what they spoke about, and what the next action items are have to do with hitting this year's number? The answer is *very little*. How does an up-to-the-minute forecast report affect the outcome of a sale? It doesn't. Yet salespeople are asked to divert valuable selling time to activities that do not capture the reality of their account planning or aid in their ability to close deals. In some sales forces, it is more important to keep the boss informed of what is going on than it is to get contracts actually signed.

Frustrated with the poor quality and relevance of the data reported up the line, some CEOs ask for a greater quantity of data, hoping that somewhere buried in a mountain of sales statistics will be meaningful numbers to which the sales leader can be held accountable. The CEO's pressure for more and better sales information demands a level of sophistication and comfort with data for which the head of sales is rarely prepared. Companies often agree to invest in technology systems such as sales force automation or customer relationship management tools to solve this problem. They seek to automate the sales process as much as possible because the field sales reps complain about how much time reporting takes. The company spends millions of dollars purchasing such a system, weeks or months training the sales force on how to use it, and guess what happens? They automate a broken process and the system ultimately brings no value. The garbage-in, garbage-out problem still exists, but the only difference is that the garbage can now be viewed in nifty dashboards and in special colors. The problem remains unsolved and the cycle repeats itself.

In a last ditch effort before the vice president of sales loses his job, the "saviorlike" consultants are brought in. The so magical white knight salespeople-turned-sales-gurus are expected to "fix" the sales force productivity issue. The company spends large sums of money on learning tools and multiple in-person training sessions, yet the outcome is still the same—failure. Why? The consultants themselves do not implement data-driven decision making. They may have been very successful in prior careers and have entertaining "tribal knowledge," but they do not boast a systematic method to solve the most vexing sales problems.

Regardless, the company may enjoy a small increase in volume in a few isolated territories and raise the victory flag so that the head of sales is spared his job for another quarter or two. Then, when the numbers revert to poor form, the CEO adds up all the money wasted with little discernable return and realizes that no independently verifiable improvements were made and no new disciplines are in place; instead, the changes implemented were more "sales artistry." At this point, the CEO is left with two choices: accept responsibility and report to the board that he has no sales answers, or search for a scapegoat while initiating a search for a new vice president of sales. Which do you think he chooses? The result is another story of a well-intentioned sales leader who lost his job with no real understanding as to why it happened.

TO REVIEW

- The average sales leader responsible for a 100-person sales force will replace 38 sales professionals each year.
- Many sales organizations fail because of the old mind-set that there is a "golden secret" to sales that cannot be measured.
- Charisma and a strong work ethic are not enough. Hard work and discipline are important, but to be successful, you have to *work hard and work smart*. Sales benchmarkers combine hard work with intelligence to produce outstanding results.
- Quality and price are no longer at the forefront of competition. Sales force execution is one of the last remaining sources of competitive advantage.
- Salespeople are historically judged on intangible attributes, not specific key performance indicators. A salesperson's W-2 can be a very reliable piece of recruiting information.
- In some sales organizations, it is more important to keep the boss informed of what is going on than it is to actually get contracts signed.

CHAPTER 4

WHAT'S IN IT FOR THE SALES EXECUTIVE?

"A corporation's responsibility is to the shareholders, not its retirees
and employees."

—BEN STEIN, WRITER, ECONOMIST, ACTOR

The importance of benchmarking lies in its ability to increase profits and positively impact *each business function* within the organization. There is nothing different when it comes to sales.

The application of benchmarking to the sales function can be so transformative that it should be a matter of interest from the individual sales reps all the way up to the corporate boardroom. Sales benchmarking covers the full ground—it provides a strategy-centered technique to quantify results that help build shareholder wealth; it arms the CEO with a proven tool to help the company reach its numbers; it helps the vice president of sales hit targets quarter after quarter; and it enables sales reps to make more money. Everyone has something to gain by adopting sales benchmarking.

FEAR OF REPLACEMENT

Competition in the labor market encourages managers to perform in the best interest of shareholders. In the same fashion as with sales representatives, so too with sales managers—there is always a capable, motivated manager both outside and inside your organization who is able and willing to replace you. Such contenders, both those who reveal themselves and those "waiting in the wings," will make the case to your executives that only they have the ability to do more with less, generate higher returns on each sales dollar, achieve impossible revenue targets, open new markets, and so on. The reality of this job competition requires a sales executive, at a minimum, to consistently satisfy shareholders. More often than not, the bar has been raised to a point where managers feel the pressure to demonstrate that the sales force specifically has made vital contributions to corporate financial performance.

Those firms willing to pay sales talent the most will lure the best sales managers; these companies are also usually the ones that compensate managers based on value creation. Any sales executives, managers, or even quota-bearing representatives who desire to work for firms that pay in a way most closely tied to performance realize they must deliver results. In fact, such performance often has to come first to provide the justification for premium pay. But this is the type of challenge that motivates the best in the sales profession. They flock to the value creation companies and, conversely, they avoid the ones where sales contribution is minimized and relatively unrewarded. This is a point well known in the sales industry but often downplayed in the boardrooms, as it conflicts with a cost-cutting executive mentality. The fact is, though, that when companies stop rewarding superior performance with superior pay, they send out powerful marketplace signals as to what they want in their sales professionals and managers. They usually get it in spades.

WHY SHOULD THE BOARD AND THE SHAREHOLDERS CARE ABOUT SALES BENCHMARKING?

Shareholders determine the membership of the board of directors by voting. Thus, the shareholders control the directors, who in turn select the management team. Contracts with executive management and their compensation arrangements, such as stock options, are structured in such a way that management has an incentive to pursue shareholder goals.

If the price of a firm's stock drops too low because of poor management, the firm may be acquired by another group of shareholders, another firm, or even an individual. As a result of such a takeover, especially a hostile one, the top management members of the acquired firm may find themselves out of a job. This ever-present threat to job security puts added pressure on management to make decisions in the shareholders' best interest. Bottom line—this takeover fear provides managers the motivation they need to act in such a way as to maximize stock price.

A BRIEF REVIEW OF MARKING CAPITALIZATION

One of the most commonly used financial metrics to evaluate the value of stock is the profit-to-earning (P/E) ratio. Figure 1 shows the calculation for the P/E ratio as follows:

$$\text{P/E ratio} = \frac{\text{Price per Share}}{\text{Earnings per Share}}$$

By relating a stock's price per share (PPS) to its earnings per share (EPS), one can understand the value the market places on the stock relative to the wealth the company creates. The historical P/E ratio of the Standard & Poor's (S&P) 500 Index across all industry types is about 15. This means that the average stock trading for $15 per share has an EPS of $1. Assuming the P/E ratio of a stock represents "fair value" and remains relativity constant over time, an increase in EPS will increase PPS and vice versa.

Market capitalization (market cap) is the current stock price multiplied by the number of shares outstanding. In a situation where additional equity is not distributed, the number of shares outstanding remains constant. This means that an increase in share price drives an increase in market cap and a decrease in share price drives a decrease in market cap. In the above example, for instance, if the "average" S&P company was able to double its earnings from $1 to $2 and its P/E ratio remained at 15, its stock price would double to $30.

Assume in the above example that there are one million shares outstanding for this company. Thus, with a $15 share price, it would have a $15 million market cap. Doubling earnings to $2, which drives share price up to $30 per the P/E ratio formula, will raise the company's market cap to $30 million. The additional $15 million in shareholder wealth represents a 100 percent return on investment. Gains like this would satisfy even the most critical shareholder.

HOW DOES SALES BENCHMARKING IMPROVE SHAREHOLDER VALUE?

So what does this have to do with your best interest? No matter who you are in a public firm—salesperson, sales leader, CEO, CFO, or board member—shareholder value affects you. Shareholders control the firm and are focused on maximizing shareholder value. Therefore, a board of directors focused on sales performance should embrace sales benchmarking because it improves shareholder value.

How might sales benchmarking improve sales performance? For example, it may help determine that a firm is overspending on sales training because it relies on live, classroom-based sessions when a Web-based, on-demand curriculum would be more effective with costs lower than those of the relevant peer group. Or perhaps a firm is failing to leverage virtual sales calls and spending significantly above the benchmark for travel expenses related to unqualified calls. Or maybe the labor expenses for base pay are too high because the compensation plan is not sufficiently leveraged and the company is paying the 40 percent of the sales force that fails to hit its number and contributes only 20 percent of the total top line almost as much as the 60 percent who are successful and making 80 percent of the revenue contributions.

Conflicts between management and shareholders arise when corporations pursue managerial goals at the expense of shareholder goals. Sales benchmarking helps realign them again. As you will see below in the example of Consolidated Inc., the second largest expense on a company's financial statements is usually the category of selling general and administrative (SG&A). In this example, the sales component (the "S" of the SG&A expense item) is well over half of the total—a situation not out of normal. Data-driven decision making enabled through sales benchmarking allows the board of directors to determine if selling expenses are dedicated to increasing shareholder value. Many other examples of possible overspending in the sales department can be revealed through sales benchmarking. The key point is that significant opportunities will be revealed when you unleash the power of sales benchmarking and effectively apply its concepts.

CONSOLIDATED INC.—OUR FIRST EXAMPLE OF THE POWER OF SALES BENCHMARKING

Let's look at an example of the fictional company Consolidated Inc., to see the power of sales benchmarking.

First, let's review Tables 1 and 2, which are derived from Consolidated's most recent financial projections:

Table 1: Income Statement Projections		
Income Statement	**Amount (millions)**	**% of Revenue**
Revenue	$1,100	100
Cost of Revenue	$495	45
Operating Expenses	$539	49
SG&A	$440	40
Cost of Sales	$220	20
G&A Expense	$220	20
R&D	$99	9
Other Expenses	$11	1
Earnings	$55	5

Table 2: Financial Metric Projections	
Financial Metric	**Value**
Shares Outstanding	50 million
Share Price	$22
Earnings per Share (EPS)	$1.10
P/E Ratio	20
Market Cap	$1.10 billion

Additionally, we need to make the following assumptions about Consolidated:

- Revenue has been growing on average 10 percent annually over the past five years.
- Expenses have remained constant as a percentage of revenue.
- Its P/E ratio of 20 is consistent with similar companies, and market forces are unlikely to change it in the near future.

Based on these assumptions the data in and Tables 1 and 2, Consolidated will generate $1.1 billion in revenue during the next fiscal year, and will have earnings of $55 million, an EPS of $1.10, and a P/E multiple of 20. This will translate into a share price of $22 and a market cap of $1.1 billion. The historical average return for the S&P 500 is 10.4 percent—a rough benchmark for companies like Consolidated. Based on the projected numbers, however, Consolidated expects to enjoy a return of only 10.0 percent—already 0.4 percentage points behind average. And this is the return they hope to get if they hit their numbers!

This is where the sales-benchmarking discipline can be used to improve Consolidated's situation and improve shareholder satisfaction, even in the first year it is deployed.

REDUCTIONS IN COST OF SALES

Let us examine the financial metric known as *Cost of Sales,* which is defined as the percentage of revenue dedicated to sales expense. Table 1 shows Consolidated is projecting a 20 percent value for its cost of sales. We shall assume that Consolidated has selected a relevant peer group for its sales channel and sales force size and has used them to compute a world-class performance benchmark for this metric of 17.5 percent of revenue. (We will discuss the importance and derivation of world-class status in Chapter 12.) This means that Consolidated is overspending by 2.5 percent (20.0%–17.5%), which equates to $27.5 million per year (2.5% × 1.1 billion). Can anything be done to safely reduce the sales cost without significantly impacting top-line sales production? How can Consolidated know what performance area is weakest and what to do about it? The answer, as we shall see, is to perform a more granular benchmark.

Consider if, in the first year, Consolidated cuts back on those expense items that are least likely to impact negatively the top line. Using this low-risk, cherry-picking approach, Consolidated is able to reduce its cost of sales by $22 million, from 20 percent of top-line revenue to 18 percent. Since there is no impact on revenue, nearly all of the 2 percent savings (with the exception of some taxes) will fall directly to the bottom line. The result will be an earnings growth of nearly 7 percent rather than 5 percent.

Based on Consolidated's projected sales of $1.1 billion, this approach would generate a total of $77 million in earnings (as compared to the previous estimate of $55 million). With the same fifty million shares outstanding, EPS will now be $1.54 (up from $1.10). With a P/E ratio of 20, the stock will now be valued at $30.80 per share, driving market cap up to $1.54 billion. The result of this seemingly low-impact sales expense reduction effort is over $440 million in increased shareholder wealth ($1.54–$1.1 billion)! Tables 3 and 4 display the positive results of a *cost-of-sales*–driven approach.

This is worth repeating. *Through the P/E leverage, a $22 million savings in the area of sales produces a twenty-times return, generating $440 million in shareholder wealth.* This is too large an opportunity for a company like Consolidated to ignore.

Table 3: Updated Income Statement Projections Based on Cost-of-Sales Improvements				
Income Statement	Original Amount (millions)	Updated Amounts (millions)	Original % of Revenue	Updated % of Revenue
Revenue	$1,100		100	
Cost of Revenue	$495		45	
Operating Expenses	$539	$517	49	47
SG&A	$440	$418	40	38
Cost of Sales	$220	$198	20	18
G&A Expense	$220		20	
R&D	$99		9	
Other Expenses	$11		1	
Earnings	$55	$77	5	57

Table 4: Updated Financial Metrics Projections Based on Cost-of-Sales Improvements		
Financial Metric	Value	Updated Projection
Shares Outstanding	50 million	
Share Price	$22	$31
Earnings per Share (EPS)	$1.10	$1.54
P/E Ratio	20	
Market Cap	$1.10 billion	$1.54 billion

Below is a list of sales metrics against which companies can benchmark themselves to achieve top-line revenue improvements. By analyzing and then improving performance in these dimensions, companies can determine the extent of shareholder wealth that can be created. There are, in fact, many other sales metrics that can be measured and leveraged to achieve this effect; the ones below are provided for reference and because they have a track record of success in this type of effort.

- Sales productivity per sales rep
- Ramp time to full sales productivity
- Annual sales rep turnover rate
- Sales rep time allocation
- deal size
- Sales cycle length
- Deal closure percentage

PRODUCTIVITY IMPROVEMENTS

Assume, for example, that Consolidated is focused on growing top-line revenue, rather than reducing its cost of sales. In this case, Consolidated would implement benchmarks on productivity measures. Accordingly, Consolidated might institute a series of process-related, structural, and other improvements, all of which are identified with data-driven decision making. The result is that Consolidated accelerates growth in the coming year from the industry's historical 10 percent rate to one of 15 percent. Thus, Consolidated now revises its initial assumption of $1.1 billion in next-year revenue, to a new prediction of $1.15 billion in sales. With this increase in revenue growth above the industry average, the market rewards the company with a P/E multiple of 22 instead of 20. Assuming that the expenses stay at the percentages in the initial estimation, Consolidated now predicts $57.5 million in earnings for an EPS of $1.15. With a 22 P/E ratio, the stock now trades for $25.3 per share, raising the market cap to $1.265 billion. These top-line–focused changes net Consolidated $165 million in shareholder wealth. Tables 5 and 6 show the details of Consolidated's new projected balance sheet.

Table 5: Updated Income Statement Projections Based on Top-Line Improvements			
Income Statement	Amount (millions)	Updated Amounts (millions)	% of Revenue
Revenue	$1,100	$1,150.0	100
Cost of Revenue	$495	$517.5	45
Operating Expenses	$539	$563.5	49
SG&A	$440	$460.0	40
Cost of Sales	$220	$230.0	20
G&A Expense	$220	$230.0	20
R&D	$99	$103.5	9
Other Expenses	$11	$11.5	1
Earnings	$55	$57.5	5

Table 6: Updated Financial Metrics Projections Based on Top-Line Improvements		
Financial Metric	Projection	Updated Projection
Shares Outstanding	50,000,000	
Share Price	$22	$25.30
Earnings per Share (EPS)	$1.10	$1.15
P/E Ratio	20	22
Market Cap	$1.10 billion	$1.265 billion

REDUCTIONS IN COST OF SALES AND PRODUCTIVITY IMPROVEMENTS

Now, let's assume Consolidated uses benchmarking to reduce costs while at the same time accelerating revenue. The result of combining the two examples above is that Consolidated now plans on generating $1.15 billion in top-line sales but also, through cost cutting, achieving profitability of 7 percent. This translates into earnings of $80.5 million, or $1.61 on a per-share basis. With a P/E ratio of 22, the stock is now trading at $35.42, which translates to a market cap of $1.77 billion. Tables 7 and 8 show the marked improvements to Consolidated's projected balance sheet when simultaneously pursuing cost-cutting and revenue-enhancement opportunities.

Table 7: Final Updated Income Statement Projections			
Income Statement	Original Amount (millions)	Final Amount (millions)	Final % of Revenue
Revenue	$1,100	$1,150.0	100
Cost of Revenue	$495	$517.5	45
Operating Expenses	$539	$540.5	47
SG&A	$440	$437.0	38
Cost of Sales	$220	$207.0	18
G&A Expense	$220	$230.0	20
R&D	$99	$103.5	9
Other Expenses	$11	$11.5	1
Earnings	$55	$80.5	7

Table 8: Final Financial Metrics Projections		
Financial Metric	Initial Projected Value	Final Projected Value
Shares Outstanding	50,000,000	[no change]
Share Price	$22	$35.42
Earnings per Share (EPS)	$1.10	$1.61
P/E Ratio	20	22
Market Cap	$1.10 billion	$1.77 billion

CONCLUSION FOR CONSOLIDATED

Consolidated's improvements have created $670 million in shareholder wealth ($1.77–1.10 billion). Investors will be delighted to see that the share price at the end of this fiscal year is worth $13 more than initially anticipated—an increase of 77 percent! Such twelve-month growth in share price will put the company squarely in the eyes of the media. A few times a week, the firm will be profiled on the Internet, TV, talk shows, newspapers, and trade magazines. Because of the free press being generated and demand for the company's products and services increasing, subsequent fiscal years will look even brighter. The board and management team celebrate, thanks in large part to the early adoption of sales benchmarking.

WHY SHOULD A CEO EMPLOY SALES BENCHMARKING?

Jim Collins, author of the bestselling books *Built to Last* and *Good to Great*, is a world-class practitioner of benchmarking. In his book *Good to Great: Why Some Companies Make the Leap . . . and Others Don't*, he used benchmarking to sift through mountains of data to present a case for how mediocre companies can achieve enduring greatness.[1] In his study, Collins explained the key determinants of such "greatness." The most important determining factor, according to Collins, is that "great" companies are led by *Level 5 Leaders.*

Using Collins's definition of organizational success—Level 5 Leadership—as a guide, let's analyze how sales benchmarking can help the CEO at each level of leadership. Such an approach can help a CEO as well as the chief sales officer determine at what leadership level he or she is operating and how benchmarking can support personal improvement.

Level 1: The Highly Capable Individual—Makes productive contributions through talent, knowledge, skills, and good work habits.

Most CEOs did not rise through the sales function. As a result, they don't really understand sales. A recent Sales Benchmark Index study found that only 7 percent of Fortune 500 CEOs spent all or a portion of their career in the sales function, which explains why many struggle to apply analysis, problem-solving, and decision-making skills to the sales department. This is one reason why sales force execution remains a largely unrecognized aspect of competitive differentiation for many companies despite the fact that it can dramatically increase performance. Further, with sales benchmarking, CEOs can accelerate their knowledge of the sales department's capabilities. By applying data-driven decision making to the sales force, a CEO can quickly get to the root cause of any potential issue or opportunity, thus being able to impact the sales function instead of being an isolated and uninformed outsider. Sales benchmarking increases a CEO's Level 1 effectiveness by increasing his or her knowledge of sales force management, principles, issues, and deficiencies—all without the need for formal training. This is particularly valuable for the 93 percent of the CEOs who come to the position without formal experience in a sales role.

Level 2: Contributing Team Member—Contributes and Works effectively in a group setting.

Much like CEOs, however other functional leaders—key members of the leadership team from finance, operations, HR, legal, manufacturing, IT, and others—also often have no experience in sales. This lack of knowledge and experience from the executive team prevents many members from contributing to the overall effort of growing revenue. Sales benchmarking provides the CEO with a tool to educate other leaders in the organization in a language that everyone can understand—numbers. With sales benchmarking, the CEO is better equipped to more clearly frame the goals for the other functional leaders as they relate to sales growth. The CEO is empowered with the use of benchmarking because he or she is in a position to educate the other departments on the issues facing the sales force.

Level 3: Component Manager—Organizes people and resources toward the effective and efficient pursuit of predetermined goals.

The leaders of the other business functions within an organization all want to help the company grow revenue, yet they typically do not understand how they can make a contribution to the sales department. Often, they are unsure as to the best way to provide support without being intrusive, and some cannot help but be intimidated by the sales leader, who can be a commanding presence. As a result, vital collaboration between departments does not occur and both the sales force and its companion departments suffer, all for the lack of a common modeling language for performance. Benchmarking can provide much of this missing lingua franca. As a common data-based parlance, the language of benchmarking is one that everyone can understand. When reduced to and expressed in certain performance metrics, especially those that have cross-departmental implications, it is much easier to determine how assistance can be rendered from the nonsales business functions. Thus, when a CEO is armed with an objective analysis of the sales department, he can better direct other parts of the company on exactly how to enable the sales force to grow new sources of revenue.

Level 4: Effective Leader—Catalyzes commitment to and vigorous pursuit of a clear and compelling vision, stimulating higher performance standards.

CEOs often struggle to create a vision that each and every employee can support, let alone one about which they can become passionate. Typically, a missing element in selling this vision is the ability to explain to employees their role in executing the vision. Salespeople and sales leaders are often the biggest resisters. They frequently translate such vision statements into wall posters not worthy of adherence or even serious consideration. A sales force that is not thoroughly supportive of the corporate vision will flounder, particularly because the sales staff is the key liaison between the corporation and its customers. Sales benchmarking allows CEOs to explain to a sales force its specific role in bringing the corporate vision to life. It gives the CEO the chance to convince the sales force why the vision is viable, and calculates the payoff for the sales department if they are able to successfully execute it.

Level 5: Executive—Builds enduring greatness through a paradoxical blend of personal humility and professional will.

Sustained corporate success is difficult enough for the CEO to achieve because sales execution (i.e., increased revenue) is based partly on the richness of personal client relationships, which are largely owned by the sales force. Even worse, when a salesperson leaves a company, he takes these relationships with him. Because turnover in the sales force is 40 percent per year, CEOs can be forgiven for their concern. Sales benchmarking transforms the sales department's capabilities from tribal knowledge to a bastion of intellectual property embedded in company systems. This reservoir of data—both historical and comparative—forms the basis for a new sales culture and more predictable sales behavior patterns. Level 5 leaders posses "personal humility and professional will," according to Collins. Yet haven't we all encountered CEOs who feel that sales force execution is beneath them? This is an important distinction, given the vital role the sales force plays in the corporate bottom line. Level 5 leaders are able to check their egos and utilize sales benchmarking as a source of sustained competitive advantage.

WHY SHOULD THE VICE PRESIDENT OF SALES TRY SALES BENCHMARKING?

The vice president of sales has a complex job with an average tenure of only nineteen months. In this type of environment, what can sales leaders do to enhance their chances of survival?

Sales leaders either hit their numbers or miss them. This black-and-white aspect of the job allows for a very clear understanding of performance during the annual review cycle. When the sales leader hits his numbers consistently, one of three things happens: He gets promoted to CEO, gets poached by a competitor for more money, or retires because he has made enough money to satisfy even the most ambitious of appetites. Top sales leaders are savvy and smart enough not to remain idle. When they miss their numbers consistently or by a large margin, one of two things happens rather quickly: The sales leader begins to seek a sales position in another company or he gets fired. Again, the sales leader is not idle.

THE FIVE OUTCOMES FOR EVERY SALES EXECUTIVE

If you are a sales leader, therefore, you have *five possible outcomes* available to you in the coming years:

1. Get promoted to CEO
2. Get recruited to a different organization for more money
3. Retire
4. Sell yourself into a similar job
5. Get fired

Let's look at how proficiency in sales-benchmarking positions you for these five eventualities.

OUTCOME #1: PROMOTED TO CEO

If this is your desired outcome and you are coming up through the sales ranks, you have your work cut out for you. Historically, boards of directors have not looked favorably upon former sales leaders as CEOs. The marketplace stereotype that sales leaders are temperamentally, experientially, and organizationally unqualified for the CEO role will hamper your efforts. Your ability to convince the board that you have what it takes to lead the entire organization must address and overcome this resistance. To even gain active consideration for an open CEO slot, a sales leader would need to be able to answer the following questions:[2]

- *What do you like or dislike about your current position?* The board is looking for skills you will transfer from your current position as sales leader to a new one as chief of all the other business functions. To answer this question successfully, you must talk about why your current job is interesting, what specific aspects you find stimulating, and what you wish you could be doing in addition to your current responsibilities. You will need to deliver specific examples that the board will remember without difficulty. For instance, explain that you enjoyed taking inherited sales force effectiveness (i.e., tactical execution measured in sales as a percentage of a quota goal) to a high-performing business function (i.e., one measured in overall market share gains from one year to the next). A rich discussion of how being 120 percent of quota was great, but what was even more rewarding was going from 10 percent of the market to 13 percent of the market will go a long way toward alleviating board fears that a sales leader cannot transcend the sales-centric perspective of the business to more strategic issues. Looking at the big picture is something the sales leader should actually be able to do even better than his or her peer group based on an understanding of the competition, customers, and the marketplace. It is just that the average sales leader does not usually get the opportunity to put those skills on display.

- *What are the most challenging aspects of your current position and how did you approach them?* Resist the temptation to discuss a long list of complaints; instead focus on how you both made and saved your company money. Sales benchmarking provides the numbers behind your case for the top spot. It will be compelling to demonstrate that you reduced selling expenses from 30 percent to 28 percent of revenue, drove new account business 28 percent higher year over year, or captured competitor market share due to sales force expertise. Speaking to board members in the language of verifiable data will help bolster your case. Further, your ability to demonstrate that sales performance was favorable vis-à-vis a relevant peer group will add the credibility necessary to your claim of future excellence.

OUTCOME #2: RECRUITED TO A DIFFERENT ORGANIZATION FOR MORE MONEY

If it appears you have stagnated where you are and the road to the CEO spot is not available to you, you will need to make yourself attractive to the open marketplace. The job market is filled with impostors—sales leaders who have great résumés but inconvincing proof of accomplishment. Sales benchmarking will demonstrate your track record and separate you from a crowded field. Your willingness to subject yourself to outside comparison will increase the confidence of a potential new employer who will see you are not only comfortable with but also desirous of inspection. In all likelihood, the hiring executives at another company will be somewhat surprised to select a sales leader who accepts industry-standard sales metric definitions, adopts leading (not lagging) indicators of accomplishment, and rejects the notion that selling is an art.

OUTCOME #3: RETIRE

Simply put, sales benchmarking will ignite your sales performance, so much so, in fact, that it will energize your entire retirement schedule. Compensation plans for sales leaders are a blend of base pay and a commission/bonus system, the latter of which is usually relatively unrealized. Typically, this variable pay component is based on a flat fee and some sort of accelerator that kicks in following performance in excess of quota. The real money—retirement money—is made when a sales professional has reached these accelerators, well over goal. That is where sales benchmarking will make its mark and influence your retirement expectations. If practiced with consistency and excellence, sales benchmarking will put you into accelerators *every year.* Therefore, it will take years off your savings calendar, getting you to retirement much more quickly, if that is your objective.

OUTCOME #4: SELL YOURSELF INTO A SIMILAR JOB

Missing your numbers, especially when it is clear that the miss is not an anomaly, is a difficult fact to overcome, even for veteran salespeople. Benchmarkers avoid this unpleasant scenario, particularly due to their focus on leading indicators and the knowledge of what relevant sales force peers are doing. Others who have not yet adopted benchmarking can still turn to sales benchmarking to provide a plausible answer to the facts of below-quota performance. Benchmarking can help in two ways. First, it can demonstrate that, possibly, expectations were placed too highly on your sales force as the peer group might very well not have performed any better. Without the external data and a willingness to collect and compare your own organization, there is no way to determine if the chances for your success were slim from the start. Second, you can use sales-benchmarking data to underscore any number of successes in the various sales processes, some of which may have produced verifiable, quantifiable successes. These successes may yet yield some change in the revenue picture, though the link may be tenuous. In any case, if you do not have the external comparison data, you will not be able to defend your tenure at all.

OUTCOME #5: GET FIRED

This is a result that no one wants, including the employer, even though it happens with alarming frequency in the sales profession. Sales benchmarking is the best insurance policy for the vice president of sales. As discussed previously, the marketplace is filled with sales leaders running their sales forces on gut instinct. With sales benchmarking, you run your sales force with data-driven decision making. Your team will thrive and outperform the competition *every day*. Still, corporate politics, mergers, acquisitions, and market-related collapses can all lead to the loss of position, even for a dedicated sales benchmarker. So what to do? Once you get to the level of vice president, the supply-and-demand imbalance exerts its powerful effect. There are a limited number of available executive positions and a continuous surfeit of job seekers to fill them. There are hosts of mediocrities who clutter the sales talent selection process. However, there remain for any one sales executive position usually a host of relatively well-qualified candidates anxious to present their bona fides. In some cases, it may come down to two well-balanced résumés—yours and the other person's. Sales benchmarking can be the coin that tilts the scale to your side. Use the discipline of sales benchmarking to differentiate yourself in the talent race just as you do to enable your sales force to win in its marketplace.

RECAP

These five different "career options" represent the real options for most vice president level sales positions. Many years will pass before a significant number of executives are promoted to CEO who also possess some sales experience. Until that time, the hire-fire dynamic described above will hold sway.

But in the interim, it is showtime!

Sales benchmarking is a tool designed for today's battlefield. Strive to understand it first, practice it second, and perfect it eventually. In the process, you will best your competition, increase your personal net worth, and intelligently engage senior executives. You will be far ahead of the game as the first executive team sales player who can also address boardroom-level issues.

TO REVIEW

- Sales benchmarking increases profits and positively impacts every role in an organization.

- Significant executive opportunities exist if you understand the power of benchmarking and can effectively apply the concept.
- Benchmarking can be used to drive top-line revenue by analyzing metrics such as sales productivity per sales rep, ramp time to full sales Productivity, annual sales rep turnover tate, sales rep time allocation, deal size, length of sales cycle, percentage of prospects, or deal close rate.
- The second-largest expense on a company's financial statements is SG&A. Data-driven decision making enabled through sales benchmarking allows the board of directors to determine if selling expenses are ultimately creating or destroying shareholder value.
- Use of sales benchmarking enables CEOs to accelerate their knowledge of the sales department's capabilities, quickly getting to the root cause of any potential issue or opportunity.
- Sales benchmarking arms the vice president of sales with the language required to compete and speak intelligently to senior executives about key issues.

CHAPTER 5

WHAT'S IN IT FOR THE SALES PROFESSIONAL?

"He who refuses to embrace a unique opportunity loses the prize as surely as if he had failed."

—WILLIAM JAMES, AUTHOR, PHILOSOPHER, PSYCHOLOGIST

A MACRO LOOK AT THE NUMBERS OF SALES PROFESSIONALS

What do AFLAC, AT&T, Schering Plough, PepsiCo, and Microsoft all have in common? The answer isn't obvious. An insurance company, telecommunications provider, drug maker, beverage company, and technology giant would seem to be very different, at first glance. However, each of these companies employs over 10,000 salespeople. In fact, there are an estimated 20 million people in the United States who claim "sales professional" as their primary occupation.[1] This represents 6.6 percent of the United States' total 300 million population, according to the U.S. Census Bureau. Salespeople from the manufacturing industry drive $3.2 trillion in revenue, and 615,000 salespeople from the services sector contribute close to $2.2 trillion in annual revenue.[2] Clearly, the role of sales professional is an important one with strong demand trends in which quality is recognized and rewarded.

Just because there are a lot of people in the sales profession, why would any of them be interested in sales benchmarking? The answer to this question lies in demographics.

THE COMING SALES-RELATED LABOR SHORTAGE

A projected shortage of skilled salespeople will eventually tilt the supply-and-demand balance in favor of the rare top sales producer. Due to an aging population, the U.S. Bureau of Labor Statistics projects that, by the year 2010, there will be a shortage of over ten million workers. Assuming that the percentage of workers in the sales profession remains at the current 6.6 percent, this implies there will be a shortage of some 660,000 salespeople in just a few years. This shortage represents raw numbers and does not take into account the skills gap—a gap caused by the fact that the retiring sales professionals are those with the greatest subject matter expertise, longest careers, and the deepest skill set. When this gap is considered the supply shortage is more acute for those industries where quality is just as important as quantity.

Few salespeople have begun to leverage this employer predicament. Consequently, those reps who prepare for this new hiring environment will achieve a brighter future. Those who ignore the coming crunch will end up mismanaging one of the most important trends impacting their career. They may very well find themselves settling for employment with companies that invest little in recruiting, training, and, most importantly, premium compensation.

Employers today are worried, as they always have been, about the economy, customer retention, marketplace dynamics, competitive threats, and a host of other strategic considerations. Many healthy companies, like the ones listed at the beginning of this section, will face risk due to the coming sales-related labor shortage. This creates an opportunity for salespeople to reposition themselves as top producers—through the use of sales benchmarking—to take advantage of the opportunity as it materializes over the coming decade.

This book is meant to be a wake-up call for just such salespeople.

The concepts presented here are vital for those sales professionals who feel a keen sense of responsibility for managing their future success. Until this point, most salespeople have not even considered evaluating their performance objectively against peer groups. One cannot entirely fault them, as the techniques, infrastructure, support, and track record of others doing this have not previously been widely known. This shroud of ignorance is lifting as sales benchmarking concepts are gradually gaining mind share. Failure to leverage the discipline of sales benchmarking will consign a generation of sales professionals to a spectator role in the drama of their own careers.

TAKING ADVANTAGE OF THE LABOR SHORTAGE

How does competency in sales benchmarking enable a salesperson to take advantage of this shortage when it comes? Many salespeople have become used to a corporate support infrastructure that has enabled them to take much for granted. Organizations provide sales support resources in myriad ways—office assistants, product collateral, sales support staff, marketing departments, presales engineers, sales administrative staff, sales technicians, sales automation tools, and other techniques. Taken together, these resources help the individual sales professional achieve success. With such a generous level of support, many salespeople, especially those who work in the larger companies, have not felt the need to assess themselves nor take into account the larger macroeconomic factors that bear on their profession. But the leading companies of the future, the ones that will create the best opportunities for salespeople, will be different.[3] Such companies are likely to be more decentralized in nature than current corporate behemoths; they will provide no-frills environments, stripped of many of these support perks.

HOW DOES SALES BENCHMARKING HELP INDIVIDUAL SALES REPRESENTATIVES?

Data-driven decision making allows salespeople to transform themselves in preparation for the future. As a quota-bearing salesperson, waiting for others to make decisions is a strategy for failure in the fast-paced business environment of the twenty-first century. In a corporate world now influenced by Google, eBay, and Yahoo, as opposed to one previously dominated by AT&T, IBM, and GE, it will be very important for salespeople to know exactly how they rank against peer groups and how their skills match market demands. Techniques like benchmarking, thought previously to be the sole province of corporate number crunchers, are really tools of use to the individual as well.

Sales benchmarking allows salespeople to better manage their most precious resource—time. It allows salespeople to focus on those opportunities with the highest probability of success. Data-driven decision making enables sales reps to eliminate nonvalue-adding activities that consume selling time. Furthermore, it can assist individuals in making more informed decisions about which types of companies and for what kind of sales leadership to work. Overall, benchmarking in the sales profession allows the salesperson to put some truth in the slogan,

"Work smart as well as hard," with "smart" now providing leading indicators of potential future success.

SALES BENCHMARKING AND ADVANCEMENT

Opportunities for advancement and achievement in the sales profession will be plentiful in the future, but they will be different in nature and in kind from the ones we have today. Salespeople who make the time to take multiple looks at their role, who are comfortable with change, and who express self-confidence about the decisive advantage sales plays will be well positioned to exploit these future opportunities. Salespeople of the future should be willing to step away from the crowd, understand the facts of future sales situations, and act accordingly. This is where the focus of sales benchmarking for the individual can be found.

Benchmarking at the sales rep level has some advantages. Individuals can cut through the daily clutter better than corporations. With technology available at the fingertip through Web services, Internet portals, and SaaS offerings, sales benchmarking is now affordable—particularly for the individual sales rep. Even when working for a company or a boss who does not recognize the value of benchmarking, there is still fertile ground for the salesperson to benchmark. As individual sales representatives gain confidence in and demonstrate mastery of their sales benchmarking skills, the ability to document performance versus a peer group will yield increases in personal pay. Benchmarking is a skill too valuable to outsource or ignore, at least not for those interested in success.

The coming shortage of workers, combined with the mastering of sales benchmarking, will enable the individual salesperson to differentiate his or her skills. One by one, employers will become aware of the reality that sales force execution can be a source of sustained competitive advantage. When this happens, they will make it a priority to distinguish between average and above-average salespeople. They will vote with their dollars by paying more for *verified* exceptional performance. Sales benchmarking provides just such a measuring stick. Other sales professionals, however, will remain mired in their current comfort zone and miss this opportunity. Pay-for-performance will be the default approach; indeed, it has already begun to transform the sales compensation industry. A small measure of how far this trend has come is the personal pay calculator found at www.salary.com. What started out as a tool for individuals to benchmark their pay compared to a relevant peer group (established by location and profession) has now begun replacing compensation consultants inside corporate America.

SALES BENCHMARKING FOR THE INDIVIDUAL AT THE CORPORATE LEVEL

The benefits of working for a large corporation are diminishing, as are the opportunities. In the past, it was generally easier to sell for a large company than to work for yourself or for a smaller firm. Yet working for yourself or a smaller firm oftentimes produces a greater return. Over time, working for a large corporation will increasingly take on the attributes of a start-up, but without the upside. To become leaner, such companies are requiring employees to assume added responsibilities, even as they reduce support resources. And when market conditions dictate that these companies lay off employees to conserve cost, those who remain will find themselves saddled with more responsibility for customer care, administrative minutiae, and seemingly endless demands for management status updates—but without appreciable improvement in compensation.

A salesperson skilled in benchmarking will be better prepared to succeed inside larger firms, if that is the type of organization for which they chose to work. Additionally, sales benchmarking can reduce the risk of accepting a position with a smaller firm that promises a greater upside—a risk-reward calculation that is difficult to make without the aid of prior benchmarking. Data-driven decision making at the rep level can replace support previously received from headquarters. For instance, individuals can free themselves from over-dependence on the marketing department for leads, tools, or competitive information. Benchmarkers demonstrate a degree of self-sufficiency unique in the marketplace.

A SPECIFIC EXAMPLE OF BENCHMARKING FOR THE INDIVIDUAL SALES REP

Here is how a fictional salesperson, Jane Doe, can use sales benchmarking to improve personal productivity using the Sales Benchmark Index Formula for Sales Success. To begin, Jane needs to apply the model to her individual professional situation. To do this, the following four questions have to be asked and answered:

1. What is her Annual Sales Projection?
2. Is she on track to meet her quota?

3. How do her metrics compare to her peers?
4. On which inputs should she focus going forward?

To answer the first question, Jane checks and determines that, based on her current performance, the input values needed to calculate her Annual Sales Projection are:

- Outbound activity: *Ten calls/day*
- Close rate: *5% close/call*
- Deal size: *$8,000/close*

Using the formula's calculation, Jane's *Annual Sales Projection* should be $960,000, calculated as follows:

To answer the second question, "Is she on track with her quota?," we first need to know how big a bag Jane is carrying. Jane has a $1 million quota so, with $960,000 in projected sales, she is already $40,000 off pace. And she hasn't even started making sales calls yet. How can Jane close the gap?

Jane could increase the *Outbound Activity, Close Rate, Deal Size,* or some combination of all these three inputs. Below is a representation of what happens when each variable is impacted.

Increase Outbound Activity. Look what happens when Jane adds just one more call per day (from ten to eleven) to her task list. That change alone gets her over quota by $60,000.

Increase Close Rate. Look what happens when Jane uses a slightly higher close rate (5.5 percent vs. 5.0 percent). This change also gets her over quota by $60,000.

Increase Deal Size. Look what happens when Jane ups the average deal size by about 12 percent (from $8,000 to $9,000). That change gets her over quota by the most—$80,000.

Increase All Three. Look what happens when Jane assumes the trifecta of improvement—outbound (call) activity, close rate, and deal size. Taken together, these changes would probably get her into accelerators, as they put her $300,000 over goal.

As can be seen from each scenario, being able to optimize time across multiple dimensions is critical. In each case, Jane is able to see how making one change or another gets her closer to her goal.

With the data in hand from exploring the scenarios to close the gap, it is now time for Jane to answer the third question, "how do her metrics compare to her peers?" Jane should start by doing some internal comparison, asking those working within her organization what their outbound activity, close rate and deal size are. She should explore how a peer is performing better in a given area. Sharing best practices, even in a nonsystematic fashion, can really boost sales performance. Once Jane obtains this internal sample set, she should begin looking outside the organization for comparison. One way to do this is to contact her internal sales operations group and ask for their support in obtaining relevant data. Or Jane might network through formal sales associations like Sales & Marketing Executives International (SMEI) or participate in any number of Internet-based affiliate groups focused on the sales profession. Once this external data is in hand, Jane can go through another round of comparison and also collect more best practices on how to close the gap.

With all of that accomplished, Jane now faces the fourth and final question, "On which input(s) should she focus going forward?" Based on the scenarios Jane ran, she knows what needs to be done to close the gap to quota. Based on speaking with peers or reaching out to gather external data, she knows how her data stacks up against others. Now it is time for Jane to reflect on all the data gathered to determine which inputs to focus on—outbound activity, close rate, and deal size—and what actions she needs to take to improve her success rates. The variables selected should be a combination of ones that will help her over-achieve quota, but also should be ones for which the effort she will expend in making improvements will be met with the biggest relative impact on her annual sales projection.

WRAP-UP

In summary, sales benchmarking deployed at the sales rep level allows individuals to better allocate their time, focus selling activities on the best opportunities, select the best companies for which to work, self-assess skills areas and improve on weaknesses, provide insight quickly on customer buying cycles, make decisions based on actual market performance rather than on generalizations, and test ideas with instant feedback. These types of skills will be in high demand in the future and will ultimately result in greater income for the salespeople who utilize them.

Through this, you can gain an in-depth understanding of sales benchmarking as it applies to the overall organization, as well as the specific roles within it. Remember, benchmarking is not new. It has been used and applied for years in other business functions. But it is new to sales, and you can be a pioneer, setting your team up for success, if you take the time to understand this powerful discipline.

TO REVIEW

- The U.S. Bureau of Labor Statistics forecasts a shortage of some 660,000 salespeople in just a few years.
- Sales benchmarking will position salespeople to take advantage of this shortage by focusing their energies on those opportunities with the highest probability of success.
- Sales benchmarking is not just for the executives and the sales leader; sales

representatives can use the skills and techniques of sales benchmarking to advance their careers.

- Sales representatives are encourage to apply macro formulas, such as the Sales Benchmark Index Formula for Sales Success™, to their own territories and circumstances.

CHAPTER 6

WHAT IS BUSINESS BENCHMARKING?

"All successful companies are constantly benchmarking their competition. They have to know what they have to match up with day-in and day-out if their company is going to be successful."

—JAMES DUNN, CHIEF INVESTMENT OFFICER
AND BUSINESS WRITER

BENCHMARKING FOR OTHER BUSINESS FUNCTIONS

Benchmarking is one of the most universally effective management disciplines available in business today. It has demonstrated an ability to consistently produce quantum performance improvements in the functional areas where it has been adopted—finance, manufacturing, human resources, supply chain management, warehouse management, distribution, and so on.[1] What is of further significance is that benchmarking has registered these positive results regardless of an organization's size, industry, business model, or location; in other words, its application requires no order-of-magnitude scale or any other precondition to achieve its impact. Benchmarking is a truly democratic approach to corporate self-improvement—it works for everyone. Having said that, benchmarking is not for the faint of heart. It is often tempting to say, "We are so unique that no comparison is valid," or "They are different from us that any attempt at learning from them would be a waste of time." These variations on the "not in my backyard" excuse can damage, even completely derail, a promising benchmarking initiative.

Despite these notes of caution, the universal appeal of benchmarking has sped adoption and implementation across most corporate business functions. In fact, it has spread so far and fast that a whole cottage industry has arisen to support, advance, and enable benchmarking. Just a few of these organizations include the following:

- American Productivity & Quality Center—www.apqc.org
- Recruitment Industry Benchmarking—www.ribindex.com
- The Benchmarking Network, Inc.—www.benchmarkingnetwork.com
- Global Benchmarking Network—www.globalbenchmarking.org
- International Government Benchmarking Association™—www.igba.org

WHY IS BENCHMARKING SO POPULAR?

Benchmarking is a powerful change-management tool because it challenges thinking and extends performance indicators beyond the insular environment that exists inside the organization. It helps overcome organizational resistance to improvement as it drains the argument for change of much of its emotional content and makes it more difficult for change resisters to defeat initiatives because there is no historical track record internally to support such an effort. Further, benchmarking clearly indicates where current practice falls short of best practice, not to mention world-class practice.

Benchmarking may be a single exercise or it may be an ongoing practice. The latter approach yields the most value, as a continuous process enables organizations to challenge practices that may be sufficient one day but stale the next. For those organizations who adopt best practices benchmarking, the end game is to transcend the competition.

WHAT DOES BENCHMARKING DELIVER?

Benchmarking is not a panacea; it will not correct a flawed business model nor will it force an organization to make the necessary changes—that is the job of the leader. It does, however, serve up a wealth of positive possibilities. The following are just some of the reasonable expectations you should have for a successful benchmarking effort:

- Awaken competitive drive by providing a clear vision of what is attainable
- Disclose and display the hidden links between process and result
- Stimulate an objective review of practices, systems, and metrics
- Raise questions and challenge business methods that merit greater scrutiny
- Provide evidence to support business cases for change
- Provide a means to help overcome barriers to change adoption

BENCHMARKING WORKS—BUT WHY?

We have discussed the promise and popularity of benchmarking. Indeed, the realization of its promise and the reason for its popularity lie in one key aspect of benchmarking—it works. So many corporate strategic change initiatives sound enticing and often come with expectations of major impact to the balance sheet. Somewhere, somehow, though, the effort fatigues and the results are not obtained. In these cases the sponsoring executive develops some selective amnesia and the project is quietly buried, if possible, given the increased scrutiny of shareholders, and all parties move on to the next *big thing*. Not so with benchmarking. Benchmarking initiatives do not create dashed hopes and ruined careers. They merely deliver results—usually in a low-key, almost surreptitious fashion. But why is this so? Below is a list of some of these reasons why benchmarking works, no matter what business function is using it to drive superior performance:

- *Unbiased and Viable Context.* Benchmarking produces objective findings that uncover the reasons why some organizations succeed while others fail at the same task. Benchmarking results are used objectively to identify, quantify, and prioritize improvement opportunities while also highlighting areas of risk. Benchmarking findings serve as the unbiased support for creating business strategies that drive effective change. There are many aspects of what businesses do that are similar enough to merit comparison. The "we are so unique" argument is not supportable given the high degree of commonality of process, approach, and technique within each business function.

- *Effective Emulation.* With thousands of companies attempting to address similar problems, innovative practices are oftentimes found by looking outside an organization or even outside the industry for proven, new ideas. This tendency to look far and wide for best practices due to common process or function but not common industry is a well-established practice. If you want to emulate the best supply chain go to Wal-Mart; if you want to emulate the best made-to-order process, study Dell; if you want to emulate the best direct business-to-business sales force, copy EMC. And so on. In the end, it does not matter much what industry in which you compete, if you have a function shared by other companies, find the best in the business in that function and start comparing. Thus, benchmarking opens the avenue to identify and locate the most effective and applicable practices, regardless of their source.

- *Data-driven Decisions.* Companies are driven by the need to grow revenue, shorten business cycles, improve quality, and contain costs. Consequently, they cannot afford to expend effort and resources on activities that do not yield demonstrable value, as evidenced by increased revenue, improved products/services, and more efficient processes or cost savings. Oftentimes, improvement initiatives, especially those directed at the sales department, are light on the financial details and lack convincing business justification. Benchmarking, at its core a data-oriented quantitative discipline, leapfrogs over these other, more qualitative approaches. It provides executives with the ability to make decisions based on a flow of high-quality empirical data, enabling more proactive and defensible approaches to the board. This data-rich decision-making environment may seem a luxury to sales leaders in the current environment, but it is a reality well within reach.

- *Risk Mitigation.* Benchmarking gives management the assurance it needs to focus on action that drives substantial change with the reasonable expectation that results will be achieved. Why is the risk premium so low? Because the benchmarking discipline has a long pedigree and a substantive footprint. It can be cited, leveraged, and deployed with the knowledge that its techniques will work. No matter the field some other organization or business function has already used benchmarking to unearth opportunity and then drive performance improvement. With this experience as a backdrop, corporate auditors usually assess a benchmarking project as low risk compared to the alternatives.

- *Future Focus.* Benchmarking has a relatively unique focus on the future in its prognostication. It uses leading indicators to help point the way to expected future performance, even when change is not yet adopted. This represents a break with typical past practices, which focus on lagging indicators and straight-line projections. The ability to be reliably predictive helps underscore benchmarking's inherent veracity.

- *Compatibility with BSM.* As discussed previously, business leaders face increasing global demands and more vigorous competition. Part of the mantra to cope with this new dynamic is that organizations should seize growth and improvement opportunities wherever they exist. A recent development along these lines has been the emergence of business service management (BSM), a strategy for linking key internal service components (e.g., IT, human resources, legal) to the goals of the business. It enables organizations to understand and predict how changes in these service components will impact the business. Those who have adopted BSM have aligned their internal support infrastructure to such an extent that the business functions as an integrated whole. BSM requires a process-centric view of the organization so that each service component can be assessed cross-functionally. Benchmarking fits this strategy like a hand in glove, as it too enables organizations to compare one internal process to another and therefore lead the way to improved productivity, profitability, and competitive positioning for an individual business function.

- *Growth Opportunity Identification.* Executives are starving for good ideas. They might hear a tidbit here and another there from consultants, colleagues, and staff. What they lack, though, is a comprehensive means to expose all the possibilities and establish a framework within which to view them. Benchmarking provides this. In the existing hyper-charged globalized business environment, executives are demanding that each functional discipline come to the table with a whole raft of ideas, not just a fait accompli project as the only way to achieve success. Above all, benchmarking yields a wealth of options.

CHARACTERISTICS OF ORGANIZATIONAL BENCHMARKING

Is your organization ready for benchmarking? Does it have the traits necessary to support such an effort? What follows below are some of the basic corporate "personality traits" conducive to a good benchmarking organization. Is your company:

- *Process friendly?* Benchmarking is a process that drives value from measurement, focused action, and transference of best practices. But it is a process and if you are an organization that rejects structured process as a means of improvement, benchmarking would not be for you.

- *Dynamic?* Benchmarking is an interactive, ongoing, and volatile activity that rests on a constant update of data—new metrics, fresh comparisons, changing peer groups, etc. Benchmarking cannot succeed if it remains static. Organizations use benchmarking to invent, improvise, and learn each day. To be effective, organizations that benchmark should be flexible and dynamic.

- *Open to continuous improvement?* Benchmarking works best when it is continuous. Some may choose to apply benchmarking techniques periodically as a diagnostic tool, and only when the problem becomes painful. But benchmarking is most effective when it is woven into the fabric of the organization and its operational culture. In this way, the early warning radar is always on—issues are identified, raised, and addressed before they become problems.

- *Willing to learn and change?* Everyone usually answers, "yes," to this question, but they should probably spend more time being honestly self-critical. A lively desire for overcoming challenges and an openness to accept difficult news are at the heart of successful benchmarking. Benchmarking only transforms an organization when it is willing to act on the results and demonstrates an ability to resist the "not invented here" syndrome.

THE THREE PHASES OF BENCHMARKING

There are three basic phases in the discipline of benchmarking.[2] These phases do not represent a formal methodology, but are provided to help readers understand that there are some prerequisites to enable the benchmarking project to flow smoothly.

Assess Current State. To begin a benchmarking process an organization must first understand its operating environment and its conduciveness to benchmarking. Sponsoring executives should ensure that the proper infrastructure is in place prior to supporting the planned benchmarking project. Such infrastructure might include senior management endorsement, sales training capabilities, various information technology systems, a culture of learning, requisite funding, specific support staff (i.e., sales operations or administration), third-party sales consultancy, benchmarking expertise from an association or paid membership, and enough time to be successful. Another aspect to this phase is the need to focus on one specific business function—sales, finance, marketing, whatever—as the target of the benchmarking. This is necessary to establish a baseline, to measure against a best-in-company standard, and to become knowledgeable about the processes and inputs specific to that function.

Selecting a Peer Group. The second phase of sales benchmarking focuses on performance and outputs. For benchmarking to be of use to an organization, it requires the existence of a relevant peer group, a term that represents the universe of other organizations against which it can be validly compared. What is a relevant peer group? In a nutshell, a relevant peer group is a collection of organizations that share one or more attributes such that when they are measured, the results show a degree of dispersion and clustering. For instance, when benchmarking financial-services organizations on their performance, a relevant peer group may be established based on attributes such as product or service category, customer type, geography, and sales model.

In order to determine whether an attribute should be used to bound a peer group, first remove it as a defining variable of the sample data set. If the results on a given metric do not change appreciably in a data set ordered by the attribute from one not defined by the attribute, it is not a significant variable. If, however, the results do change, the attribute may be used to form your peer group. With regard to the sales function, Sales Benchmark Index has found that the two most important attributes in determining a peer group for sales benchmarking purposes are sales channel and sales force size. When normed for these attributes, organizations can be compared against each other, even if they are in different geographies or industries.

Performing External Comparison. During this stage, a company begins to look outside of its own walls. The standard upon which it measures itself is the industry in which it competes. To succeed in benchmarking, a company must compare its business activities with others.

Aspiring to World-Class Comparison. The third phase of sales benchmarking concerns itself with strategy. The focus of this phase is to compare a company's sales productivity against best-in-world or, what some refer to as, world-class status. During the strategic phase, a chief sales officer looks for breakthrough improvements after already having captured incremental improvement during the first two phases. Acquiring and customizing best practices from unrelated industries provides strategic benefit that is difficult to replicate. We will discuss the specifics of World-class comparison, calculation, and application is discussed in Chapter 12.

BENCHMARKING FRAMEWORKS

There are a variety of proprietary and free frameworks that govern and guide benchmarking efforts. Some of these arose from individual corporations, such as Xerox, that were early benchmarking advocates. Others stem from academia. Table 9 provides a comparison of three of the better-known benchmarking methodologies and summarizes their multistep approaches.[3] The progenitors of these methodologies—Robert Mann, Robert Camp, and Sylvia Lodling—are published authors and longstanding benchmarking experts. None of their approaches, though, is specific to sales; in fact, most are oriented to other business functions such as manufacturing or information technology. Later in the book, we will describe a sales-specific methodology for benchmarking.

Table 9: Benchmarking Methodology Comparison			
Step	Mann's TRADE Methodology	Camp's Methodology	Codling's Methodology
1	Terms of reference (plan the project)	Identify what is to be benchmarked	Select subject ahead
2	Research (research the current state	Identify comparative companies	Define the process
3	Act (undertake data collection and analysis)	Determine data collection method and collect data	Identify potential partners
4	Deploy (communicate and implement best practices)	Determine current performance 'gap'	Identify data sources
5	Evaluate (evaluate the benchmarking process and outcomes)	Project future performance levels	Collect data and select partners

Step	Mann's TRADE Methodology	Camp's Methodology	Codling's Methodology
Table 9: Benchmarking Methodology Comparison			
6		Communicate benchmark findings and gain acceptance	Determine the gap
7		Establish functional goals	Establish process differences
8		Develop action plans	Target future performance
9		Implement specific actions and monitor progress	Communicate
10		Recalibrate benchmarks	Adjust goal
11			Implement
12			Review/recalibrate
13			

LAGGING VERSUS LEADING INDICATORS

Many organizations measure lagging indicators of sales performance against internal data alone. While this is better than not measuring anything, it stops short of the end goal. For example, stack ranking your sales force, best to worst, using the metric of *Percentage Quota Attained* would be a lagging internal indicator. It is lagging because it tells you what has already taken place inside the organization. Although this is helpful, it may not be an indicator of future performance.

Proactive sales leaders will want to understand what factors are predictive and causal. Their sales management process should support measurement of such leading indicators of internal sales performance and comparison against external data. An example of this is the sales metric known as *Pipeline-to-Quota Ratio*. This leading indicator allows sales leaders to understand the breadth and depth of opportunities in which they are currently engaged. If this ratio trails the historical external average, it may suggest that quota may not be attainable in future quarters. If this ratio is superior to historical external averages, it may suggest overachievement is possible. Sales leaders should ask themselves how many of the indicators they view look forward and how many backward.

BENCHMARK VERSUS BENCHMARKING

Since the discipline of benchmarking has been in existence for some time but readers may just be learning about the concept, it is important to distinguish between a benchmark and benchmarking. A benchmark is a sighting point from which measurements can be made or a standard against which others can be measured. Think of it as a specific value for an operating statistic specific to a metric. It should establish a norm. For example, in the sales field there are many possible metrics one might use to assess performance; examples include *Sales Cycle Length, Pipeline Ratio*, and *Customer Churn Rate*. The benchmark for one of these metrics would represent a point of reference—it could be an arbitrary value or a median value from a peer group, or even a certain quartile. In this case, "benchmark" is a noun; you might ask if a sales rep exceeded the benchmark for pipeline ratio this quarter. Benchmarking, in contrast, is the ongoing search for best practices that produce superior performance when adapted and implemented in one's organization.[4] It is in every sense a verb—it requires investigation and discovery, application and effort. One might say that the business needs to adopt the discipline of benchmarking right away, and change its operating procedures accordingly. It is the latter with which we are concerned almost exclusively throughout this book.

TO REVIEW

- Benchmarking is a powerful change-management tool because it challenges thinking and extends performance indicators across relevant peer groups.
- Benchmarking may be a single exercise or it may be an ongoing practice. The latter approach yields the most value, as a continuous process enables organizations to challenge practices that may be sufficient one day but stale the next.
- Benchmarking is not a panacea; it will not correct a flawed business model nor will it force an organization to make the necessary changes—that is the job of leadership.
- A benchmark is a sighting point from which measurements can be made or a standard against which others could be measured.
- Benchmarking, in contrast, is the ongoing search for best practices that produce superior performance when adapted and implemented in one's organization.

CHAPTER 7

FIRST GLIMPSE INTO SALES BENCHMARKING

"He that will not apply new remedies must expect new evils; for time is the greatest innovator."

—Sir Francis Bacon, English lawyer and philosopher

BENCHMARKING + SALES = NEW COMBINATION

Into the turmoil and uncertainty of today's business environment has arrived the discipline of sales benchmarking—a new technique to help diagnose what ails a sales organization. Sales professionals respond differently when exposed to the concept of benchmarking. Some never accept the notion that it can be applied to sales. Others are almost tortured by its exercise, spending all their time gathering data and analyzing it but never taking any real action. Still others, the most successful disciples, gain comfort from combining data orientation with street smarts. When benchmarking is used properly, an accurate picture can be drawn and from that picture sales managers can judge exactly what resources they need to make their numbers.

Sales benchmarking helps organizations understand how to use data to uncover the *root cause* of individual sales problems, drilling down to the real issue preventing success. It should be noted, though, that the adoption and application of benchmarking to the sales function have been slow, slower than expected, and certainly slower than warranted. The concept of sales benchmarking was not developed by a single organization, nor is it owned by a sole entity.[1] Even the sales-benchmarking entry in Wikipedia is brief (en.wikipedia.org/wiki/Sales_benchmarking), a mere page with little detail to inform.

Many organizations, including a few sales improvement, consultancy, and training firms, offer sales-benchmarking assistance to complement their other offerings. These companies have deployed aspects of benchmarking into the sales profession in various forms and fashions. None, though, other than Sales Benchmark Index, has developed a specification that defines the metrics, processes, formulas, and relationships necessary to constitute a complete taxonomy for sales benchmarking. Thus, we are at an early stage of the evolution in the dissemination of benchmarking expertise throughout the field.

THE CASE OF SALES HEAD COUNT

Only 57 percent of sales managers will make their quota this year.[2] This alone suggests a new approach should be welcomed as well as needed.

How often has the vice president of sales received head-count targets from the CEO that are then applied like peanut butter (all the same to every territory) across the field sales force? Endless rants then follow from sales managers convinced their "unrealistic" quota merits more sales staff than their peers. Is quota attainment the best approach to use to determine staffing levels? How many is too many reps? How about too few?

Winning is contagious; nothing destroys morale and momentum more quickly than denying staff to those managers making their numbers. Should the most productive sales managers and reps get more staffing or those who are falling short?

SALES BENCHMARKING—A SOLUTION TO HEAD-COUNT ALLOCATION?

Is starving the winners while you feed the weak the best staffing policy? No; instead, benchmarking can point to a different approach. Relying on conventional head-count-planning average values such as revenue per head, number of reps per manager, number of reps per account, sales rep–support employee ratio does not work. When executives make top-down decisions based on averages alone, executives will typically assign either too many reps per territory or too few. The key to success is not in managing a static head-count allocation, but instead in managing staffing using a unique concept known as sales workload.[3] By switching to this bottom-up method, one that factors in how many of each account type exists in each territory, the results are a more accurate headcount distribution, greater revenue generation, reduced turnover, improved sales manager morale, and more rational basis for staff allocation. To use the sales workload approach, the following two formulas must be solved:

Total Calls per Year = (# accounts) × (# calls per year)

Optimum Sales Force Size = (# calls required per year) / (# calls per rep per year)

In order to calculate these formulas, you must first group your customers by size based on annual sales revenue. Many use a simple designation like enterprise accounts vs. small and medium-sized businesses (SMB); others go for more granular categories (e.g., Platinum is > $1 billion in revenue, Gold is $100 million to $1 billion, etc.). Once accounts have been segregated in this fashion, the calculations can be performed.

AN EXAMPLE (DIVERSIFIED LTD)

In order to better demonstrate this concept, we have included values from a fictional company, Diversified Ltd. Diversified has segmented its customers into three categories—A, B, and C, and Table 10 shows the following sales activity:

Table 10: Diversified Ltd's Activity Input Data		
Account Type	Number of Accounts	Number of Calls per Year
A	1,000	36
B	2,000	12
C	4,000	4

Based on the formula above, Diversified can make 76,000 *Total Sales Calls per Year:*

(1,000 × 36) + (2,000 × 12) + (4,000 × 4) = 76,000 sales calls

Diversified has also determined that, since there are 240 selling days in a year and their sales reps can make only 1 call per day on average, they can assume 240 sales calls can be made per rep per year. Therefore, Diversified's *Optimum Sales Force Size* is as follows:

$$76,000 / 240 = 317 \text{ sales reps}$$

Diversified now knows the number of sales reps it needs to support the activity it can generate. What results is a fact-informed decision that avoids emotional leverage—something that makes sense and can be defended.

STUCK IN THE STATUS QUO

Head count is just one example of how benchmarking can be applied to a sales organization to increase revenue and strengthen a sales force. So why don't more sales organizations adopt the practice of benchmarking for their own sales teams? The best organizations work hard to understand how past performance metrics affect future and present success. Mediocre organizations will continue to fail most of the time because they stay in their comfort zone.[4] Assuming that all sales leaders want to hit their number, and they are open to the concept of sales benchmarking, one of the most glaring stumbling blocks to its more widespread acceptance is the lack of easy-to-use methodologies.

BENCHMARKING METHODOLOGIES

Such proprietary methodologies are the staple practice of a consulting business. In some cases, their thought capital is adopted so widely that it becomes industry standard. One example might be PRINCE2—a project management methodology for implantation of information-technology–process improvement. These methodologies help organizations put into practice the principles of an industrial theory. Sales Benchmark Index has developed several useful methodologies applicable to sales benchmarking. As one would expect, these methodologies share similar characteristics and concepts with other methodologies, especially those used to perform benchmarking in other, nonsales business functions. Sales Benchmark Index has developed the following proprietary sales-benchmarking methodologies:

- 5 Step Sales Benchmarking Program
- Sales Management Maturity Model
- Formula for Sales Success

In developing these proprietary approaches, we have helped sales leaders to implement this management discipline. Each methodology speeds deployment cycles, increases project success rates, improves execution quality, and delivers results. They are described below.

5 STEP SALES BENCHMARKING PROGRAM

Sales Benchmark Index's 5 Step Sales Benchmarking Program is available to the public for the first time in this book. The unique application of benchmarking to the sales force required development of this robust approach. It was through much trial and error, over many implementations, that this methodology was refined and commercially tested. The five steps are as follows:

1. Metric Identification (Step 1)
2. Data Collection (Step 2)
3. Compare and Contrast (Step 3)
4. Focused Action (Step 4)
5. Sustained Improvement (Step 5)

The details of this methodology are explained in Section III of this book.

SALES MANAGEMENT MATURITY MODEL

Sales Benchmark Index also introduces to the public in this book its proprietary Sales Management Maturity Model. This model draws from the extensive benchmarking work previously performed in the information technology industry. It enables a sales leader to assess his or her organization across two dimensions: maturity and productivity. The details of this methodology are explained in Chapter 12.

FORMULA FOR SALES SUCCESS

Two key principles that influenced Sales Benchmark Index's Formula for Sales Success were reverse engineering and process benchmarking.[5] In using this formula sales leaders solve for their annual sales revenue "in reverse," understanding the impact each variable has on the output. By testing performance variations for each of these variables, a sales leader can simulate future quarters. As for process benchmarking being applied to the sales process, the formula considers various key sales activities as inputs to a more strategic process, and transactions are an output. Annual revenue is the ultimate reflection of customer satisfaction for it indicates the degree upon which the market accepts the company's sales process. Let's study a detailed example.

A PRACTICAL APPLICATION FOR THE FORMULA FOR SALES SUCCESS

Since understanding this formula is elemental to later concepts with regard to sales benchmarking, we offer below a fictional example, the eponymous company of Acme, Inc., to help explain the concept.

Let us assume that the CEO of Acme has been asked by its board to increase sales by 20 percent in the next fiscal year. The CEO comes to the Acme sales leader with a revenue target 20 percent greater than last year's and tells him that he must meet this number. The sales leader tries diligently to debate the validity of this increase, but is unsuccessful because he doesn't have the necessary information to support his claims.

If sales benchmarking was a best practice in this firm, the board, the CEO, and the sales leader would be made aware of the five variables that drive a sales number,[6] which can be expressed in a formula. This formula illustrates the relationship each variable has on the output.

The formula is as follows:

An example:

In this simple scenario, the board has asked for a 20 percent increase in sales next year. How do the five variables impact annual sales revenue? First, look at calls per day. If the number of sales calls per day doubled, annual sales revenue would also double:

Now look at the impact of success rates. If the success rate increased from 10 percent to 20 percent, again, the annual sales revenue would double:

Deal Size increased from $100,000 to $150,000, annual sales revenue would grow by 50 percent:

Now, look at how the number of salespeople affects sales outcome. If the number of salespeople increased from fifty to seventy-five, annual sales revenue would increase by 50 percent:

As you can see, there are five variables that affect annual sales volume and only one of them—the number of days per year—is fixed.

With understanding the Formula for Sales Success and how to use it, the CEO, the board, and VP of sales would now be engaged in a much different conversation. They would be discussing *which* of these variables they could most positively affect. Data-driven decision making, enabled by sales benchmarking, can help answer this and other questions by looking at additional metrics to uncover the root cause of such sales problems.

Benchmarking is not new, but its applicability to sales is, which represents a clear and distinct opportunity for those organizations that adopt it. Applying a proven concept to a new area is a low-risk path to delivering exceptional results. Sales benchmarking, if executed correctly, can enable your sales force to become a source of sustained competitive advantage.

Now that you understand benchmarking as a sales function and the obstacles you may face in your attempts to implement it within your sales force, you are ready to move on to the challenges of implementation. Section II will provide you with a blueprint on how to execute the practice of sales benchmarking in your organization.

TO REVIEW

- Benchmarking is not new, but its applicability to sales is. This provides a clear opportunity for organizations that adopt it to experience exceptional results.
- Sales benchmarking is a generic process that means different things to different people, but these patterned approaches should accelerate the speed of adoption in sales benchmarking.
- Benchmarking uses data to uncover the root cause of individual sales problems (like head-count allocation) and drill down to the real issue preventing success.
- Sales Benchmark Index has developed the following proprietary sales-benchmarking methodologies built on the foundation of the benchmarking body of work: 5 Step Sales Benchmarking Program, Sales Management Maturity Model, and Formula for Sales Success—all of which have been built on the foundation of the benchmarking body of work.[7] These methodologies are proprietary.

SECTION II

DIVING DEEPER INTO SALES BENCHMARKING

CHAPTER 8

WHAT SALES BENCHMARKING IS NOT

"The more opinions you have, the less you can see."

—WIM WENDERS, GERMAN FILM PRODUCER,
DIRECTOR, AND PLAYWRIGHT

N ow that a case has been made to support the need for sales benchmarking, we will explore the topic more deeply. One way to do this is to describe what it is not. Otherwise, you may come to believe some solution or another reflects good sales-benchmarking practice when, in fact, it does not.

PREREQUISITES FOR SALES BENCHMARKING

For those in the hunt for someone to assist in conducting a sales benchmark or training in the discipline of sales benchmarking, four key assets must be evident from the offering to ensure that it will support your initiative effectively. These assets are:

- Sales-benchmarking taxonomy
- Sales-benchmarking repository
- Sales-benchmarking automation technology
- Sales-benchmarking subject-matter experts

These assets, long available to the finance, manufacturing, IT, and HR departments, are now commercially available to sales leaders. Excellence in the sales function can now be defined, measured, and attained with assurity. In order to better understand each of the assets, we shall consider them individually.

SALES BENCHMARKING TAXONOMY

At its most basic, taxonomy is a term used to describe the application of certain metadata (data that describes data) in a process of classification. Originally, biologists created taxonomies that applied to living organisms (genus, species, etc.). Now, however, taxonomy captures a much wider set of objects; the term is applied to almost anything—places, concepts, events, properties, and relationships—concept that benefits from better definition. Such classification includes not just the items themselves, but also the principles underlying them and the processes supporting them. With regard to sales benchmarking, a taxonomy should cover, at a minimum, definitions for all data inputs, definitions for all metric formulas rendered from these inputs, and definitions for all sales processes into which these metrics are grouped.

With any taxonomy, definition is just the first step; adoption is the second. For a specific taxonomy to be successful in the long run, it must achieve a critical mass of adoption by the using community. There can be more than one acceptable taxonomy for a given subject matter, particularly if each can be reconciled or cross-referenced. It is often easier, though, if all parties in a community adopt a common taxonomy, much in the same way that technology companies often coalesce around a standard (usually published by the American National Standards Institute) that may have originated from just one member organization. Sales Benchmark Index publishes a sales-benchmarking taxonomy of its own, some of the details of which are presented in Appendix B.

One aspect of taxonomy worth noting here is the difference between strategic sales benchmarking and process sales benchmarking. Chapters 8 and 9 delve into these differences in more detail, but for now, it is important to note that any successful taxonomy for sales benchmarking should establish a demarcation between the two. Strategic metrics are those that provide big-picture guidance while process-related ones are more tactical in nature. In some cases, too, strategic metrics have an organizational focus, while process-related ones apply to individuals.

SALES BENCHMARKING REPOSITORY

Without data, sales benchmarking is impossible. The challenge, though, is not so much *data vs. no data,* but what kind and how much data. The amount of sales data that has been collected via automated systems (SFA and CRM mostly) has grown exponentially in the past decade or so. Even though many rollouts of these systems have encountered resistance from sales forces meant to benefit from them and still others have had rocky or failed implementations they have succeeded in digitalizing sales performance. At this point decision makers have significantly more raw sales data at their fingertips than ever before. Raw sales data on an internal company computer system is not, however, a sales-benchmarking repository. Several intervening steps are necessary to transform and migrate the data trapped within the corporate walls so that it can contribute to an independent, multi-organizational sales-benchmarking repository. These steps include validation of the data by a third party, application of necessary meta data, transfer off-site, and in some cases translation to an acceptable standard format (as defined by the taxonomy).

Several other aspects to the population of a sales repository must also be considered. First and foremost is that the data collected must be empirical. In other words, it must represent a factual representation of reality, not someone's opinion or estimation. This typically prevents the inclusion of survey data in a sales-benchmarking repository. Such survey data, usually collected via e-mail, phone conversation, or interview represents, at best, informed opinion. Many times, however, respondents to these surveys are ill informed, forgetful, and occasionally deliberately misleading. Another risk to the acuracy of a sales-benchmarking repository is posed by data collected from the wrong system. In these cases, the data is not derived from an opinion survey but it is not the correct source.

An example of how this plays out during a benchmarking exercise might help explain the point. When a company is benchmarking its sales force there are several data inputs needed that relate to compensation. There is a tendency for the company populating these metrics to draw this information from its sales system because that system is the most familiar to them. In reality, though, the best system to use as the source for compensation data is the HR system—it is ground zero for all personnel payments. Using the CRM system, for example, might lead to use of innacurate input data, which generates in an erroneous metric, and therefore leads to poorly supported conclusions.

In addition to excluding of survey information and incorrectly sourced data, the sales-benchmarking repository should boost a wide variety of defining attributes, including:

- Industry segments (e.g., consumer products, retail, financial services)
- Geographical areas (e.g., America, Europe, Asia)
- Sales channels (e.g., direct, indirect, telesales, e-commerce)
- Sales force/organization size (e.g., <100, 100–1,000, 1,001–5,000)
- Public, private, and even NGO
- History (for annual trending)

The bottom line is that the sale repository should be a robust, extensive, layered, archival, verifiable, and integrated data resource. Almost certainly this requires the owner and manager of the repository to build multiple different data sources and ensure their regular integration and refresh. This is clearly something that takes time to assemble and effort to maintain. But, without the repository, meaningful comparison, peer group selection, trend analysis, and other statistical sampling techniques cannot be performed.

SALES-BENCHMARKING AUTOMATION TECHNOLOGY

Once the definitions are captured in a taxonomy and a repository built and populated, half the battle has been waged. One additional requirement is the need for some tool that enables the many and oftentimes manual processes to be automated. What are these manual processes? The first is the actual identification and collection of the data inputs necessary to support calculation of sales metrics. Once data is collected, it should be stored in an interim state while it is validated by a third party. The actual formulaic calculation of the metrics for the organization should be automated as well as the selection of a relevant peer group from the repository and determination of world-class status for all metrics. Last, comparison of the organization's metric scores against that of the peer group and world-class status should result in the automatic generation of a series of visual graphs that tell the story of the data. Such graphs should encompass each individual metric, comparisons in all related sales process areas, and overall performance across the organization. It may also be advantageous to automate the integration of the organization's sales data with an external sales-benchmarking repository via some enabling technology such as extensible markup language (XML). This integration provides an additional labor savings and allows a bidirectional flow of information—not just to the repository but also back from it. With this return of information, organizations can plug sales-benchmarking comparison information into their own corporate dashboard systems.

SALES-BENCHMARKING SUBJECT-MATTER EXPERTS

With the taxonomy in place, the repository available, and automating software in place to enable the free flow of information, the last asset needed is a cadre of sales-benchmarking experts. Such experts may be "quants"—those individuals trained in business statistics generally and specifically in the discipline of sales benchmarking. Whether quants or more traditional sales analysts, sales-benchmarking experts perform a wide variety of tasks, including the following:

- Conducting needed statistical interpretations
- Developing new metrics from existing input data
- Identifying new input fields required to build new metrics
- Building compound metrics from existing ones to provide a fresh look (much like Billy Beane built new baseball metrics from old ones)
- Determining how to extrapolate organizational performance from a ground-up metrics view
- Mining year-over-year data for trends
- Interpreting the relevance of gaps between peer group and world-class scores
- Providing consultative expertise based on a unique combination of hands-on sales background and knowledge of data analysis

Without these experts, the fruits of sales benchmarking would largely go unrealized. They are literally the glue that holds together the other three sales-benchmarking assets, ensuring that a solution results from the benchmarking process.

WHAT ORGANIZATIONS ARE LIKELY SPONSORS OF SALES-BENCHMARKING INITIATIVES?

Since sales benchmarking is still a developing discipline, there is not yet a large number of companies that possess the four assets just described, although some may boast of after. Below is a list of the types of organizations that can provide assistance to those wishing to engage in sales benchmarking, even though they may not yet possess all of the necessary four assets:

- Survey firms
- Benchmarking firms
- Talent management firms
- Associations
- Sales consultants
- Dashboard software companies
- Technical benchmarking firms

SURVEY FIRMS—LACKS EMPIRICAL DATA

As mentioned earlier in this chapter, there is a significant difference between sales-related survey information and sales-related benchmarking data. In addition to the obvious difference—surveys are little more than compilations of individual opinion—the use of survey data as a substitute for benchmarking data can be problematic and even dangerous.

As noted by Regis McKenna, "there are several reasons not to trust market research surveys":

- The environment in which the research is done is different from the actual decision-making environment.
- Trends and changes can be understood only historically. Research focuses on history, not the future. Predictions based on opinions (as opposed to leading indicators based on empirical fact) cannot even boast of being directionally correct.
- Communication is so instantaneous and information so prolific on any given event that attitudes and opinions change on a daily basis.[1]

In fact, there are even more reasons to distrust any conclusions based on a survey, even if survey results have held steady or shown year-over-year trends. These surveys rely on volunteer participation, which immediately excludes a statistically significant portion of the target population. No studies available in the benchmarking field suggest that the opinions of those who choose not to participate in surveys are statistically equivalent to those who do. On the contrary, there is good reason to believe that they are substantively different. Even worse, the survey techniques that are at least more comprehensive and accurate (phone) are usually dropped in favor of those that are faster and cheaper (Internet-based methods).

So, if surveys pose such a danger to accurate prognostication, why are they so popular? The clearest explanation is that the necessary assets to support sales benchmarking have only recently come into existence. Prior to that time, sales benchmarking could not be conducted with appropriate due diligence. Accordingly, some companies filled the benchmarking void with survey data, arguing that some information was better than no information. But this nationale no longer suffices as a justification for the use of survey data to inform strategic decision making.

BENCHMARKING FIRMS—DON'T ADDRESS SALES COMPREHENSIVELY YET

Previously mentioned, benchmarking is a discipline with a long pedigree in other business functions. As the concept has matured and deepened in adoption in these other areas, an ecostructure of benchmarking firms has developed to support it. Thus far, these firms have not focused on the sales function; however, that gap in coverage is likely not to last. For instance, there are a number of benchmarking firms that support the call center industry, marketing, and customer service. While none of these functions is equivalent to sales, they all have a healthy overlap with it. It would not be surprising if some of these firms began the process of collecting data for sales-related metrics in order to extend their offering in the sales direction.

TALENT MANAGEMENT FIRMS—LIMITED TO HUMAN RESOURCE AREAS

Probably the richest reservoir of firms claiming sales benchmarking as an offering can be found in the talent management industry. This industry has given birth to a whole host of companies that employ behavioral scientists, data analysts, sampling techniques, and other tools to amass repositories of human resources—oriented information. These firms then mine this information and combine it with the expertise of industrial psychologists to derive various personal indicators of performance on pay, environmental prodivities, and job satisfaction. This has been most helpful to the call center industry, whose adherents need to make numerous accurate hiring decisions on call center support staff.

Talent management firms use terms like *comparison data, taxonomy,* and *evaluation experts.* This all smacks of benchmarking; however, these firms are focused on HR issues and do not delve into the operational, financial, or productivity sides of sales performance beyond the call center and customer service.

ASSOCIATIONS—TOO IMMATURE

At first blush, one would think that associations, whether profit or nonprofit, might be the best means of providing the critical mass necessary to engage in sales benchmarking. There are many sales-related associations, forums, groups, and the like but, so far, none have adopted sales benchmarking as a feature of their memberships. To fill this gap, some emerging benchmarking-related associations are attempting to serve as one-stop shopping for collateral, advice, events, and ideas. Examples include the Sales Force Effectiveness Benchmarking Association (www.sfeba.com) and the Sales Forecasting Benchmarking Forum (www.sfbf.com). These organizations focus more on the sharing of best practices though, a technique discussed in greater depth in Chapter 11. Once the number of organizations that have gone through a successful cycle of sales benchmarking has increased to a tipping point, these associations may be able to serve as repositories of information and expertise, possibly even as holders of a common taxonomy. For now, though, they are providing primarily a means for networking among like-minded professionals.

SALES CONSULTANTS—DELIVER EXPERTISE, NOT DATA

The number of sales-related trainers, consultants, speakers, and advisers is almost too large to count. One can find sales experts in large consultancies, in regional or specialized firms, and in solo practices. They cover the gamut, from providing training on how to use SFA or CRM software to implementing any number of proprietary sales methodologies. Sales consultants specialize in areas such as lead management, territory planning, sales management, talent management, and so on. Their skills range from serving as a tactical staff augmentation to delivering strategic advice to the boardroom. One thing they all share is that none of them, as of yet, are performing sales benchmarking as we describe it in this book. Part of this may be the conflict in business models; consulting requires a thick stream of projects for personnel to perform while sales benchmarking is based on collecting data, then delivering comparative analyses at various points—not a labor-intensive activity.

DASHBOARD SOFTWARE COMPANIES—PROVIDES INTERNAL NOT EXTERNAL DATA

Many software firms in the market space have created some form of a dashboard report based on the data collected by CRM and/or SFA systems. These reports use color to show areas of weakness or urgency. They are based on empirical data drawn directly from corporate systems and so do not suffer from any of the defects of survey data. What such reports typically lack, however, is any external data against which to compare the internal results. That may be an acceptable trade-off for data reported on a daily or even weekly basis. However, the reality check provided by external comparison (sometimes known as baselining) is an invaluable and necessary ingredient to calculating where the gaps are between median practice (shown by the relevant peer group) and best practice (shown by the world-class results). Some of the dashboard software firms have been working to incorporate streams of external sales-benchmarking data into their offerings. When and if this occurs, these firms will have a compelling offering for their clients.

TECHNICAL BENCHMARKING—NOT APPLICABLE TO A BUSINESS FUNCTION

Probably the largest number of firms or organizations that engage in benchmarking are actually test beds for the comparison of one technology against another. They create a lablike set of conditions where various technologies (hardware, software, firmware, or some combination) are literally clocked against one another. The benchmark they publish then becomes a standard against which future configurations must meet or exceed. This is an entirely technical exercise and has no relevance to a business function like sales.

A SUMMARY OF SALES BENCHMARKING

This chapter has provided some clarification on what sales benchmarking is not so that we can spend the rest of the Section II discussing what it indeed is. Table 11 helps summarize our points.

Table 11: What Sales Benchmarking Is and What It Is Not	
Sales Benchmarking Requires:	**Sales Benchmarking Is NOT:**
A detailed taxonomy	Valid without accepted definitions
Empirical and validated input data	A series of opinion-based answers from only those who decided to respond to a survey
Comparison of your performance against a relevant peer group	A simple comparison of your current performance against past performance
A statistically valid sample set significant dimensions	A summary of survey results
Coverage of all the major sales processes and subfunctions	Limited to one subfunction (such as compensation planning)
Strategic and tactical sales metrics	A list of qualitative questions
Tools to automate the series of steps from data collection to analysis to display	Accomplished manually without Herculean effort
A living repository with sufficient data and OLAP-like (online analytical processing) functionality to enable multidimensional and trend analysis	A collection of disparate data sources, surveys, and spreadsheets that lack integration, consistency, and analytic functionality
Subject-matter experts with specific expertise in comparative data analytics	Possible with ex-salespeople trying to perform data analytics without applicable training

TO REVIEW

- There are four key assets that any organization purporting to offer sales-benchmarking services should be able to demonstrate: a Sales-benchmarking taxonomy, a sales-benchmarking repository, sales-benchmarking automation technology, and sales benchmarking subject-matter experts.
- Sales-benchmarking taxonomy covers, at a minimum, the definitions for all data inputs, metric formulas rendered from these inputs, and sales processes into which these metrics are grouped.
- A sales-benchmarking repository is a robust, extensive, layered, archival, verifiable, and integrated data resource that possesses a series of attributes, including industry segment, geography, sales channel, sales force size, company type, and history.

- Sales-benchmarking automation technology enables a series of steps from data collection to analysis to display to long-term integration.
- Sales-benchmarking subject-matter experts perform a wide variety of assessment and analytical tasks.
- Other types of organizations are attempting or might soon attempt to perform sales benchmarking. These include survey firms, benchmarking firms, talent management firms, associations, sales consultants, dashboard software companies, technical benchmarking firms.
- Sales benchmarking requires the calculation of sales metrics from empirically verified input data that reflects a sales reality. It is not possible to accomplish this using survey data.

CHAPTER 9

PROCESS SALES BENCHMARKING

"If you can't describe what you are doing as a process, you don't
know what you're doing!"

—W. Edwards Deming, American statistician,
lecturer, author, and consultant

W hen trying to improve performance in a corporate business function it is
necessary to understand what work is being done, as well as when, why,
and by whom. The answers to those questions tell you what your processes are. Once these processes are documented in some fashion, process
engineers can begin breaking down tasks into workflows, swim lanes, decision
points, and so on. With this current-state reality literally mapped out, efforts can
be taken to find various means of improving these processes. The whole discipline of process reengineering arose in the 1990s, spearheaded by two management consultants,[1] who successfully argued that corporations could achieve
competitive advantage by engaging in sustained reengineering efforts of core
business functions. A prerequisite of any such reengineering effort is to define
and formalize the processes for the functions being improved.

WHAT IS A BUSINESS PROCESS?

Assuming that the connection between improved business processes and improved business performance is valid, the next step is to ensure that the concept of business process itself is well understood. There are six key characteristics of a business process.[2]

1. *Definability:* A business process must have clearly defined boundaries with recognized inputs and outputs. For sales an input might be a lead delivered by Marketing, and an output might be a forecast report viewed by management.

2. *Order:* A business process must consist of activities that are ordered according to their position in time and space. For sales, such order is well defined; for example, the sales pipeline funnel flows from initial contact, prospect education, objection handling proposal, and final order.

3. *Customer:* There must be a recipient of the process's outcome. In the case of sales, this is usually the customer of the product or service sold. However, there are some ancillary sales processes where sales is serving an internal customer. For instance, sales often provides detailed input on product development requests that it collects from its customer base. In this case, the customer would be the marketing department (assuming it owns the product development function).

4. *Value-adding:* The transformation taking place within the process must add value to the recipient, either upstream or downstream. Sales adds value to the process primarily in terms of its interaction with existing customers or future prospects. Such value-add activity might include delivering presentations, conducting education sessions, or responding to request for purchase justification.

5. *Embeddedness:* A process can not exist in itself; it must be embedded in an organizational structure. All the sales processes are firmly located within the corporate infrastructure.

6. *Cross-functionality:* A process regularly can, but not necessarily must, span several functions. Sales processes occur with the input, support, and approval of other business functions. Examples of such cross-functional cooperation include contract negotiations (with legal), competitive intelligence–gathering (with marketing), existing customer upselling (with customer support), and enhanced client interaction and automation (information technology).

WHAT DOES A PROCESS LOOK LIKE?

Now that we have described some of the characteristics of a process, let us briefly describe the artifacts and attributes of a process. In other words, what does the documentation of a process "look like"? When trying to capture all of this on paper, many sales managers and operations staff confuse process with procedure and policy. Accordingly, when they try to capture their own internal disciplines, the result is a jumble of documents that do not fit together well, do not establish common operating methods, and do not offer the opportunity for continual improvement. The difference between process, procedure, and policy and how they interrelate can be explained as follows:

> *Process*—A process tells why. All processes, even those informal undocumented ones, boast several features: They describe a series of activities or tasks performed by people in a defined role; these people use various inputs (e.g., information, reports, data) to make decisions, which result in the creation of outputs used by other groups inside or outside the process. Throughout this life cycle, various dependencies, exception conditions, specific metrics, best-practices references, templates, and tools govern and guide the process tasks. Typically, this is all captured in a workflow document that clearly demarcates the who, what, and how. Examples of sales processes are provided later in this chapter.

> *Procedure*—It provides a step-by-step set of instructions on accomplishing a task. A procedure should be a "step" identified in a process workflow that is complex enough to merit its own documentation. For systems-related procedures, the documentation might contain screen shots for visual understanding scripts, operational guidance, and settings—anything necessary to a systems-implementation step. An example of a procedure might be how to overcome a prospect's objection to purchasing a product. A procedure tells how to do something.

> *Policy*—A policy tells the what of doing something. It is a statement, rule of thumb, or specifications that sets forth measurable guidelines on what to do and not do. Invoked either in a process or in a procedure, a policy helps other business functions and sales staff members understand where the parameters of operation and the lines of decisionmaking exist. Some people refer to policy

as business governance. An example of a sales policy might be the requirement that all accounts with greater than $1 million in revenue be managed by the strategic accounts group.

POOR PROCESS DESIGN

The majority of sales professionals find themselves working for organizations that have poorly designed processes rather than no process at all. Poor process design manifests itself in inaccurate workflows, bad governance, inadequately defined roles, and insufficient standard operating procedures. This is felt most keenly in the inability to support large volumes of support activity, manage sales-related digital-process knowledge, automate interfaces between interdependent sales processes, and track the life cycle of various transactions (such as sales orders or sales leads). Deficiencies in both process and design are evident when evaluating performance against specific objectives known as key performance Indicators (KPIs). KPIs typically cover areas such as the following:

- Comparison to past process performance
- Input costs to indicate the decline of operating expenses in process delivery
- Output quality to measure the effectiveness of the process production
- Timeliness to reflect optimum responsiveness in supporting required actions
- Ease of data collection to support the KPI

Process-related KPIs are not to be confused with benchmarking metrics. The former describe the overall area of measurement specific to a given sales process. The latter are the specific measurements themselves, with the required data input fields, formulas, and measurement frequencies.

IMPROVING PROCESSES

Upon hearing about the idea of formalized process, some sales managers' first reaction is to say, "We have some good procedures and great people, isn't that enough?" In order to achieve world-class sales status, the answer is simply no. To benchmark against peers and adopt their best practices, you must have something upon which to pattern future improvements. Grafting one company's process onto another usually does not work unless adjustments and accommodations are made. How are such changes made? For instance, if those who are performing a task cannot clearly articulate a compelling reason for a step, it may be unnecessary. The desired result of each step is defined so that sales reps can determine where they are in the process and what progress has been made. This type of analysis is possible when there is a culture of support or, at a minimum, recognition that process is necessary for achieving excellence. An improvable process will possess the following qualities:

- *Repeatable*—It lends itself to multiple iterations of the same complete life cycle of steps/actions in the same order and enables multiple people to perform different roles.
- *Consistent*—It has no logical contradictions or any requirements that cannot be accomplished.
- *Reliable*—It produces the same results when it is followed correctly.
- *Trustable*—It describes and defines all the process activity. In other words, there are no hidden steps that occur in reality but are missing from the defined workflow.
- *Measurable*—It contains metrics that enable the measurement of work within the process (e.g., if a given step was performed correctly or on time) as well as the output of the process itself (e.g., a completed sales order).
- *Comprehensible*—It contains instructions and guidance that are understood by all roles within the process. Further, it should define sufficiently any inputs so that the process responsible for producing the input can do so without error and should define any outputs so that the recipient considers that they meet the requirements specified.

WHY HAVE SALES PROCESSES?

Processes seem tailor-made for manufacturing lines or distribution units or warehousing facilities—lots of workers doing relatively the same thing most of the time. But do they apply to sales? Establishing process discipline seems to demand a lot of work and formal documentation—not a subject that excites the imagination of a sales leader trying to hit a number or a sales executive trying to transform a failing organization. Some might be tempted to ask, "Why have any defined sales processes at all? Why not just provide a working environment, laptop, customer list, cell phone, and morning coffee, and ask them to make the number?" Amazingly, this approach represents the de facto condition for a large number of sales forces. At its core sales process helps sales staff by removing uncertainty and unpredictability in their decision making, training them on what to do, when to do it, and why, and introduces a measure of auditability for management. To become world-class, you must be able to get your arms around your sales processes. Period.

DIFFICULTIES IN DEFINING SALES PROCESSES

Process is the road map by which sales gets things done. Sales, however, has often found it difficult to describe, measure, and verify the various activities that support its role as corporate revenue generator. Sales, like most of the other business functions, is complex, and requires a wide number of roles (including executives, managers, quota-bearing representatives, indirect sales representatives, partner managers, channel managers, sales operations staff, customer service, controllers, sales support engineers, lead generation staff, business development, telesales, and sales administration). It has multiple touch points in other key departments—marketing, product development, manufacturing, operations, and finance—each of which has its own unique interface requirements. Finally, sales has many discrete functions. These functions are the core tasks that need to be accomplished in order for the sales department to achieve its mission. Sales managers who say, "Too many deals fail to progress from upside to forecast" or "why does it seem that it takes so long for new hires to become productive?" are giving voice to the fact that their process is insufficiently defined or poorly controlled.

WHAT ARE THE COMMON SALES PROCESSES?

Many focus almost exclusively on the primary sales process—the one that starts with first contact of a potential customer and eventually leads (sometimes) to a sale. Though this is the key process within the sales function, it is far from the only one. Some choose to group various sales functions into categories in which they share common attributes. They then consider these sales categories as defacts processes. Below is a partial list of these sales processes.

Automation enablement	Presentation development
Basic account planning	Product development input
Client management	Proposal development
Closing	Prospect identification
Cold calling	Prospect qualification
Compensation planning	Relationship development
Competitive intelligence gathering	Sales analytics
Contract modification	Sales call execution
Cross-selling	Sales candidate hiring
Customer council support	Sales candidate interviewing
Customer education	Sales candidate sourcing
Customer/prospect research	Sales management
Customer support for billing	Sales meeting management (internal)
Forecasting	Sales meeting management (external)
Internal resource management	Sales partner management
Lead identification	Sales plan development
Lead qualification	Sales reporting
Negotiation	Sales training on methodology
Objection handling	Sales training on product/service
Obtaining customer feedback	Strategic account planning
OEM channel management	Territory design
Order taking	Time and expense reporting
Order tracking	Upselling
Post-implementation/delivery follow-up	Win-loss analysis

SALES METHODOLOGIES

The devil is certainly in the details in terms of defining sales process. Some of the processes listed above arguably overlap with others, either wholly or in part. Many call a similar process by another name (e.g., talent management instead of candidate sourcing). Still others argue that there are some missing processes or that some of these processes are not even the proper responsibility of the sales department. In fact, due to such diversity of opinion, a vibrant and varied industry has grown up around the concept of sales methodology. There are many firms engaged in the sale, promotion, education, and certification of clients in accordance with a particular sales methodology. These methodologies provide a formal structure that identifies which processes are important, how they can be accomplished, what automation technologies are available to support them, and how compliance can be measured. Organizations are increasing adoption of these proprietary approaches because they provide at least some means of standardizing an approach to the sales function. Sales process and sales methodology are inexorably intertwined. The more intimately a sales force has adopted one of these formal approaches, the better defined their sales processes will be.

SALES BENCHMARKING AND SALES PROCESS

Sales benchmarking can and does measure overall sales performance, a concept covered in the following chapter. To be effective, though, sales benchmarking should extend to a level or two lower than the strategic. Since sales processes capture where and how work is done, this is the prism through which sales benchmarking can be used to more granularly assess performance. The purpose of process sales benchmarking, therefore, is to identify the "most effective operating practices from many companies [in a peer group] that perform similar work functions".[1] When an organization is able to elevate an entire sales process so that it attains world-class status, it can achieve breakthrough performance improvements. The question is how?

WHICH PROCESSES MATTER?

After a long period of study and experience, Sales Benchmark Index identified a subset of sales processes that more consistently deliver improved bottom-line results. In addition, because these processes are widespread, they are more amenable to the identification of relevant peer groups from which external data samples can be taken. These twelve sales processes and a brief definition of each follow:

- *Account Planning*—Covers strategic, target, and tactical account planning. It encompasses the tasks necessary to prepare to sell to customers and prospects, and to learn their pain points, buying habits, and influencers. It produces a series of artifacts to reflect this knowledge acquisition and preparation effort.

- *Budgeting*—Captures all the steps necessary to perform proper fiscal management of the sales force, advanced financial planning, and headcount determination. Some sales organizations do not have this within their control, but those that do find great opportunities for improvement here.

- *Channel Optimization*—Encompasses all the reconciling, optimizing, and managing of the various external sales channels. Such channels might include formal business partners, resellers, original equipment manufacturers (OEMs), informal business partners, franchises, and licensees.

- *Compensation Planning*—Covers the planning and implementation of compensation design, quota development, incentive programs, accelerators, new product introduction ties to compensation, and variable pay for nonquota-bearing sales executives.

- *Expense Allocation*—Captures all the steps necessary to track how and where money is spent to support sales efforts. All items that fall under the "S" of SG&A expenses are reviewed in this process category.

- *Sales Management*—Encompasses the entire discipline of sales management—leadership, accountability, training, motivation, knowledge transfer, nurturing, mentoring, and so forth. This is a crucial process for many sales organizations.

- *Sales Methodology*—Addresses the degree to which the organization has adopted and is following established sales methodology. Independent of any specific proprietary methodology, this process captures the take-up rates of the core functions relevant to a basic sales methodology.

- *Staffing*—Covers a range of activities relevant to sales support, operations, presales, administration, and customer service staff. This process also incorporates sales rep and manager staffing challenges.

- *Talent Selection*—Captures the complete process for finding, fixing, and hiring new sales staff as well as career management/enhancement for existing sales staff. This process also includes measuring third parties that provide support to talent management activities of both executives and front-line sale leaders.

- *Technology Infrastructure*—Addresses the adoption, implementation, and applicability of a series of sales support systems to the sales force. Such systems include SFA, CRM, lead management, mobility, virtual conferencing, and knowledge management.

- *Territory Design*—Covers the effort necessary to analyze, segment, and manage the sales territories in accordance with product line, customer orientation, geography, vertical industry, and buying habits.

- *Training*—Covers the training for sales staff on sales methodology as well as on internal product and service offerings.

WHICH SALES METRICS BELONG IN WHICH SALES PROCESSES?

Now that each of the twelve processes has been identified, the next step is to determine which sales metrics should be included in each process area. This is a critical decision as all subsequent measurement, analysis, and follow-up action rests on the applicability and accuracy of these metrics to that process. The first prerequisite is that the process (and any subprocesses, which are often present) must be well mapped out so that all the decision points, workflows, roles, inputs, outputs, and dependencies are known. Armed with this information and some insight into sales dynamics, the metrics that best measure the activity relevant to the process can be selected. It is acceptable to have the same metric fall into more than one sales process area. This reflects the fact that sales processes are inherently interdependent; therefore, one metric may capture performance information important to more than one process. For instance, the sales metric for *Forecast Accuracy* could be assigned to both the sales management and the training process areas.

A complete list of every process area, and all metrics contained within it, is proprietary, as it reflects the comprehensiveness of the metrics database, the completeness of the taxonomy, and the thoroughness of the sales process diagnosis. Nevertheless, in an attempt to help clarify this concept, below is a complete list of the fifty-eight sales metrics Sales Benchmark index has assigned to the process area of *Territory Design:*

Account maintenance time allocation	Accounts per executive
Administrative time allocation	Breakeven point
Close rate	Cost per appointment
Customer acquisition cost	Customer breakeven point
Customer churn rate	Customer share
Customers	Customers per sales rep
Deals issued via RFP	Direct sales lead contribution rate
Discount levels	Existing customer sales
Inbound lead ratio	Third-party lead contribution rate
Inside sales close contribution rate	Third-party close contribution rate
Internet lead contribution rate	Lead generation time allocation
Leads	Leads per sales rep
Market demand	Market growth rate
Market share	Market share gain
Marketing to sales lead follow up compliance	New business sales ratio
New customer gain	New customer sales
No decision deal ratio	Open positions
Outbound lead ratio	Outside sales close contribution rate
Pipeline ratio	Potential leads per sales rep
Quota-bearing sales force size	Sales activities to close a sale
Sales appointments per sales rep	Sales calls per sales rep
Sales deal size	Sales force size
Sales force size—executive	Sales head-count increase
Sales per existing customer	Sales per new customer acquired
Sales productivity per sales rep	Sales proposals per sales rep
Sales quota per executive	Sales quota per sales rep
Sales rep to sales manager ratio	Sales rep to sales support ratio
Traditional marketing lead contribution rate	Selling time allocation
Telemarketing lead contribution rate	Sales turnover rate

MEASURING PERFORMANCE IN A SALES PROCESSES

It is easy to envision how performance is calculated, both on an internal score and against a peer group benchmark, based on a given metric. What is harder to grasp is that there must also exist a method to determine performance across a sales process overall. In other words, how does one roll-up performance on all the metrics contained within a process area into some aggregate view of performance in that metric?

Any number of statistical techniques can be used to normalize the results of sales process benchmark. Sales Benchmark Index has developed a concept called a *Relative Index* (RI) to do just that. The RI measures relative performance of an organization for multiple metrics to arrive at a performance factor for a given process area. This is useful for determining overall performance on a process-by-process basis. In the RI calculation, all the scores on a given metric are plotted and the percentiles calculated based on median scores. From this, a scale of 0–2 is used such that a score of 2 places an organization at the level of world-class performance (top quartile), and a score of 1 places them on par with the median average of the relevant peer group. A score of 0 places the organization as the worst performer in the entire peer group. Figure 4 provides a graphical depiction of this normalization. It shows scores for three sales metrics (*Customer Churn Rate, Customer Lifetime Value,* and *Customer Share*) within the account planning process. Each score has been normalized from the actual value (in this example, the customer churn rate was 18 percent, the customer lifetime value was $896,000, and customer share was 29 percent) into a score of 0–2. This allows an organization to account for the score of each individual sales metric within a process area on a common basis so that an average can be taken. This average indicates the organization's process area performance so it can be compared to both peers and world-class organizations.

Figure 1 provides an illustration of the RI for the account planning sales process area.

In this chapter we have defined and reviewed the importance of sales process and sales methodology to sales benchmarking. We have described the relationship between sales metrics and sales process and given some examples on how this can be measured.

To be effective at sales benchmarking, an organization should have some form of sales processes, should be willing to improve these processes as part of

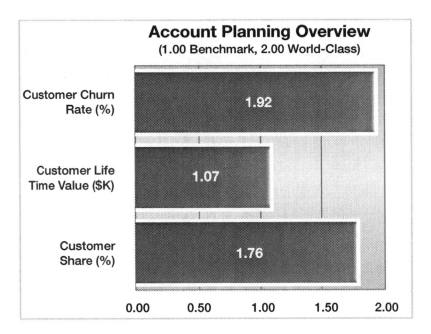

the benchmarking effort, and should look to these process areas as the prism through which to analyze their sales operations more granularly.

TO REVIEW

- A *business* process must be definable, ordered, have a customer, add value, and be cross-functional.
- When sales organizations try to capture their own internal disciplines, they can generate a jumble of documents that do not fit together well, establish common operating methods, or offer the opportunity for continuous improvement. This is because process, procedure, and policy are not well understood. Processes tell why to do something. Policies tell the what of doing something.
- Poor process design hampers efforts at analyzing its defects and improving a process when these gaps are known.
- Defining sales processes is necessary in order to achieve world-class status through benchmarking.
- There are twelve significant sales processes—account planning, budgeting, channel optimization, compensation planning, expense allocation, sales management, sales methodology, staffing, talent selection, technology infrastructure, territory design, and training.

- Sales metrics need to be assigned to each of these process areas to capture the most meaningful activity.
- Sales Benchmark Index's Relative Index (RI) is a technique that can be used to measure performance across many metrics within a process area so that an organization can be compared to a peer group and world-class status.

CHAPTER 10

STRATEGIC SALES BENCHMARKING

"Strategy without tactics is the slowest route to victory. Tactics without strategy is the noise before defeat."

—SUN TZU, CHINESE GENERAL AND AUTHOR

Now that we have completed our discussion on process sales benchmarking we need to take a step backwards, or more appropriately upwards, to understand how benchmarking fits with the "big picture." Whereas process benchmarking involves a detailed examination of the minutiae of activity within a given business function, there is another approach that yields performance comparison, and should precede any process benchmarking: strategic benchmarking.

WHAT IS STRATEGIC BENCHMARKING?

In general terms, strategic benchmarking examines how companies compete. It involves considering high-level aspects such as core competencies, development of new products and services, and improved capacity for dealing with changes in the external environment. This type of benchmarking is useful for realigning business strategies that have become ineffective.[1] Strategic benchmarking is seldom industry focused. Instead, strategic benchmarking helps identify winning approaches that have enabled world-class companies to succeed in their respective marketplaces.[2] The author of what is probably the preeminent book on this topic, Gregory Watson, noted that strategic benchmarking is a "deliberate search for a plan of action that will develop a business's competitive advantage and compound it. For any company the search is an iterative process that begins with recognition of where you are and what you have now.[3]

WHAT ARE THE FOCUS AREAS OF STRATEGIC BENCHMARKING?

Strategic benchmarking covers the full gamut of business functions and looks for those areas where applying an organizational change effort will yield the greatest gain. Typical focus areas for strategic benchmarking include:

- Acquisition strategy
- Business partnerships and strategic alliances
- Competitive dynamics
- Core competencies
- Foreign markets
- Marketplace segmentation
- Outsourcing, offshoring, and insourcing opportunities
- Process capabilities
- Product offerings and product development
- Service portfolio
- Strategic intent
- Technology enablement

It is the portability of strategic success in these areas that provides strategic benchmarking with its power and promise. This portability exists largely independent of industry segment and, therefore, provides an opportunity to any organization constrained by competitive fears from accessing best practices from others in its marketplace.

POTENTIAL DRAWBACK TO STRATEGIC BENCHMARKING

One of the drawbacks to strategic benchmarking is that strategic information from other companies typically is held closely and not released to the general public, even when competitive considerations are not operative. This is a tough obstacle to overcome because the most dangerous competitors are those firms most similar to yours. The differences between you and them are the basis of your advantage. Your objective is to enlarge the scope of your advantage, which can happen only at another's expense.[4] That is what makes *direct* strategic benchmarking—the borrowing of practices and performance from close competitors—difficult, almost impossible. But this is one of the advantages of metrics-based strategic benchmarking. Instead of seeking to copy the stated strategic policies of a peer group or world-class organization, the first step is to compare actual performance across a series of strategic measures. Once accomplished, the areas of greatest gaps represent the biggest opportunities for shareholder gain. The process of closing those gaps involves best-practices adoption—the topic for the following chapter. Suffice to say that, for strategic benchmarking, the most effective approach is first to apply focused metrics and then later adopt best practices that may or may not originate from within your industry.

STRATEGIC SALES BENCHMARKING

The assembly of a list of sales metrics that could be deemed strategic has to be culled from the complete list of sales metrics for which comparable external data exists. From this list of metrics, the next step is to determine which ones might best measure the *points of leverage* within the sales function. These points of leverage constitute indicators of excellence or lack thereof that have impact and significance well beyond the internal workings of a given sales process. In addition, these metrics represent leading indicators of future success. Companies want to measure and adopt those strategies will produce the most dramatic results and if necessary enable them to make mid-course corrections. In addition, strategic sales-benchmarking approach should be broad and measure all key areas that might impact sales success. Focusing narrowly on a single process may result in improvements in that area at the expense of in poor overall performance in other areas. Instead, strategic sales benchmarking should raise the level of performance across the board and produce optimal returns. To do so means first selecting what macro effects are desired.

Examples of some macro effects include the following:

- Existing customer retention
- Greater pipeline value
- Higher activities that lead to future business
- Increased revenue per transaction

- Market share improvements
- New customer acquisition
- Opportunities for cost savings
- Shortened sales cycles
- Talent improvements and skills efficiencies

The goal is to choose only those sales metrics that, when measured and compared against an external sample set, will expose which areas are most weak and provide definitive direction with regard to these macro effects. By definition, therefore, closing the gap in these areas of weakness will yield the greatest benefit.

SUGGESTED STRATEGIC SALES-BENCHMARKING APPROACH

In the course of our deliberations, analysis, and scenario testing, Sales Benchmark Index established a series of these leading metrics. Table 12 provides the list of the forty strategic sales metrics we selected and grouped them across all twelve sales process areas.

Table 12: Sales Benchmark Index's Strategic Sales Metrics	
Sales Process Area	**Sales Metric**
Account Planning	Customer churn rate
	Customer lifetime value
	Customer share
Budgeting	Break-even point
	Gap to goal
	Net income per sales rep
	Return on sales
Channel Optimization	Outside sales contribution
	Outbound lead ratio
Compensation Planning	Sales quota attainment
	Total available income
	Variable compensation rate
Expense Allocation	Cost of advertising
	Cost of marketing
	Cost of sales
	Cost per sales rep

Table 12: Sales Benchmark Index's Strategic Sales Metrics	
Sales Process Area	**Sales Metric**
Sales Management	Sales quota per sale Sales productivity per sales rep Forecast accuracy Pipeline ratio
Sales Methodology	Sales activities to close a sale Sales cycle length Sales deal size
Staffing	Ramp time to full sales productivity Sales rep to sales manager ratio Sales rep to sales support ratio
Talent Selection	Sales turnover rate Interview pool needed Sourcing pool needed Time to backfill a sales rep
Technology Infrastructure	Sales growth rate Technology CRM/SFA system utilization Technology lead source system utilization Technology mobile system utilization
Territory Design	Close rate Customer acquisition cost Customers per sales rep Potential leads per sales rep
Training	Training budget Training hours per sales rep

Armed with this list of the best indicators, organizations can conduct a strategic sales benchmark, the results of which will indicate both the metrics *and* the process areas that are most deficient. The former helps provide a sort of fiduciary triage, helping organizations get to work immediately closing the gaps in the areas farthest from their peers. The latter helps by indicating where next to turn the benchmarking microscope. Which process areas are most in need of improvement? By performing the strategic sales benchmark as the first major benchmarking effort, organizations avoid the mistake of prediagnosing their problem areas, which can lead to decisions to conduct process benchmarks in processes that do not offer the best opportunity for significant return.

The strategic benchmark also serves as a barometer that should be revisited frequently to recalculate-baseline performance. Sales variables are largely interdependent; so a change in one area may impact another area. By constantly keeping your finger on the pulse of your strategic benchmark, you should stay attuned to the overall opportunities that exist and keep your team focused on the big picture.

PULLING IT ALL TOGETHER

So what does the fruit of a strategic sales-benchmarking effort produce? At its most basic level, there is usually some sort of summary indication of which process areas are deficient (relative to the peer group) and by how much. Sales Benchmark Index generates such a report for its members and uses the RI approach to norming the metrics within a given sales process areas. Figure 2 depicts the summary chart for a sample strategic sales benchmarking effort. It shows that there are five sales process areas that are in the bottom quartile vis-à-vis the peer group, four that are in line with the peer group, three that are approaching the top quartile, and none that have achieved world-class status (indicated by a RI score of 1.75 or greater). This stoplight comparison chart leads to a deeper investigation of the magnitude of the revenue and cost-savings opportunity in the five most deficient process areas. This detailed financial analysis is covered in Section IV.

Priority	Category	Rating	Rating
1	Territory Design	0.41	☐
2	Sales Methodology	0.54	☐
3	Account Planning	0.62	☐
4	Sales Management	0.62	☐
5	Staffing	0.64	☐
6	Compensation Planning	1.08	○
7	Channel Optimization	1.09	○
8	Technology Infrastructure	1.10	○
9	Budgeting	1.17	○
10	Training	1.30	☆
11	Expense Allocation	1.33	☆
12	Talent Selection	1.49	☆

Figure 2: Overall Relative Index Performance on a Sample Strategic Benchmark

WRAP-UP

This chapter has discussed the need for strategic benchmarking, some of its focus areas, and how to accomplish this within the sales function. The next step is to address the very in-depth and important topic of best practices—how to identify, share, adopt, and leverage them to close the gaps unearthed through benchmarking.

TO REVIEW

- Strategic benchmarking examines how companies compete. It involves considering high-level aspects such as core competencies, the development of new products and services, and improved capacity for dealing with changes in the external environment.
- A drawback to strategic benchmarking is that the information organizations attempt to obtain from other companies is typically held closely and not released to the general public. This drawback is overcome through use of metrics-based strategic benchmarking.
- The goal of strategic benchmarking for sales is to develop a list of metrics that represent points of leverage within the sales function. These points of leverage are indicators of potential excellence that will have a financial impact of significant magnitude—well beyond a minor payback from a tweak to the internal workings of a given sales process.
- Sales Benchmark Index has provided a list of forty strategic benchmark metrics for the sales function and has cross-referenced these to the twelve process areas discussed in Chapter 8. These metrics represent the points of leverage for sales.
- A relative index (RI) stoplight chart is one means to display the results of a strategic sales benchmarking effort to expose the process areas that represent the greatest opportunity.

CHAPTER 11

BENCHMARKING AND BEST PRACTICES

"Old Truth: Thou Shalt Not Steal"
"New Truth: Though Shalt Steal Non-proprietary Ideas Shamelessly"

1988 MOTOROLA PUBLIC INTEREST ADVERTISEMENT

Best-practices benchmarking is about understanding and improving the processes within the business, not about comparing sets of numbers. It is what comes after you have diagnosed the problem areas and quantified the magnitude of the opportunity for financial gain. Best-practices benchmarking is the *how* of closing the gap in current performance to an improved one. Interestingly, the organizations from which you select a best practice to emulate may or may not have been in the peer group used for metrics comparison. In fact, many times they are not.

Best-practices benchmarking can take many forms, but it always contains a strong component of process-based mimicry. Knowledge gained through the study of an organization known to be world-class in a particular area is distilled into a set of guidelines, habits, processes, and policies that can be introduced, with suitable emendations, into the organization seeking improvement. This series of steps—identify, capture, analyze, extract, modify, and implement some other organization's best operating practices as your own—is the essence of best-practices benchmarking.

THE INTERSECTION OF BEST PRACTICES AND BENCHMARKING

The literature on best practices for benchmarking is expansive and deepening.[1] It is not hard to see why—imitation is the sincerest form of flattery—and, when possible, companies want to learn from their noncompetitive peers in as rapid and nondisruptive way as possible. One way to accomplish this is to hire a strategic consulting firm that can leverage a large client list, many engagements, and a cadre of experienced staff who act as the conduits through which best practices can flow. The downside to this approach is that it requires an arbitrator (the consultancy), which is limited to a third party's thought leadership and content, and can be expensive. An alternate approach is internal best practices benchmarking. Best-practices benchmarking encompasses the effort necessary to:

- Identify those companies that are known for excellence in a certain discipline or process.
- Gain agreement from them to study their unique set of policies, operating environment, and techniques.
- Determine if and how this discipline should be modified so that it can be imported into your organization's unique culture and systems.
- Make those modifications.
- Implement the new discipline/process and enter into a cycle of continuous improvement.

It is important to understand that any effort at best practices benchmarking should follow a metrics-driven benchmarking exercise. Why is this so? The effort to import such best practices is a difficult one, and can be expensive and time-consuming. Accordingly, it should not be undertaken until your organization has proven that, when adopted, such best practices will impact an area that shows a significant gap between current-state and world-class status. This gap is revealed first through the metrics-driven analysis of sales benchmarking. Table 15 lists best practices and the sales metrics with which they are associated that were identified during a strategic sales-benchmarking effort of a client of Sales Benchmark Index. Performance in each of the sales metrics listed in the table was determined to be deficient as compared to world-class and peer-group status. The next step was to list what best practices were available that pertained to this metric and could be patterned from other companies. Such a list formed the basis for a best-practices implementation follow-up effort.

Table 13: Partial List of Best Practices Relevant to Sales Metrics		
Best Practice	**Process Area**	**Sales Metric**
Establish a break-even volume Approach to Sales cycle	Sales methodology	Sales activities to close a Sale
New-hire productivity acceleration techniques	Staffing	Ramp time to full sales productivity
Identifying turnover risks upfront	Talent selection	Sales turnover rate
Setting effective sales growth targets	Technology infrastructure	Sales growth rate
Implementing measurements for rep closing capabilities	Territory design	Close rate
Quantifying hidden customer acquisition costs	Territory design	Customer acquisition cost

SEVEN LEVELS OF BEST PRACTICES BENCHMARKING

Before launching an effort in best-practices benchmarking, it makes sense to understand the topic a bit better. A good way to do this is to explore the different types of benchmarking. As one would expect, there are several levels of benchmarking that relate to best practices.[2] These levels begin at the most basic and proceed to the most involved (but also most effective) form. In reading about the definitions and activities of each level of best-practices benchmarking, some might be tempted to think that seems so simple. Where is the complexity found in most corporate programs? If your thoughts tend to this direction, you are not alone. And yet most organizations are not putting energy and commitment to these areas, so even if the concept is basic, the execution is lacking. In fact, as the goal of a best-practices benchmarking effort is improvement, the "dogma of any particular benchmarking approach [is] unimportant. [Best-practices] benchmarking is a business practice or skill with countless forms and applications".[3] With that said, each level of best-practices benchmarking is described below.

LEARN FROM PAST SUCCESS

Organizations should perform the technique of *success analysis*. This encompasses the habit of documenting what went right as well as what went wrong on any number of corporate-specific tasks. Oftentimes, such places of success reveal the existence of *Centers of Competency* that can be exploited by other areas of the business. Virtually anything—meetings, reports, projects, programs—can be captured and assessed using some form of success analysis. There are even software programs in the knowledge management industry that perform this function. The first step is to recognize when there is success and document it. The more difficult follow-up actions of publicity, sharing, and emulation are where the value is obtained. This is the most elemental form of best-practices benchmarking; it is surprising that so few companies practice it.

BORROW GOOD IDEAS

"Small companies tend to be especially skilled at idea importation. . . . Starved of resources, small companies naturally develop a beg, borrow, and creatively imitate [sic] mentality that enables them to leverage others' experience and learnings."[4] The important concept is that these ideas originate from outside the organization and are freely available. Ideas can come from research (a far more realistic activity in today's open Internet search society), observation, and inference. The source is not especially important as it comes from the public domain. What is important is the fact that the idea is already working for some other person, company, or organization. There is some creative adoption and recognition necessary to perceive that another best practice can and should be applied to your own. For example, an experience with a cutting-edge customer service system might inspire an IT executive to revamp her internal support center. As with the "learn from past success" technique, it is relatively easy to find good ideas, but more difficult to implement them into areas of the company where they do not yet exist.

BEST IN COMPANY

This type of benchmarking captures the follow-up activity that occurs in those companies collecting large amounts of data through CRM or other sales-related systems. Through the collection, assessment, and display of this data in various dashboard systems, sales executives can spot the best performers. The trick that many miss is not simply to identify who scores highest in one or more significant sales metrics but, instead, to systematically study those top performers. What are they doing, why, and when that helps them excel? What are their habits and attitudes? How do they differ from the median quota-bearing sales representative or sales manager? Answering these questions allows a company to assemble a list of "best in company" practices that can then be disseminated throughout the organization.

INDUSTRY STANDARD

This type of benchmarking, and the next three that follow, all require comparison of internal performance to external performance. What differs in each is the degree of excellence represented by the external sample set. In "industry standard" benchmarking, the goal is to bring some aspect of the organization up to the level of the relevant peer group. This may not seem like it will result in much accomplishment, but such comparisons are relative. The gap between your company's current state and the peer group in one process area might be great and the financial payback large. However, this does not imply that the current state of your organization in a different process area might very well exceed the same peer group.

INDUSTRY LEADERSHIP

This type of benchmarking is not greatly different from the previous one, but it captures an element that sometimes can be missing from industry-standard benchmarking. As discussed previously in this section, the definition of a peer group for purposes of benchmarking may or may not contain companies that are directly or even indirectly competitive. It may be a valid sample set and not even contain members from the same industry. This is because the effort is benchmarking a sales force, not a company, and there is enough common among sales forces of similar size, channel, and geography that industry is not necessarily determinative. This is where "industry leadership" benchmarking becomes an attractive option. Here the goal is clearly to exceed competitors' performance in the function being benchmarked. The ability to demonstrate this superiority rests heavily on the discipline of competitive intelligence.[5] In the end, the fruit of achieving such industry-specific excellence is the confidence that the function being benchmarked is contributing more to business than all of the relevant competitors. This does not imply that the function (sales, for instance) has achieved a competitive advantage for the company, even though it has attained industry-leadership status. It may very well be that the sales abilities of all market participants are limited. If so, it clears the way for the final two forms of best-practices benchmarking.

BEST IN COUNTRY

Achieving this designation may or may not have significance to the organization based on its customer base, market, and geography. Those selling to government organizations or those in relatively closed economies will value this highly. Being the best in a nation in a critical business function can assist in advertising, talent recruitment, and even marketing. "Best in country" can be demonstrated if the data exists to support it and the organization considers it relevant to compare a business function across many industries, services, and companies.

WORLD-CLASS

The urge to be the Babe Ruth of benchmarking is irresistible. Sales leaders particularly are always on the hunt for the "Big Idea" that is easily adopted and yields breakthrough results. These do exist, but they are a precious few. Most successes achieved through benchmarking are a series of modest improvements—singles, steals, bunts, and the occasional double—that, taken together, enable a sales organization to achieve world-class performance. To attain world-class status in benchmarking requires a deep and longstanding commitment, resources, patience, and a willingness to persevere through many obstacles. One of the most difficult experiences for those who embark on a world-class-benchmarking effort is the humbling experience of comparing their performance against the best in the world. Oftentimes the gaps are large enough as to be discouraging, even humiliating. The sheer possibility of this is enough to give pause to even the most self-confident sales leader. Still, making the investment in becoming world-class is the best way, in truth the only way, through which sales can become the source of sustained competitive advantage. The operative word is "sustained" because today's new idea is tomorrow's standard operating procedure. "To give some idea of the difficulty in achieving these sort of performance levels it is worth mentioning that in . . . the United States out of the [many] hundreds of applicants for the Malcolm Baldrige Quality Award up to the year 2006, only 60 have [reached this designation]."[6]

OVERCOMING HURDLES TO BEST PRACTICES BENCHMARKING

The first common difficulty faced when attempting to do best-practices benchmarking is ensuring that you possess sufficient knowledge of internal IT systems and business processes to enable meaningful comparison. That can be overcome with diligence, budget, and introspection. Another hurdle to best-practices benchmarking is a simple one—knowing in what companies such best practices can be found. Industry reputation is sometimes undeserved. How many times, in fact, have we read a press release or some other publicly available story about our company that spurred us to think, *That doesn't sound like my workplace!* The same holds true for the many other forms of media that trumpet organizational excellence. There has to be confirmation using empirical data or at least verifiable information. Even if you are relying on word of mouth to find best practices worthy of emulation, seek corraboration from multiple sources within the target organization who hold different roles, experiences, and motivations. As one would expect, the most significant obstacle is the difficulty in obtaining information from external organizations, whether they be competitors or not. There are some common techniques and channels to get this done (e.g., publicly available white papers, books, peers, employees with past history of competitors, former business partners of competitors, research companies, trade associations, online forums, chat columns specific to the industry). Much can be learned from plying all these sources, but it is typically not enough to establish a comprehensive, detailed, empirical source of information against which to glean best practices. And, even when you are able to extricate the key details of a best practice from an industry leader, there is the challenge of importing it into your environment. The first part of this effort is determining if a particular practice is even suitable for your situation; the second part is determining what modifications need to be made to the practice and which ones to your organization so that the technique/process is adopted rapidly. The last, and most significant, hurdle is the most difficult to overcome—resources—the time, talent, and budget over which so many corporate initiatives compete.

CONNECTION BETWEEN BEST-PRACTICES BENCHMARKING AND WORLD-CLASS STATUS

"Best practices are those practices that have been shown to produce superior results; selected by a systematic process; and judged as exemplary, good, or successfully demonstrated. These practices are then adapted to fit a particular organization. *Best Practice Benchmarking* is the most powerful type of methodology for identifying best practices and involves comparing the performance levels of organizations for a specific process or activity and capturing, analyzing, and implementing best practices."[7] The idea is that by adopting these "best practices" across its business functions, an organization can transform itself and radically improve the business relationships it enjoys (e.g., partners, customers, shareholders). Some see world class in terms of a specific business function, as we do with sales. Others argue that best practices must be deployed across all the functions to merit the title of world-class organization.

Most organizations are just searching for better practices that they can quickly identify and implement. Robert Camp, the modern-day father of benchmarking stated, "the point of best practices is to discover and close performance gaps, so defining 'best' might be as simple and subjective as what an executive instinctively feels is best, knowing the business and its competition. Adopting this process does not necessarily mean aiming for world-class."[8] But what is the definition of world-class? In terms of metrics-based business benchmarking and best-practices benchmarking, the term "world-class" has been defined many different ways. Overall, it can be thought of as organizational excellence—established via de facto recognition by a community of users/customers, a de jure award by an impartial third party, or an empirical assessment through benchmarking.

This leads us to the final topics of this section—defining world-class for the sales function and describing how a self-aware sales force will be able to determine its maturity level as a preparatory step for benchmarking.

TO REVIEW

- Imitation is the sincerest form of flattery and, if it is possible, companies want to learn from their noncompetitive peers in as rapid and nondisruptive ways as possible.

- Best-practices benchmarking is the effort necessary to emulate the business processes operated by top organizations.
- There are seven levels of best practices benchmarking as follows:

  1. Learn from past success
  2. Borrow good ideas
  3. Best in company
  4. Industry standard
  5. Industry leadership
  6. Best in country
  7. World-class

CHAPTER 12

THE IMPORTANCE OF BEING WORLD-CLASS

"We are what we repeatedly do. Excellence, then, is not an act, but a habit."

—ARISTOTLE

Every organization has the potential to field a *world-class* sales force, regardless of list size, history, or market. To get there it takes is a firm commitment to deploy a continuous benchmarking habit. How else will you know when you have achieved world-class status? Such comparisons point to what the successful companies inside and outside your industry, are doing. World-class organizations know how to master change; they are able to weather the vicissitudes of marketplace change, competitive dynamics, and product portfolio overhauls, and still hit their numbers. You learn from their experiences and then adapt them to your environment. Imitation is the sincerest form of flattery—and the easiest.

It is no surprise that benchmarking has emerged as a major force for corporate change and renewal. The fact is that companies, public and private, want to improve. They seek to maximize their shareholder or owner wealth and are constantly on the lookout for new ways to do so. Through that wide door enters benchmarking—a discipline that offers the prospect of unearthing improvement opportunities of many different magnitudes. Through benchmarking, organizations can understand how they compare to peers that are similar enough to them in geography, size, and sales channel that such a comparison is meaningful. These comparisons can be high level, as discussed in Chapter 10 or they can be rather detailed, as discussed in the process benchmarking Chapter 9. However, comparison to a relevant peer group really only leads to the extreme possibility of mediocrity. On a personal level, we do not seek merely to exceed the average; high-achieving students do not bring home C grades with joy, nor do A players revel in making a wage just a bit more than everyone else. No. Instead, at the individual and the organizational level, we desire excellence. The search for excellence at the corporate level is equivalent to attaining world-class status. Just what world-class status is, how it relates to benchmarking, and what are the benefits of obtaining it are the subject of this chapter.

NUMBER 1 OR NUMBER 2 OR GET OUT

Influenced by management guru Peter Drucker, Jack Welch, former chairman and CEO of General Electric, decided in the 1980s that all the businesses under his control had to have as their strategic objective to be #1 or #2 in their market segment.[1] The goal, of course, was not just to be the top first or second in a market; instead the real goal was improve the value of the company. Drucker convinced Welch that this technique of business unit selection was the way to do it. Welch's decision to embrace this approach and adopt the mantra of "fix, close, or sell" led to an explosion of value for GE shareholders. GE's success resulted in this wealth-maximization strategy becoming part of corporate received wisdom. There continue to be management theorists who argue that business model diversity yields value over and above what is lost by not being #1 or #2. There is an American linguist from the early twentieth century who would disagree with them.

ZIPF'S LAW OR "WINNERS TAKE ALL"

Zipf's law, named after George Kingsley Zipf (1902–1950), a philologist and professor at Harvard University, can be summarized as such:

> *The probability of occurrence of words or other items starts high and tapers off. Thus, a few occur very often while many others occur rarely.*

He discovered that the most popular word in the English language ("the") is used ten times more than the tenth most popular word, one hundred times more than the one hundredth most popular word and one thousand times more than the one thousandth most popular word. Figure 3 shows a logarithmic-by-logarithmic Zipf plot for words on a given day on the popular Web site Wikipedia. It shows, as you would expect, that the most common occurrences are "the," "of," and "and."

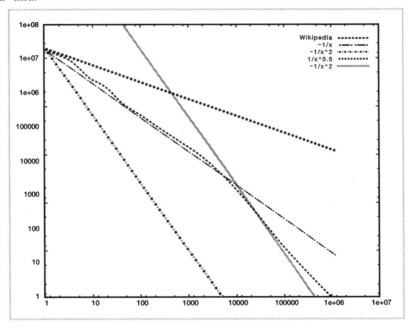

Figure 3: Zipf Distribution for Word Frequency on the Wikipedia Web site (November 27, 2006)

So what does this have to do with benchmarking or sales or the concept of world-class?

Marketing maven Seth Godin has applied this statistical law to the way in which we propagate and receive ideas. Godin noted that Zipf's law applies to any number of frequency distributions, including market share for software, soft drink sales, automobile production, candy bar consumption, and the frequency of hits on Web site page hits. The point, Godin made, is simply this:

> *In almost every field of endeavor, it's clear that being #1 is a lot better than being #3 or #10. There isn't an even distribution of rewards, especially in our networked world.[2]*

It may seem more than obvious that it is better to be #1 than #3 in a given market, but what Zipf's law tells us is that the punishment for not being #1 in a market segment is much more severe than you might initially assume. Fifty percent of the market might as well be a monopoly, because the drop-off is so steep. What that means for those who do not hold the #1 position in their market is that the price of strategic inactivity is corporate death. Attempting to become best in class, another moniker for world-class, in all business functions is the way up and out for those not privileged enough to dominate their market at the top of a Zipf distribution. The way to obtain this world-class status is through benchmarking—using the techniques of comparative analysis to find the gaps and best-practices implementations to close them. So, now that we know world-class is the goal, how do we know if we have reached it?

DEFINING WHAT IT MEANS TO BE WORLD-CLASS

World-class can be a loaded term, meaning many things to many people. In our research we have found it used, largely without specific attribution or definition, to define companies that are very good at what they do. Moving beyond that, though, to a concrete definition is when the arguments begin. However, it is vitally important to arrive at a proper definition of world-class, one that is open, understood, and consistent. The remainder of this chapter seeks to do just that. But before diving into the details, let us first establish a taxonomy of sorts with regard to the term "world-class."

WORLD-CLASS FOR A SPECIFIC METRIC

Within benchmarking, there are several different perspectives on what it means to be the best, to be world-class. These perspectives are probably best understood first by looking at the benchmarking's microcosm—the individual metric. At its core, benchmarking is an exercise of comparing one organization's "score" against others on a series of metrics. Sometimes, especially when undergoing a process benchmark, there may be as many as one hundred individual metrics against which an organization will compare itself to a peer group. Sales executives often want to know, for each individual metric, how they compare against peer group and world-class organizations. Take the sales metric *Ramp Time to Productivity*,[3] for instance. Showing world-class status for this individual metric level can be done in three basic ways:

1. Take the average of the "highest" scores (top quartile, for instance) in this metric from only those organizations in the peer group.

2. Take the average of the scores in this metric from those organizations in the peer group that have been declared to be world-class via a macro technique.

3. Take the average of the scores in this metric from those organizations, both inside and outside the peer group, that have been declared to be world-class via a macro technique.

Of the three, the first technique always yields a higher score for world-class than the second one, because it includes only those who scored the best in that specific metric.

WORLD-CLASS OVERALL

Another way to view world-class status is from the macro level. Because some metrics are mutually exclusive (i.e., scoring well on one prevents you from scoring well on another), some prefer to look at world-class from a top-down perspective. There are several ways to calculate an overall world-class status as well. Each of these approaches can be applied to all organizations in the peer group or all organizations in a sales-benchmarking repository or an amalgamation of both. Three different approaches to determine macro world-class status are as follows:

1. Choose a handful of metrics (no more than five, to be practical) that are determined to be indicative of superior performance. Determine who scored "best" (top third, for instance) in each metric. Choose only those organizations that scored best in all metrics. This usually yields a very select crowd.

2. Determine a way to "norm" the scores for each individual metric. In other words, since metric values are represented in many different terms (e.g., $ per person, days, $ per order) it is necessary to establish a common scale so that a score for the metric *Sales Turnover Rate* can be compared to *New Customer Gain*. In doing this, an organization's actual metric score (say, their *Sales Turnover Rate* was 34 percent) is converted into a simple number (a 3.1 on a base scale of, say, 1–5). There are several different statistical techniques that can be used to accomplish this; the key is to publish the norming technique used so all concerned can understand it. Using this norming approach, calculate the total average

normed score across all metrics and choose the highest (again, say top) quartile.

3. Another approach is a combination of the first two approaches. In this approach you still cherry-pick the top five or so metrics, but also norm the scores as in the second approach. Once normed, choose those organizations that score highest (again, say, top quartile).

WORLD-CLASS FOR A PROCESS

Business processes describe where the work gets done—they capture the roles, the workflows, the dependencies, the tasks, the documentation generated, and the automation tools needed. An organization wanting to improve itself by emulating a world-class one is going to want to mimic the latter's processes. Accordingly, some believe that the most meaningful unit of measure in establishing world-class sales status is the process area, not the metric. How one would measure world-class status for a process requires a combination of the approaches used in the bottom-up metric view and the top-down overall view. First, all metrics within a process area would need to be normed. Next, the best performers (top quartile, again) in the normed metrics would be selected as world-class. This straightforward approach is helpful to those who must follow a benchmarking-measurement effort to accomplish the real work of improvement.

MORE THOUGHTS ON WORLD-CLASS

We have described so far different means of calculating world-class status based on a bottom-up (i.e., metrics-driven) view of performance. There are those in the best-practices community, however, who consider that using only metrics as a means of determining world-class status is too limiting, even when bounded by dimensions like sales channel, geography, and sales force size. Advocates for a more holistic determination of world-class advance the following arguments:

- Aggregate sales excellence is not captured by sales-specific process that do not map well to overall performance. Therefore, a sales force categorized as world-class must prove, in a sense, that its contribution was determinative to organization performance. Therefore, world-class status much correlate to measures like net profit, shareholder wealth, market share, and so on. Although it is possible for a world-class sales force to be saddled with a set of subpar business functions whose performance is so bad that their negative impact on the bottom line overwhelms the positive contribution from sales, this is indeed a rare occurrence. It is so rare, these proponents argue, as to be statistically insignificant.

- Others note that most measures of world class performance tell only how other organizations have already performed, not necessarily how they are going to perform. Therefore, the metrics that should be selected for inclusion in the set that determines world-class are leading indicators, not lagging ones. This would ensure that those who wish to emulate world-class sales organizations do so with an element of future predictability in their plans. We find this a compelling argument and one that should inform future sales benchmarkers especially when they elevate their sights to achieving world-class status.

- Others believe that in addition to looking at leading indicators, a track record is equally important. Year in and year out, those organizations that remain world-class are truly the elite. How far back should one go to determine whether this consistency has been established? Three years? Five years? More? Such questions are worthy of debate. Either way, we find this observation to be valid as well. When choosing whom to emulate, an unbroken track record of sales excellence vis-à-vis a peer group is compelling.

WORLD-CLASS IN SALES

There are those, us included, who believe that the quantitative and productivity-oriented sales metrics we have been discussing do not capture all that is relevant about an organization. Such metrics enable organizations to determine the specific areas where performance improvements will yield the most significant results. Failure to consider the productivity dimension will result in improvement efforts that do not move the revenue or cost needle. However, there is another, equally important, aspect to characterizing sales force excellence and that is maturity. By maturity we mean a favorable systems support, and culture environment that enables an organization to improve and, more important, to sustain any sales performance successes. Failure to accommodate this maturity dimension will result in improvements that are short-lived, if at all.

In their measurement of current state and in application of best practices to close gaps in performance, sales benchmarkers need to address both of these dimensions. Figure 4 below represents a magic quadrant display of maturity and productivity mapped out on a standard scatter plot. The designation of world-class in this sense can be captured at this intersection of the top quartile in both dimensions. "Up and to the right" is an old dictum of the sales profession and it applies here, too.

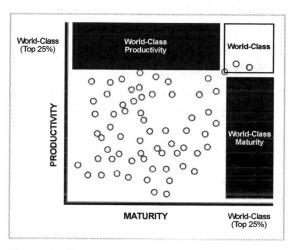

Figure 4: World-Class Magic Quadrant

WRAP-UP

We have discussed the concept of world-class in this chapter and have explained how it differs from a peer group comparison. As the old saying goes, a picture is worth a thousand words. Accordingly, Figure 5 below graphically depicts what confronts the Acme benchmarkers when they plot their performance against a relevant peer-group world-class status. The gaps between Acme and a world-class company are immediately apparent in this approach. Such is the clarity that sales benchmarking brings.

TO REVIEW

- There are many different techniques to measure world-class status— a bottom-up approach through individual metrics, one that focuses on the sales process, and one that takes an overall view. All are potentially valid.

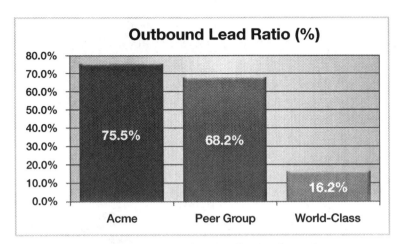

Figure 5: Sample Comparison for the Outbound Lead Ratio Sales Metric

- Zipf's law, when applied to the current global marketplace, provides a stern warning to those companies that are comfortable with mediocrity. The penalty for not being #1 is severe.
- Using a quantitative approach, you can objectively define, measure, and evaluate your sales force's performance relative to other, world-class sales organizations that rank in the top 25 percent based on maturity and productivity measures.
- The intersection of the productivity and maturity dimensions—at the point where the top quartile in each can be identified—represents compelling definition of world-class.
- Once your sales organization has been benchmarked against your peers and world-class sales performance, you can then develop a plan to consistently outsell the competition.

CHAPTER 13

THE SELF-AWARE SALES FORCE

"He who knows others is learned;
He who knows himself is wise."

—Lao-tzu, Tao te Ching

We have spent the majority of Section II covering many of sales benchmarking's more intimate aspects—strategic sales benchmarking, process sales benchmarking, world-class sales organizations—all terms that should now be lodged firmly in your lexicon. What remains to be discussed, though, is what steps a sales leader needs to take to prepare his or her organization to begin a sustained benchmarking effort. That preparation and self-assessment activity is the focus of this chapter.

THE NEED TO SELF-ASSESS YOUR SALES FORCE

Sales benchmarking is not a one-size-fits-all proposition. Organizations and their sales forces have distinguishing characteristics that influence whether and how they should be compared against each other. The results of sales benchmarking—metrics, scores, gaps, comparisons—all need to be evaluated when they are finally produced. This evaluation step must be performed in the context of what type of organization is being assessed, into what markets it is selling, in what geographical areas it is selling, what sales channels it is using, and so on.

These various attributes are used to place the statistically significant results in the proper context. All these attributes taken together enable you to determine what sales force *category* applies to your organization. Once you understand which category applies to your sales force, you can then take the next step of determining the maturity level at which your sales force is operating.

SIX CATEGORIES OF SALES FORCES

Sales forces can best be characterized by their dominant trait, which typically falls into one of the following six different categories:[1]

1. Delivery
2. Order taking
3. Missionary
4. Technician
5. Demand creator
6. Solution provider

Each category is discussed in its turn with examples and an indication of how this category of sales force should be treated when sales benchmarking.

DELIVERY

The primary task of a *delivery* sales force is to deliver the product or service. This type of salesperson is commonly found in distribution companies where the value creation happens as a result of moving a product from point A to point B. Examples of a delivery sales force might be courier services, FedEx delivery staff, or a local beer distributor. Sales benchmarking can help *delivery* sales forces accelerate cycle times, improve vendor-managed inventory turns, and decrease customer service defect rates.

ORDER TAKING

The primary focus of *order takers* is to fulfill demand. Generally, the prospects for order-taking sales forces have already determined that they need the product or service being sold. They may need a small amount of advice on what version of the product to buy (premium or regular package, color, size, etc.), but they are not comparison shopping when they reach the order-taking salesperson. Oftentimes, the clients of order-taking sales forces will use the Internet or a toll-free number to place an order. This approach is best suited for products and services sold in high volume at low prices. Examples of order-taking sales forces include all those supporting online retail and e-commerce. It is a large category indeed. Sales benchmarking can help order-taking sales forces lower order errors, improve repeat business, upsell new product lines, and increase average order size.

MISSIONARY

The role of *missionary* salespeople is to educate the marketplace to build brand awareness. Usually, these salespeople do not actually take the order, but influence the prospect to choose their products and services. If they have direct contact with a prospect, they typically direct them as soon as possible to a fulfillment provider. Examples of missionary salespeople include those who offer tastes of free food in retail grocery stores, speakers who tout books, and those in the more active marketing departments who go "on the road" to tour new product launches. Sales benchmarking can help missionary sales forces expand their prospect reach, improve the quality of their education efforts, and broaden portfolio penetration across the customer base.

TECHNICIAN

The *technician* sales force is characterized by a preponderance of technical sales reps or sales reps who cannot complete a sale without the direct assistance of a presales engineer. These sales forces are commissioned to sell a product or service that is technically advanced and hard to understand without expert assistance. The engineering "consultants" who fill this sales role can explain the key differentiated attributes of their products or services. Examples of the technician sales force can be found in electronics, aerospace, certain pharmaceuticals, and select defense-industry providers. Sales benchmarking can help technician sales forces shorten typically long sales cycles, differentiate from competitors, and produce more compelling value propositions.

DEMAND CREATOR

Demand creators are the classic transaction-based, business-to-business sales force. They focus on creating demand where none previously existed or at least where desire for their product and service was low. Demand creators are responsible for managing pipelines, prospecting, creating customer-specific value propositions, nurturing relationships, and closing deals. Virtually the entire business-to-business sales community falls into this category. Sales benchmarking can help demand-creator sales forces improve their close rates, build better pipelines, reduce sales cycle lengths, and increase average deal size.

SOLUTIONS PROVIDER

Solutions Provider sales forces are focused on solving customer problems. These solutions often involve many products and services cobbled together by several different companies that have been seamlessly pieced together for the client. Sometimes, solutions providers represent one massive company (say, IBM) that is attempting to provide all aspects of a solution themselves. Typically, though, solutions providers stitch together a series of products and services from various vendors into an apparent seamless whole. This type of sales force is often faced with longer sales cycles and extended client engagements. Examples of solutions-provider sales forces include consulting companies, value-add resellers, and rich media producers. Sales benchmarking can help solutions-provider sales forces improve solution-to-customer match, establish more accurate customer expectations, and decrease dissatisfaction resulting from unresolved problems.

DETERMINING YOUR SALES FORCE CATEGORY

Determining which category best fits your organization and business culture depends on your go-to-market strategy and the type of services and products you sell. In order to help determine which of the six categories of sales forces best applies to your particular organization, each sales leader needs to ask, "What is the specific objective of my sales force?" Here are a few sample questions you should ask so as to understand and appreciate which of the six categories most closely applies to your sales force:

- Do you segregate your sales force between hunters and gatherers?
- Do your sales reps also provide customer service?
- Do your sales people have much control over price?
- Do you sell a product or solution or a service?
- How much time do your sales reps spend in educating your prospect vs. fulfilling the order?
- Does your sales team actually deliver the service or product, too?

- Does your sales team include technical support or presales engineers necessary to explain the solution or product?

WHAT IS THE VALUE OF KNOWING YOUR SALES FORCE CATEGORY?

As discussed in Chapter 11 on best practices and again in Chapter 17 on focused action, the fruit of a benchmarking program is change. Based on the comparative analysis performed and the gaps identified, an organization will choose any number of possible remediation plans to achieve the desired sales force transformation. Typically, these strategic efforts involve software implementation, training, third party assistance, internal staffing resources, budgetary adjustments, and other project-management aspects normally required when trying to change organizational practice/behavior. Much is at stake in these projects and risk reduction is a key goal. That is a key benefit of determining your sales force category. Designing an implementation plan aimed at the wrong category will lead to a failed project. The sales leader will rapidly become frustrated, both with sales benchmarking and with the efforts to bring about improvement. In addition, if the project managers sheperding these sales transformation efforts do not adjust their plans based on the sales force category, they will be unable to achieve success, likely feeling as though they were trying to pound a round peg into a square hole. Therefore, we advise sales leaders to use the questions above and the category descriptions to determine the appropriate sales force category so as to orient your benchmarking-inspired solutions.

HOW MATURE ARE YOU?

With the sales category now determined, the next step prior to initiating a benchmarking effort is to perform a snapshot analysis of your sales force maturity. Knowledge of both sales force category and sales force maturity will ultimately inform and guide your benchmarking implementation plan. Once you appreciate these two internal sales force characteristics, you can better understand how your group compares externally. This will allow you to plan your organization into a magic quadrant that measures world-class status.

USING A METHODOLOGY

The effort to assess maturity can be performed in a perfunctory manner or with the due diligence of a formal consulting project. In either case, you will need a measuring stick—some device against which to provide a rating scale. Such scales are found in the family of maturity models. The most well established is Carnegie Mellon's CMMI methodology (which measures software development program maturity). This approach spawned a whole host of imitators, each of which varies only by industry and activity being measured. Examples include the Six Sigma Maturity Model, Business Process Maturity Model, the IT Service Capability Maturity Model, and so on.[2]

THE SALES MANAGEMENT MATURITY MODEL

In this book, Sales Benchmark Index introduces the Sales Management Maturity Model, a formal methodological model for measuring sales force maturity. To our understanding, it is the first maturity model designed to be applied to the sales business function. This methodology uses a scale of Level 1 to Level 5, each of which is clearly defined, to assign maturity scores. According to the Sales Management Maturity Model, adoption of benchmarking will move a sales force through the following seven "value points": understanding past successes, borrowed ideas, best in company, industry standards, industry leadership, best in class, and world-class.[3] To obtain world-class status (as discussed previously) an organization must be in the top 25 percent of both maturity and productivity. Above all, the Sales Management Maturity Model Methodology helps organizations determine at which value point to initiate their sales-benchmarking improvement effort. Figure 6 below shows the name and progression of each of the five levels, which are shown as *Chaos, Defined, Reportable, Managed,* and *Predictable.*

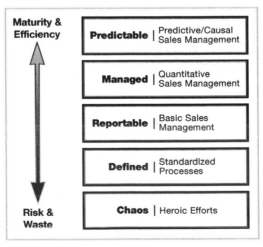

Figure 6: Sales Management Maturity Model scale

EXPLANATION OF THE SALES MANAGEMENT MATURITY MODEL'S FIVE MATURITY LEVELS

In order to better understand the characteristics of a sales force at these levels, it makes sense to provide a more robust definition for each.

LEVEL 1: CHAOS (AD HOC ACTIVITY)

At Maturity Level 1, processes, if they exist at all, are ill defined and unmanaged. Thus, the sales environment is neither stable nor predictable. Maturity Level 1 sales organizations are characterized by a tendency to overcommit and underdeliver. They demonstrate inconsistent performance and are unable to repeat successes (if they occur at all) or even provide plausible explanations for them. They thrash about in times of crisis, whipsawing from one reflexive response to another. In this frenetic effort, they often exceed expense budgets, miss cost targets, and find it impossible to predict future revenue based on a sales pipeline. Success in these organizations depends on the heroic efforts of key individuals rather than a proven system. By its nature, such success is fleeting and dependent on the few willing to exert extraordinary effort on behalf of the sales organization. In tracking performance, the management team relies on qualitative measurements that vary from person to person and team to team. A Maturity Level 1 sales force performs ad hoc execution in all twelve sales process areas discussed in Chapter 9.

LEVEL 2: DEFINED (PROCESSES DOCUMENTED)

At Maturity Level 2, most sales processes that support corporate objectives have been developed and documented. Maturity Level 2 organizations have invested in the tools necessary to support the sales force, but processes have not been adopted throughout the organization. Though past accomplishments are at times repeatable on similar sales campaigns with similar scope, sales management cannot consistently depend on such outcomes. Success in these sales organizations varies from individual to individual and team to team, depending on the level of competence and/or degree of process adoption. In tracking performance, the management team relies primarily on qualitative attributes. Though quantitative measurements may be used as well, the accuracy of analysis is often not sufficient to make sound decisions due to data inconsistencies. A Maturity Level 2 sales force demonstrates a series of formalized processes and policies governing all twelve sales process areas discussed in Chapter 9.

LEVEL 3: REPORTABLE (PROCESSES ADOPTED)

At Maturity Level 3, the sales processes documented in Maturity Level 2 have now been thoroughly adopted by the sales force. Maturity Level 3 organizations have made the commitment to drive processes and tools into the culture. The change is represented by the fact that formalized aspects of the sales process—workflow swim lanes, mission statements, value propositions, software automation, objection-handling instructions, and other process guidelines—have now been comprehensively implemented. Instead of a paper trail in formal documentation, Maturity Level 3 organizations can point to behavior changes across the sales force. Since the sales force has embraced process discipline and supporting sales tools, past accomplishments are now repeatable, regardless of campaign type or scope. Sales management can now consistently depend on their execution. Consistency in these organizations is evident as the system ensures a minimum level of performance. In tracking performance, management relies on quantitative measurements for internal and lagging indicators of success. Each member of the sales force is aware of what is being measured and management uses data to reinforce decision making. A Maturity Level 3 sales force boasts adoption of process and policy governing all twelve sales process areas discussed in Chapter 9.

LEVEL 4: MANAGED (QUANTITATIVE SALES MANAGEMENT)

At Maturity Level 4, the sales management team relies primarily on quantitative internal data to manage the sales force and achieve corporate objectives. Maturity Level 4 organizations have developed and published a series of leading indicators of sales success. They have also connected these indicators to the twelve sales process areas so that a defined series of these metrics motivate, measure, and predict sales force results. Data quality consistently improves, and data and quantity increase in depth and complexity in a Maturity Level 4 organization. Sales management sees this data as a key to unearthing future improvement opportunities and in making even more routine decisions. Problems in Maturity Level 4 organizations can often be identified by management before they significantly impact performance due to the focus on leading indicators. Best practices are proactively sought out and shared across the organization, resulting in a consistent source of sales-improvement collateral. A Maturity Level 4 sales force is characterized by improvement efforts in the twelve key sales processes based on quantitative analytics, sales managers' capability to take proactive steps using leading indicators to ward off signs of trouble, and the introduction of several new subprocesses that were not operational prior to Maturity Level 4. These new subprocesses include *Data Quality Improvement Process* and *Best-Practice Identification & Sharing.*

LEVEL 5: PREDICTABLE (PREDICTIVE/CAUSAL SALES MANAGEMENT)

At Maturity Level 5, the sales management team has advanced to the point of being able to sufficiently predict sales performance and understand causality. Sales metrics that are leading indicators of success are regularly captured and benchmarked against external data sources, ensuring that the organization is exceeding peer group medians and achieving world-class status where possible. Level 5 Maturity organizations focus on continually implementing incremental and innovative process improvements. In order to execute, Maturity Level 5 organizations leverage the participation of an empowered sales workforce aligned with stated business objectives. These motivated workers are able to optimize a series of nimble, adaptable, and innovative sales processes. The organization's ability to rapidly respond to changes and opportunities is enhanced by finding ways to accelerate and share learning. A Maturity Level 5 sales force is driven to excellence. It does not settle for improved internal performance year over year; instead it seeks quantum improvements through external best-practices benchmarking. As part of its formalized continuous-improvement efforts, these sales forces utilize a final pair of sales techniques—*Sales Process Innovation* and *Causality Analysis & Resolution.*

NOW WHAT?

We have spent some time reviewing each level in the maturity hierarchy. Some readers may also have an idea which one best describes their sales organization. Sales Benchmark Indexs Sales Management Maturity Model comes with a set of diagnostic tools that provides a more accurate and detailed means to measure sales force maturity. Use of these proprietary tools results in a more accurate assessment of your sales organization's maturity. Knowing where your organization ranks on the sales force maturity scale provides insight into which systems and processes need to be addressed and helps establish a "jumping off" point successful sales-benchmarking effort.

By knowing your sales force category and sales force maturity, you are ready to compare yourself to others. For instance, a maturity score of 3.4 excellent or merely good for a technician-style sales force in the package goods industry? Is a maturity score of 2.1 mediocre or very poor for an order-taker–style sales force in the retail market space? The answers to these questions will need to be provided by the organization assisting your benchmarking effort.

PRODUCTIVITY BENCHMARKING

As we saw earlier, the maturity and productivity measures capture separate dimensions of the benchmarking magic quadrant, but both must be known in order to determine how far away world-class sales performance lies. Therefore, resist the temptation to make radical moves to improve maturity until you also perform a productivity benchmark. The productivity benchmark is the heart of the sales-benchmarking process. This is what allows your organization to compare its performance to a relevant peer across a wide range of sales metrics—all within the twelve sales processes. This benchmarking effort will reveal which areas of investment will yield the most significant improvements.

How to accomplish that productivity benchmark is the subject of Section III.

TO REVIEW

- There are six widely deployed categories of sales forces known as delivery, order taking, missionary, technician, demand creator, and solutions provider. These categories depend on business culture and go-to-market strategy.
- Determining which category best reflects your sales organization will govern and guide the efforts to establish your maturity level.
- In order to assess sales force maturity, you should use a maturity methodology. One compelling version of this is Sales Benchmark Index's Sales Management Maturity Model.
- Once you have pegged your sales organization's maturity level and sales force category, you are prepared to address the required methods and tactics to develop a consistent, winning strategy. The next step is to perform a rigorous productivity benchmark.
- Once your sales organization has been benchmarked against your peers and world-class sales performance, you can then develop a plan to consistently outsell the competition.

SECTION III

GETTING IT DONE—
FIVE STEPS TO
EFFECTIVE SALES
BENCHMARKING

CHAPTER 14

METRIC IDENTIFICATION (STEP 1)

"The way to get started is to quit talking and begin doing."

—WALT DISNEY, FILM PRODUCER/DIRECTOR, ANIMATOR,
ENTREPRENEUR, PHILANTHROPIST

Now that benchmarking has been defined and its applicability to the sales function clearly understood, how do you get started? Where do you begin? This section will explain in detail how to implement sales benchmarking and data-driven decision making in your organization. The approach we will use is Sales Benchmark Index's 5 Step Sales Benchmarking Program.

Benchmarking is a data-intensive exercise and derives its value from comparing information at different points in time. The first step in a executing sales-benchmarking effort is to identify which key sales-related metrics to measure. An organization wanting to embark on this sales benchmarking journey must first contend with the hundreds of possible sales metrics and operating statistics. Reviewing all these metrics is daunting. What sales leaders need to select such metrics is a prism through which to view them to determine their significance. That prism is the Sales Benchmark Index Formula for Sales Success.

DEFINE YOUR TERMS

Metric identification begins with a review in Figure 7 of the Sales Benchmark Index Formula for Sales Success to determine the drivers of your firm's overall sales performance:

Figure 7: Sales Benchmark Index Formula for Sales Success

First, you must define in your company's business terms each nonconstant variable in this equation (*Activities, Conversion, Transaction, and Talent*). For example, how do you define an activity? Is it a lead? Is it an e-mail? Is it a phone call? Is it a virtual sales call? Is it a face-to-face sales call? A proposal? Is it something else? Or is it all of the above? It is important to keep in mind that the goal is to identify the key activities performed by your sales team that have the most *significant impact* on whether you win a deal tomorrow, next week, next month, or at all.

An additional area of focus—cost—lies outside the Formula for Sales Success™ equation but underscores it, too. Benchmarking your sales costs against a relevant peer group will result in a decrease to your sales-related expenses. In a similar fashion, benchmarking your measures of productivity against peers will result in increased revenue through improved sales. By doing both simultaneously (i.e., the revenue line increases and the expense line decreases) an organization will generate greater profit for each dollar of new sales generated. This boosts earnings and results in improvement of the sale metric known as *Return on Sales.*

SELECTING YOUR STRATEGIC SALES METRICS

Once you have defined each of the four nonconstant variables in terms specific to your company's sales force, it is time to select the specific metrics to measure. Appendix B lists ten common sales and marketing metrics. There are many more from which an organization can choose. These metrics range across the entire spectrum of the twelve sales processes discussed in Chapter 9. Publication of the details of such metrics in a formal taxonomy represents important evidence of the competency of a third-party benchmarking firm. In addition to the existence of these basic sales metrics, there are a virtually inexhaustible number of composite metrics that can be created by linking, averaging, combining, or otherwise integrating base metrics into proprietary metrics so that the result is a measurement that captures something unique about a sales operation.

It is unreasonable to think that any organization could (or would even want to) measure every possible sales metric. Therefore, the first step is to pare down the possibilities to a strategic list (between twenty to fifity) that are judged as the best indicators of future performance and have the most likelihood (when gaps are closed) of positively impacting the organization. Organizations can either accept the recommendations of qualified third parties as to which metrics belong in a "standard" strategic list or develop their own set. In pursuing the former approach, organizations are more likely to be able to access external data against which to compare themselves; however, they may find some of the metrics more difficult to calculate because they must accept someone else's taxonomy for data input definitions or metric formula definitions.

By using the latter (customized) approach, organizations gain control over the metrics and their input definitions, but they may find themselves without meaningful external data sets for comparison. If they do choose this approach, the process of deciding which metrics to include in such a strategic list requires an understanding of the corporation's strategic objectives, some internal measurement, external benchmarking data, frequent reviews with the sales team, and occasionally expert third-party assistance. We recommend the following selection criteria be used as a guide when deciding which strategic sales-benchmarking metrics to choose:

- Relevance to your company's overall sales performance
- Connection between corporate performance and sales performance
- Degree to which each can be a leading indicator of sales performance
- Availability of the internal data and the effort required to collect the data
- Availability of the external data that correlates to the internal data
- Conformance to a corporate strategic objective

Identifying the strategic metrics you want to measure will teach you a lot about your organization. Most companies have never thought of their sales performance in terms of the Formula for Sales Success or ever considered measuring their sales force according to the many metrics from which to choose. By simply communicating the workings of the formulas, and discussing the dimensions that will be tracked with your team and the connection between these metrics and future sales force performance, you will be able to bring focus to the types of activities that are most important to your organization. Oftentimes, this initial communication and education process leads to some discernable performance improvement even before moving on from this step in the process.

ACME CHOOSES ITS STRATEGIC SALES METRICS

We again will use the example of Acme Company, a fictional publicly traded business services firm, to inform and explain each of the steps in the Sales Benchmark Index's 5 Step Sales Benchmarking Program. Acme has been faced with the challenge of growing top-line revenue by 20 percent in the next fiscal year. The Acme senior vice president of sales has decided to adopt sales benchmarking as a means of determining how to exceed this goal.

To accomplish this, the company turns to the Formula for Sales Success to determine where this revenue growth can be achieved. Acme Company uses the criteria described in this chapter to determine the best strategic metrics to support each of the four variables in the Formula for Sales Success. Having screened these possible base metrics, Acme selects twenty-six different strategic sales metrics and arranges them in accordance with each of the four variables contained in the Formula for Sales Success. Table 14 below lists the metrics chosen by Acme.

Table 14: Acme's Selected Revenue-Based Strategic Metrics	
Formula Variable	**Sales Metrics**
Activity	Lead generation source
	Number of sales leads
	Number of sales calls
	Number of sales appointments
	Number of sales proposals
Conversion	Market demand
	Sales per call
	Sales lead to call conversion rate
	Sales call to appointment conversion rate
	Sales appointment to proposal conversion rate
	Sales proposal to close sale conversion rate
	Sales cycle length

| Table 14: Acme's Selected Revenue-Based Strategic Metrics ||
Formula Variable	Sales Metrics
Transaction	Existing customer sales Share of customer Customer churn rate New customer gain New customer sales Sales deal size Sales price variance
Talent	Sales productivity per sales rep Annual sales turnover rate Ramp time to full sales productivity Recruiting Total available income Quota-bearing sales force size Annual sales quota amount per sales rep

In addition to the formula variables, Acme decides to benchmark the cost dimension. In so doing Acme aims to exploit an opportunity to reduce SG&A expenses as well as boost revenue growth. Table 15 below lists the six additional cost-based strategic sales metrics chosen by Acme.

| Table 15: Acme's Selected Cost-Based Strategic Metrics ||
Dimension	Sales Metrics
Cost	Return on sales Customer acquisition cost Cost of sales Cost per rep Cost per call Break-even point

By conducting these benchmarks simultaneously, shareholder wealth will be generated through the ultimate increase in share price. By benchmarking itself against these metrics and determining and the relevant peer group, Acme considers that it will be able to identify where the greatest opportunities exist. With that knowledge and insight firmly in hand, the Acme vice president of sales expects to be able to drive the 20 percent revenue growth promised to Wall Street—maybe even more.

YOUR TURN?

You have seen what Acme has done in this step—it stuck a stake in the ground and began its sales-benchmarking effort. So, too, can you. Identifying your strategic sales metrics will set the stage for the next steps. Hopefully, when you complete this phase, the process of educating your team on the key metrics that will be measured will have resulted in some performance improvement of your sales force. However, any early "quick win" victories pale in comparison to the opportunities that lie ahead of you during data collection (Step 2).

TO REVIEW

- Benchmarking is a data-intensive process and derives its value from comparing information at different points.
- Organizations embarking on their first benchmarking effort are well advised to use a standard methodology. This chapter and the rest of Section II use the Sales Benchmark Index's 5 Step Sales Benchmarking Program™ to explain this process.
- The first step in executing sales benchmarking is identifying which key metrics to measure. Metric identification begins with a review of the Sales Benchmark Index Formula for Sales Success™ to determine the drivers of your firm's overall sales performance.
- In Step 1, organizations should develop a list of twenty to forty strategic sales metrics that can make the biggest impact. This selection process can be done by accepting a third-party-derived set of strategic metrics or through internal measurement, external benchmarking, and frequent reviews with the sales team.
- By simply communicating the workings of the formula and discussing the dimensions that will be tracked with your team, you will bring focus to the organization on the types of activities that are most important.

CHAPTER 15

DATA COLLECTION (STEP 2)

"Prediction is very difficult, especially if it's about the future."

—NIELS BOHR, DANISH PHYSICIST AND NOBEL PRIZE
WINNER

The data-collection step is the most labor intensive of the benchmarking process, but it is necessary in order for the organization to determine how it stacks up, both internally against past performance and externally against peers and world-class entities. As one would expect, the first, and easiest, task is to establish a detailed, clear understanding of internal performance in the selected strategic sales metrics. Assembling this data will likely be challenge enough; however, it is not sufficient. Any sales organization that has come this far in the benchmarking effort seeks to deliver to its corporate parent a sustained competitive advantage *based on the sales force*. Therefore, discovering and understanding how you are performing relative to your peers is the most revealing effort in this step of the methodology.

So what does it mean to collect data? It sounds easy. It can be (if you know what you are looking for and have the tools to find it). However, let us first examine the different types of data.

QUALITATIVE AND QUANTITATIVE DATA

Qualitative data types are categorical ones based on human judgment and, therefore, are subjective. Examples would be the descriptive impact of a CRM system rollout, assessed usefulness of sales leads, and quality of sales rep hiring practices. Qualitative data types (both discrete and continuous) are numerical ones based on empirical fact and, therefore, are normative. Examples of discrete data types are sales metrics that have no time component, such as *Sales Deal Size, Number of Transactions Closed,* and *Number of Sales Reps per Revenue Generated.* One aspect to understand about discrete data is that, even though it may not include a unit of time in its calculation, time may bound its data set. In other words, usually discrete data is expressed in terms of a time series (i.e., ordered values observed over a certain period). For example, marketing program response rates or direct staffing costs may fluctuate over time, but there is going to be a certain time cross-section from which the data to populate the metric is drawn. Examples of continuous data types are where units of time are part of the metric calculation, such as *Time to Complete a Proposal, Customer Lifetime Value,* and *Sales Reps Sourced per Year.*

SALES BENCHMARKING AND DATA TYPES

Sales benchmarking is concerned with both data types: qualitative and quantitative. However, initially sales benchmarking focuses on quantitative data, applying both time series and cross-sectional techniques. Only after the quantitative data is analyzed does it make sense to investigate the impacts of qualitative items to determine if they are related to the root causes of underachievement.

STATISTICS 101

First we need to take a detour into the world of statistical analysis. Why? Because before you begin to collect data you need to understand what you are going to do with it, how, and why. To be useful, data needs to be transformed into information and then the information needs to be converted into knowledge (and finally knowledge into wisdom). Any organization engaged in sales benchmarking will need to understand both descriptive statistics and inferential statistics. This type of an arcane discussion is not a comfortable one for the average sales leader; indeed, it can be a challenge for a finance executive steeped in the rigors of such analytics. Accordingly, we will try to present each of these aspects in a clear manner and indicate the relevance to the data collection effort.

DESCRIPTIVE STATISTICS

Descriptive statistical data, the most common technique for presenting data, is collected, presented, and described both through manual techniques (such as surveys, interviews, recorded observations, and controlled experiments) as well as through more familiar automated techniques (primarily software tools). Descriptive statistics are used to balance a checkbook, play fantasy football, price shop at the grocery store, and so on. They are woven into the fabric of everyday life, so much so that people constantly perform such mental statistical calculations without even realizing it. For business purpose, the first type of data is normally presented in charts and graphs and then summarized into categories based on calculation types such as arithmetic mean, median, mode, and variance (usually measured through standard deviation).[1] The basic idea in descriptive statistics is to compare two or more items or objects on a common value or values over some time period to determine how similar or different they are.

INFERENTIAL STATISTICS

Inferential statistics focus on helping organizations make decisions based on data, through estimation testing and hypothesis testing. Descriptive statistics explain what happened—and not much more. Inferential statistics aim to predict what will happen based on what has already happened. There are two basic techniques one uses to perform statistical inference—estimation testing and hypothesis testing. Estimation testing involves the use of sample data (the fruit of descriptive statistics) to calculate a value (or interval of possible/probable values) whose purpose it is serve as a "best guess" for an unknown population parameter. In other words, it tries to predict some future occurrence based only on the data at hand. Hypothesis testing uses sample evidence (also the fruit of descriptive statistics) to test a claim regarding some characteristic(s) of a sample population. In other words, it first establishes an explanation for a trend or attribute of some data and attempts to confirm or contradict the assumption using descriptive data. Both of these testing disciplines are accomplished via a wide variety of analytical techniques—establishing multivariable connections, discerning patterns, understanding causality, proving dependencies, drawing conclusions, and then making decisions based on what the data represents.

BENCHMARKING AND STATISTICS

Benchmarking uses both forms of statistical analysis. It uses descriptive statistics to depict raw data patterns, present scatter plots, norm metric outputs, and so on. It uses inferential statistics to leverage the power of leading indicators, confirm a hypothese about performance opportunities, and build compound metrics that do a better job of explaining patterns than the basic ones.

GATHERING THE DATA

Now that we have explored various data types and the statistical techniques used to analyze them, we can now focus on the process for gathering data on the chosen strategic sales metrics. This effort can sometimes represent a real sleuthing exercise. Here are some of the reasons why:

- Data collection relies on the organization's culture of data sharing and knowledge management.
- Data collection is highly dependent on the formal policies for data access and control, which can be severely limiting in certain government contractor and financial services firms.
- Although reproduceable information relative to each selected metric may exist in the company, it may not be found in a searchable database. It may exist only in the observable work patterns, testable responses, and behaviors of employees.
- There are often halfway houses of data—not part of a centralized database but also not limited to human behavior patterns. In these cases data exists in obscure spreadsheets and other artifacts of corporate memory. This source data can be found, albeit with a little digging, but requires substantiation.
- Formal computer systems (e.g., CRM, SFA) for sales-related data often contain unverified and even false data based on entry problems that can sometimes be traced to implementation resistance from the sales force itself.

Because these obstacles make data collection a challenge, sales leaders need to push this effort. In addition, third-party firms can help substantially with tools and techniques to access the data, determine what is good and what is not, and extract meaningful data sets from what is not being systematically captured.

Whether done through internal resources or with the help of a third party, the first place to start digging for data is in the corporate CRM system. Other important sources of input data include systems for finance, payroll, expense reporting, training, human resources, and sales management. Sometimes the same piece of data is contained in multiple systems and the source will need to be ferreted out. This aspect of the sales-benchmarking effort takes some time, especially if it has never been done before. Once it is started, though, it gets easier as the staff doing the collection improve their competency.

The lessons the sales staff, sales management, and sales operations learn while engaging in this Sherlock Holmes data-collection exercise will be significant. It is not uncommon for many sales executives to be surprised, even shocked, at what insights come from raw data collection. This is before any analysis or peer group selection occurs. Such is the value of sales-related corporate introspection—an activity impossible without a focused hunt for data. What comes next will unlock the value of its internal data—an external comparison.

POPULATIONS VERSUS VALID SAMPLE

Armed with your internal data, you now need to compare this information externally to a population or a part of a population, known as a valid sample. A population is the set of all items of interest, for example, all likely voters in the next election or all sales receipts in the month of November. A sample is a subset of the population that is statistically representative of the population to such a degree that any possible errors that occur between the sample and the population are determined to be insignificant. Sampling is used because it is less time-consuming, less costly, and more practical to administer than trying to understand an entire population. If performed in a statistically nonbiased manner, sampling can provide results with a high degree of precision. There are several sampling techniques one can use (e.g., stratified, cluster, quota, random, matched random, convenience, and selective). Examples of a valid sample might be one thousand voters selected at random for interview or every one hundredth receipt selected for audit. An entire branch of statistics is devoted to the mathematical calculation of how accurate a valid sample set actually is. We see evidence of this in the survey results from Gallup and Roper and other political polling firms that publish their results with statements like "accurate within a range of +/–3%."

DETERMINING A VALID SAMPLE

Sales benchmarking uses sampling techniques to draw conclusions about a sales population. Otherwise, an organization would have to compare itself against the universe of all other sales forces that shared its channel type and size. Such a comparison would be impossible. Choosing a sampling technique is usually the responsibility of someone in the organization already familiar with benchmarking and statistical manipulation (possibly a representative from finance) or an outside firm hired for that very purpose. For sales benchmarking, matched random sampling tends to be the preferred method, but this is not a requirement. The most important aspect to the chosen method is that it includes organizations in the valid sample population that:

- Are relevant to the organization against which they are being compared
- Are sufficiently numerous as to eliminate statistical deviations of significance
- Have verified data with the same taxonomy as the metrics being considered
- Have not been culled to remove those known to have very good or very bad scores
- Do not include inappropriate summary measures that can distort metric calculations

This step can only be successful if there is an adequate external sample against which to compare internal results.

SOURCES FOR A VALID SALES-BENCHMARKING SAMPLE

There are several ways to assemble a statistically valid external sample source specific to the sales profession. A simple Internet search will point you to thousands of sites that have pieces of what you need—Salary.com and American Customer Satisfaction Index are two examples. A business leader in your organization could join a trade association, such as the National Association for Sales Professionals or the Sales Force Effectiveness Benchmarking Association, and participate in research projects that would provide access to some of the data you need.

Universities such as Stanford University, DePaul University, and others have also begun offering courses of study and degree programs focused on sales force optimization and are publishing research papers filled with data that you may find helpful. Market research firms such as Buzzmetrics and Business Validation Resources can also be a good source of information.

A resourceful, determined sales professional committed to benchmarking his sales force should be able to find most of what he needs to support a statistical sample set for external comparison. But, to make this search easier, firms like Sales Benchmark Index have amassed proprietary databases compiling this information in one place with all the metrics built in. Having all the data in one location can significantly decrease the time burden of performing sales benchmarking while improving the inferences that can be drawn due to the ability to look at multiple metrics in the context of one another. This specialization helps companies benchmark their sales forces more rapidly, with more confidence, and by eliminating one of the more time-consuming and frustrating aspects of this effort.

To further explain this, let's use the Acme Company example from the previous chapter. Also, to make the example easier, we are going to look at their data collection process from the perspective of the effort to benchmark just one of their chosen sales metrics—sales deal size.

ACME COLLECTS ITS DATA

Before Acme Company can collect its internal data, it needs to understand what is available and where the data resides. About two years ago, the company deployed a CRM system that includes detailed sales transaction information by customer. The CRM system also includes basic information about all of Acme Company's customers including total revenue and Standard Industrial Classification (SIC) codes. It has all of the information it needs available in a single system.

Acme Company is in luck!

Now, the company needs to decide if it will analyze every sales transaction or if it will conduct a random sampling. Looking at all data points will provide the most comprehensive benchmark and prevent the firm from making the critical mistake of potentially taking a biased sample.

Additionally, the company must decide how far back to perform the analysis. Because Acme fully deployed a new CRM system two years ago, it has consistent data on its entire sales force for that twenty-four-month period. Therefore, with two hundred members of the sales force and around four thousand completed sales transactions over the last two years, the company decides to gather data on all transactions completed over the past two years. (In general, benchmarking data older than two years has a somewhat limited value. Though historical data is interesting, and occasionally helpful, it cannot provide support for leading indicators, which require more data timelines.)

Having located the data, an export is completed from the CRM system that includes key data input values for sale amount, sale close date, product and/or service sold, sale location, customer name, customer annual revenue, customer industry, new/repeat purchase, salesperson, and salesperson role. (To compute sales deal size, only the sale amount and sale close date are needed, but the rest of the information will be valuable as Acme computes other sales metrics and even as it more deeply analyzes sales deal size trends. These pieces of internal information will be used to complete Compare and Contrast (Step 3).)

It is now time to look outside the organization to locate data that will be used to compare the firm to its peers. Acme captures information in its CRM system on all wins and losses and, when possible, notes the competitor who won the bid and the amount of the final transaction. This is a good starting point to understanding peer performance. The company also uses the Web to research its peers, capturing pricing data from peer Web sites, 10–K filing reports, press releases, and other data sources.

But soon this process becomes time-consuming and the data is found to have holes in it. Therefore, Acme turns to an external data provider like the Sales Benchmark Index to complete this part of the data-collection step. Sales Benchmark Index interviews Acme Company to understand its business objectives, industry, sales force size, sales force type, key competitors, and other factors. This allows Sales Benchmark Index to better identify Acme's peer group, as well as other world-class organizations in its industry, so that the most relevant information can be pulled from its data repository. Sales Benchmark Index constructs a peer group for Acme made up of 176 individual companies that share the following characteristics:

- Same vertical industry: *Professional services*
- Same sales channel: *Direct*
- Same sales force size: *100–1,000 sales professionals*
- Same geography: *North America*

The data from this peer group, when combined with the data gathered internally, will be used to complete the next step in the benchmarking process.

The goal of data collection is to have a statistically valid sample that can be used to identify where an organization is underperforming or over-performing in relation to its peers and other world-class organizations.

TO REVIEW

- The data-collection step is the most labor-intensive part of the benchmarking process, but it is where the organization will begin to understand where it stands both internally and externally.
- There are two types of data: qualitative and quantitative. Qualitative data are categorical such as the impact of a CRM system, quality of leads, and hiring practices. Quantitative data are numerical and can be broken down into two subcategories known as discrete and continuous.
- Sales benchmarking focuses on quantitative data types, applying both time series and cross-sectional techniques to support data-driven decision making.
- The process for gathering data on the chosen metrics is highly dependent on the individual company and the systems it uses. The information is already in the company somewhere and may take a little digging to find it.
- Sales benchmarking uses sampling to draw conclusions about the population. This is less time-consuming, less costly, and more practical to administer, and if done in the proper, nonbiased manner, it can support statistical results with sufficiently high precision.
- Having all the data in one location can significantly decrease the time burden of performing sales benchmarking while improving the inferences that can be drawn due to the ability to look at multiple metrics in the context of one another.
- The goal of data collection is to have a statistically valid sample that can be used to identify where an organization is underperforming or overperforming in relation to its peers and other world-class organizations.

CHAPTER 16

COMPARE AND CONTRAST (STEP 3)

"There is none who cannot teach somebody something, and there is none so excellent but he is excelled."

—BALTASAR GRACIAN, SPANISH PHILOSOPHER AND WRITER

ACME'S PROGRESS

Acme has thus far narrowed its focus to on one of its strategic sales metrics, has collected historical data on its sales force, and has identified a statistically valid sample of relevant peers to use as the external benchmark. Much to his surprise, the vice president of sales has realized some "quick hit" improvements as a result of successful implementation of Steps 1 and 2. Momentum for the initiative is building throughout the organization. Now the time has come for the most threatening part of the benchmarking process—comparing Acme's sales metrics values against its relevant peer group. This is when the data talks; sometimes we do not like what it says.

To get started, Acme first assemble its two main sets of inputs—the internal data on the organization's sales force and the external statistically valid sample. By this point, Acme will have compared metrics results between the two in a simplistic way. Sales leaders, who specialize in cutting to the chase, may be tempted to stop here—especially because some obvious patterns may jump out. That is a natural reaction, but stopping at this point would be a mistake because any observations would not represent a thorough assessment of the data. Before drawing any conclusions, Acme will need to acquire or hire a more advanced understanding of statistical interpretation.

WHAT ACME NEEDS TO KNOW REGARDING STATISTICAL INTERPRETATION

What are the skills and concepts that Acme lacks? Acme needs to understand and be able to use the following statistical techniques:

- Central location (mean, median, and mode)
- Percentiles
- Measures of variation (range, standard deviation, and coefficient of variation)

Having mastered these concepts, Acme will be able to correctly interpret its own data and extract meaning from comparison to the selected peer group. Without it, Acme risks moving ahead based on faulty or unsupported conclusions.

CENTRAL LOCATION

Three approaches—arithmetic mean, median, and mode—attempt to capture the tendency of a group of data by providing a central location for that data. In other words, they are different techniques that, when applied to a set of data, provide some insight into the meaning and implications of the data. Acme first needs to realize how the discipline of statistics defines each of these aspects of central location, and then needs to understand how to apply central location in evaluating its benchmark data.

ARITHMETIC MEAN

The arithmetic mean is the technique most commonly used to measure central location. It is derived by summing of a set of values and then dividing by the number of values—better known as "taking the average." Below is an exact statistical definition for the arithmetic mean as follows:

$$\overline{X} = \frac{\sum\limits_{i=1}^{n} x_i}{n} = \frac{x_1 + x_2 \, \cdots \, + x_n}{n}$$

In the above formula, x stands for an observed value, n stands for the number of observations in the data set, $\sum x$ stands for the sum of all observed x values, and $\overline{x}$ stands for the mean value of x.

Figure 8 shows an example of an arithmetic-mean calculation with five observed values ranging from 1 to 10 that add up to 20. The average of these 5 values is 4 as follows:

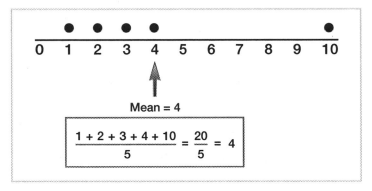

Figure 8: Example of an Arithmetic Mean Calculation

The accuracy or, better put, the relevance of an arithmetic calculation can be diminished by the existence of outliers. An outlier is statistical parlance for an extreme value. In Figure 12 the value for 10 can be considered an outlier as it "drags" the average up to an extent where the arithmetic mean is equal to or greater than all other values in the set other than the maximum value. A sales-related example might better illustrate the distortions introduced by outliers into the arithmetic mean. Assume that five salespeople produce annual revenues of $33,000, $90,000, $100,000, $110,000, and $1 million. The arithmetic mean for revenue generation of this five-person sales force is $266,600. Does this average number provide meaningful insight into the production level of the sales force? A sales manager would not take long to conclude that the arithmetic mean in this case does not provide a good indicator of overall group performance because it implies a degree of commonality of result that is not reflected in the raw data.

MEDIAN

The median is, literally, the "number in the middle." It represents the value in an ordered data set such that there is an equal amount of numbers below and above it. The median, therefore, is not affected by outliers, so is considered a better representation of central location.

Figure 9 shows an example of a median calculation on the same set of five observed values ranging from 1 to 10 that add up to 20. The median of these five values is 3 because there are two values higher than 3 and two values lower.

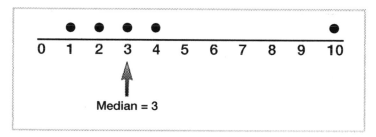

Figure 9: Example of a Median calculation

Using the sales-related example from before, the median for revenue genera-tion of this five-person sales force is $100,000. In this case, the median value of $100,000 is more representative of the overall data set than the mean value of $266,600. In other words, it is a better measure of central location. Median values themselves can be misleading when there are not many values in the data set. This is one reason why there should be a healthy number of organizations (i.e., data values) in any peer group against which a benchmark comparison will be made.

MEDIAN VERSUS MEAN

While the arithmetic mean is often used to report central location, it may not be appropriate for describing skewed distributions because it can be easily misin-terpreted. As stated above, the arithmetic mean is influenced by outliers. These distortions are revealed when the mean and median differ by a significance

extent. When this occurs, the median may be a better description of central location. A classic example of this occurs when the government reports annual
household average income. When presented with this average, many infer that
most people earn an income close to this figure. In reality, average is a good bit
higher than a significant majority of people's incomes because ultra-high-
income outliers skew the result. In contrast, the median income figure "resists"
this skewing and, therefore, is preferred by policy makers for assessing per-capita
income.

MODE

The *mode* is the value that occurs most often in a data set. Like median, mode is
another measure of central location not affected by extreme values.

Figure 10 shows an example of a mode calculation on a set of 14 observed
values ranging from 0 to 10 that add up to 62. In this case the mode for the data
set is 2 as it occurs three times and no other value occurs that frequently. As a
matter of comparison, the median for this data set is 4 and the arithmetic mean
is 4.42. So why would anyone care what the mode is, given you already know the
average (mean) and the "number in the middle" (median)?

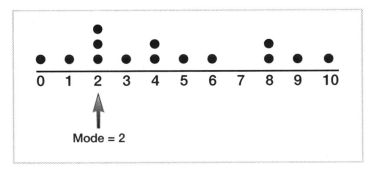

Figure 10: Example of a Mode calculation

Knowing the mode is useful where there are many of the same values in a
data set. For instance, if the Figure 10 data set had seven instances of the value of
2 and none of the value of 4, the mode would still be 2, the average would decline
from 4.4 to 4, and the median would change from 4 to 3. Not much change overall; however, with seven instances of the value of 2, the data is telling you something about a key tendency that is otherwise obscured when you average the
numbers together or split them apart to find the median. That *something* is why
the mode can be an important measure of central location.

PERCENTILES

When analyzing data, it is helpful to "chunk" it into best and worst designations. The most common way to do this is to break up data into percentiles; this aids in the understanding of data distribution and the identification of outliers. A percentile divides a set of data so that a certain percentage is above or below the given value. For instance, the median value, by definition, stands at the fiftieth percentile, since half the values are above it and half below it. The most common way to separate data in this fashion is to break it into four groupings or quartiles. For example, to locate the twenty-fifth percentile (first quartile), select the value with 25 percent of the values below it and 75 percent above it. To locate the seventy-fifth percentile (third quartile), select the value with 75 percent of the values below it and 25 percent above it.

The formula for determining percentiles is found below, where p stands for the percentile (i.e., twenty-fifth, fiftieth), n stands for the number of values in an ordered array, and i stands for the numeric point within the array that defines the point at which the quartile begins.

$$ i = \frac{p}{100} (n + 1) $$

As with all these statistical calculations, it is best to use an example to explain the concept. Figure 11 below shows a data set of 9 values ranging from 11 to 22. Using the above formula, Figure 11 displays the twenty-fifth percentile (or first quartile) as 12.5.

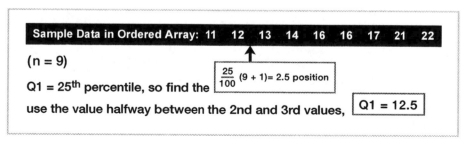

Figure 11: Calcuation of the First Quartile from a Sample Data Set

SALES BENCHMARKING AND MEASURES OF CENTRAL LOCATION

Given the statistical concepts described above, which measure of central location should organizations use in assisting analysis of their sales-benchmarking data? The answer to this question depends on the depth of sophistication and degree of complication inherent in the sales benchmarking effort. Some companies use all three measures so as to ensure that every data set enjoys the most rigorous scrutiny. Others realize the amount of effort involved in attempting to look at every set of ordered values through three different lenses, and look for a best-practices approach. It has been our experience in analyzing the distribution of sales data across both productivity and financial metrics that using the median as the central location and breaking the data at the twenty-fifth percentile (for the purpose of distinguishing world-class status) is the most effective combination of options. Focusing on this set of computations gives sales benchmarkers the benefit of simple and clean implementation while still delivering the desired result—meaningful analytics.

MEASURES OF VARIATION

Acme's sales benchmarking team chooses its measure of central location (median) and the top quartile to measure world-class status for all its sales metrics and the peer-group data set. The next step is to interpret the measures of variation. Variation indicates the degree of "spread" a set of values has around its central location. The variation helps determine the scale of the values on a chart or graph. In other words, if there is a wide variation around the point of central location, the chart will have to show a larger scale to capture all that diversity. If, however, the variation is small, the scale can be set smaller so as to magnify the differences between the data clustered around the point of central location.

There are three concepts relative to variation that are important to sales benchmarking—range, standard deviation, and coefficient of variation. Although these terms may seem academic and a little too esoteric for sales leaders who just want to hit the number, a brief foray into business statistics will be useful in becoming an effective sales benchmarker. Let's begin with defining a few key terms.

RANGE

Range is the most basic measure of variation. It is simply the difference between the largest and smallest observations. Figure 12 shows an example range calculation for a set of values from 1 to 14. Doing the simple math yields the answer of 13 for the range, as follows:

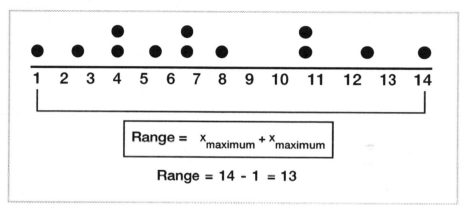

Figure 12: Sample Calculation of range

The problem with a range is that it is unable to capture any distinguishing features about the data set itself, such as the direction the data is distributed.

STANDARD DEVIATION

Based on the noted deficiencies of range in describing meaningful aspects of variation, data analysts usually turn to standard deviation to provide the necessary technique to understand variation. Standard deviation shows the statistical dispersion about the mean; in other words, it measures how broadly the values spaced in a data set are from one another around a central location point. If data points are all clustered closely around a point of central location (say, the mean), then the standard deviation is very small. If, however, there are a large number of data points far from the mean, then the standard deviation can be large. If all the data values in a set are equal, then the standard deviation is 0.

The below formula shows the calculation of the standard deviation of a discrete set of variables. In the below formula, x stands for an observed value, $\bar{x}$ stands for the mean, n stands for the number of observations in the data set, $\sum x$ stands for the sum of all observed x values, and s stands for the standard deviation of the observed values.

$$S = \sqrt{\frac{\sum_{i=1}^{n}(x_i - \overline{x})^2}{n-1}}$$

Since this formula is rather involved, we have provided a step-by-step walk-through to assist in understanding how to perform the computation for standard deviation:

1. Subtract the arithmetic mean from each observation.
2. Square each of the resulting observations from step 2.
3. Add the squared results from step 3 together.
4. Divide the total computed in step 4 by the number of observations.
5. Use the positive square root.

Figure 13 shows how standard deviation varies based on how tightly grouped the data is around the mean. In the Data A set, the data is spread between 11 and 21, leading to a standard deviation of 3.338 around a mean of 15.5. In the Data B set, the data is spread between 14 and 17 around the same mean of 15.5, but the standard deviation of 0.9258 is much less. In other words, the data in set B is almost four times more closely grouped than the data in set A. This lack of dispersion is significant in that it tells an observer that the *likelihood* of the next value added to the set being close to the number 15 is much greater in Data B set than in Data A set.

Standard deviation is a key tool in analyzing data that stems from sales benchmarking.

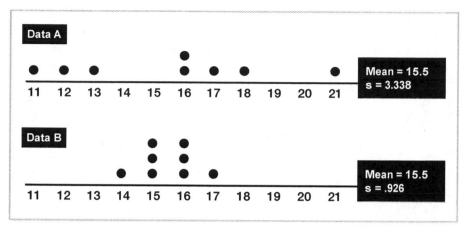

Figure 13: Calculation for Standard Deviation

COEFFICIENT OF VARIATION

Last, coefficient of variation shows the relative variation in data around the mean, expressed as a percentage. This can help add context to the standard deviation and allow variation in data sets of different units of measure to be analyzed relative to one another. The formula below shows how to calculate the coefficient of variation. In the below formula, $\bar{x}$ stands for the mean and s stands for the standard deviation.

$$CV = \left(\frac{s}{\bar{x}}\right) \times 100\%$$

The next formula provides an example calculation of the coefficient of variation to help explain this concept. Assume stock A has an average price last year of $50 with a standard deviation of $5 and stock B has an average price last year of $100 with a standard deviation of $5. Both stocks have the same standard deviation, but stock B has a smaller coefficient of variation (5 percent) than does stock A (10 percent). Using the coefficient of variation helps sales benchmarkers understand how significant their standard deviation is in relative magnitude.

$$CV_A = \left(\frac{s}{\overline{x}}\right) \times 100\% = \frac{\$5}{\$50} \times 100\% = 10\%$$

$$CV_B = \left(\frac{s}{\overline{x}}\right) \times 100\% = \frac{\$5}{\$100} \times 100\% = 5\%$$

WHERE IS ACME AT THIS POINT?

Most of this chapter thus far has been a series of explanations of various statistical terms necessary for a benchmarking beginner to be able to assess and compare data. At this point, Acme should select the median as the measure of central location for each metric calculated for the peer group. Next, Acme should determine the top quartile for the peer group scores for each metric (yielding a world-class score in that metric). Then Acme should calculate the standard deviation for each metric around the median value to determine how much spread there is around the peer group against which it is going to compare itself. Last, Acme should compare its score on each metric to the median score from the relevant peer group and to world-class to determine how large its gap is. Therefore, across the thirty-two strategic sales metrics Acme initially selected, it will now be able to calculate its own scores, peer group median scores, standard deviations, peer group and world-class scores, and the gaps. What is missing, though, is an understanding of the business value that Acme would receive by closing those gaps. Determining this "return on gap closure" is the last piece of the compare-and-contrast step.

CALCULATING THE RETURN

It is not necessarily true that by closing the gap between your and a peer group or world-class score, you can significantly reduce costs or increase revenue. To understand if such a return exists and its magnitude, you must also measure the impact that a metric has on the bottom line. Let us return to Acme and its consideration of the metric sales deal size to understand how to quantify the gap between current performance and the peer-group performance and then monetize the result to drive decision making.

UNDERSTANDING THE GAP IN SALES DEAL SIZE

For the first time in its history (because of all the sales-benchmarking computations), Acme is poised to understand the true value of each customer transaction. The next step for Acme is to complete the comparison on the internal and external data gathered during Step 2. But prior to performing this analysis, Acme must determine how to segment the data to ensure analysis will produce relevant findings that can be used to develop a performance-improvement plan.

Historically, the company has segmented its customers' annual revenue as this has been the most effective means to build sales teams, deliver sales support, and provide customer service. Acme uses four customer gradations: Bronze (< $10 million), Silver ($10–$100 million), Gold ($100 million–$1 bullion), and Platinum (> $1 billion).

Using these same segmentations, Acme then performs five different calculations on its internal data for sales deal size. These five computations are for the mean, median, twenty-fifth percentile, seventy-fifth percentile, and standard deviation. Table 16 depicts a summary of these computed values (all shown in $K) for the internal data:

Table 16: Internal Benchmark Data for Sales Deal Size					
Customer Type	Mean	Median	25th Percentile	75th Percentile	Standard Deviation
Bronze	$8.4	$7.3	$2.3	$14.9	$3.1
Silver	$43.0	$39.0	$12.0	$58.0	$11.0
Gold	$248.0	$256.0	$68.0	$367.0	$71.0
Platinum	$874.0	$749.0	$107.0	$1,681.0	$332.0

Table 17 depicts a summary of these computed values (all shown in $K) for the external data from the relevant peer group:

Table 17: External Benchmark Data for Sales Deal Size					
Customer Type	Mean	Median	25th Percentile	75th Percentile	Standard Deviation
Bronze	$12.4	$10.9	$2.9	$16.2	$3.9
Silver	$51.0	$47.0	$16.0	$89.0	$17.0
Gold	$261.0	$244.0	$76.0	$388.0	$76.0
Platinum	$822.0	$768.0	$99.0	$1,434.0	$311.0

Table 18 depicts a summary of these computed values (all shown in $K) that compares the internal value for sales deal size against the value for the relevant peer group. For instance, the value for the mean for Bronze customers using internal data was 248 (i.e., an average sales deal size of $248,000). The value for Gold customers for the peer group mean from the external data sample was 261 (i.e., an average sales deal size of $261,000). The internal value 248 is 95 percent of the external value of 261 (as can be seen below).

Table 18: Comparison of Acme Internal Data versus External Peer Group Data					
Customer Type	Mean	Median	25th Percentile	75th Percentile	Standard Deviation
Bronze	68%	67%	79%	92%	79%
Silver	84%	83%	75%	65%	65%
Gold	95%	105%	89%	95%	93%
Platinum	106%	98%	108%	117%	107%

WHAT ACME CAN CONCLUDE FROM SALES DEAL SIZE COMPARISON

The most obvious message from the data is that Acme is underperforming compared to the peer group benchmark for its Bronze and Silver customer transactions. However, the company is in line with the benchmark for Gold customers, and is even outperforming the benchmark for the Platinum customers. Beyond these simplistic assessments, though, what more can Acme learn from this data? Let us take each customer category in turn.

- *Bronze Customers.* This is the area of weakest mean performance—the internal sales deal size of $8,400 is only 68 percent of the external benchmark of $12,400. This is the area that offers the largest opportunity for performance improvement on a per-transaction basis.

- *Silver Customers.* This category is underperforming the benchmark in all categories calculated. The weakest performance is in the seventy-fifth percentile, where Acme's value of $58,000 is 65 percent of the benchmark of $89,000. This presents an opportunity for Acme to determine how to increase the larger deals with its Silver customers. One cautionary note: Acme's standard deviation of 11 is 65 percent of the benchmark value of 17. This indicates that Acme's data for Silver customers is more highly concentrated around the mean than is the data for the relevant peer group—a sign that it may be more difficult for Acme to "move the dial" on these customers since they share a more tightly concentrated tendency around the median.

- *Platinum Customers.* This is the area of strongest mean performance—the average sales deal size of $874,000 is 106 percent of the external benchmark of $822,000. While there may be an opportunity to increase Acme's performance in this area, it will be more difficult given that the firm is already outperforming its peers.

- *Gold Customers.* The median of $256,000 is 105 percent of the external benchmark of $244,000. This would be a positive sign, but there is something troubling in the data. Looking at the mean scores for Gold customers, Acme's mean of $248,000 underperforms by 5 percent the mean peer group benchmark of $261,000. This indicates to Acme that it may have some very low outlier values that are dragging its score below the benchmark. Such suspicions are confirmed when looking at the relative scores for the twenty-fifth percentile, which shows Acme's sales deal size value of $68,000 to be 89 percent of the $76,000 benchmark. This anomalous condition merits further investigation.

DETERMINING ACME'S RETURN FROM CLOSING THE GAP

To quantify revenue opportunity for improving performance, Acme needs to compute the gap between its performance and its peer group performance for the total sales for each customer segment. This will enable Acme to determine the magnitude of the opportunity presented by possible improvement in each of the customer segments. The formula below shows how to perform this calculation:

$$\text{Gap Opportunity} = \left(\cfrac{\text{Annual Revenue from Customer Segment}}{\text{\% of Benchmark}} \right) = \text{Annual Revenue from Customer Segment}$$

Table 19 shows the total revenue generated by Acme in each of its four customer segments. For instance, Acme's Bronze customers contributed $21 million of the $100 million in total revenue last year. Using the gap-opportunity formula shown above, we can calculate the magnitude of possible revenue gain Acme can obtain by matching the benchmark value for sales deal size in its Bronze customer category.

Using the mean benchmarking value, the gap opportunity is ($21 million / 68%) − $21 million for a total of $10 million. Using the median benchmarking value, the gap opportunity is ($21 million/69%) − $21 million for a total of $10.36 million. Table 19 depicts the total revenue for each customer type and the summary of "payback" possible for closing the established gaps between Acme's internal sales deal size and that of the external peer group score (all values shown in $K).

Table 19: Gap Analysis				
Customer Type	Total Revenue	Transactions (Deals)	Mean Gap	Median Gap
Bronze	$21,000	2,500	$10,000	$10,356
Silver	$14,000	326	$2,605	$2,872
Gold	$26,000	105	$1,363	$(1,219)
Platinum	$39,000	45	$(2,320)	$989
Total	$100,000	2,975	$11,647	$12,999

If Acme improves its mean performance to be equivalent to its peers in the Bronze and Silver customer segments, it will generate over $12.6 million in additional revenue. This would be a bump of more than 12 percent from what was produced the previous fiscal year. Now that it knows the size of these gaps, Acme should consider its range of options as they relate to each customer category.

- *Bronze Customers.* This is the segment with the largest potential opportunity—over $10 million is in the Bronze group. Across 2,500 total deals, Acme would have to boost its average sales deal size from $8,400 to $12,400 and, in so doing, would generate an additional $10 million in revenue. That just gets them to par with the peer group, saying nothing about achieving world-class status. The size of the prize is largest in this customer segment and Acme would be well advised to concentrate efforts here first.

- *Silver Customers.* This is the segment with the second-largest aggregate potential for gain. A closer look at the data, though, indicates that it may be relatively easier to achieve this improvement because of the significantly fewer number of transactions. In closing the gap of $10 million for its Bronze customers, Acme must make changes that impact 2,500 transactions while the $2.6 million median gap in Silver customers is related to only 326 transactions. Acme should focus on improving the average sales deal size for these customers as well, possibly even before trying to tackle the "long tail" of the smaller Bronze customers.

- *Platinum and Gold Customers.* There is not much to be gained here, at least at first blush. There are enough particularities in the data (e.g., swings in the mean vs. median outputs) that Acme would be wise to investigate further to see if there might be opportunities for improvement buried within these customer segments.

WRAP-UP

Compare and Contrast (Step 3) describes the actions necessary, after having collected the internal data and assembled the relevant peer group data, to compare them to each other. This comparison effort requires the use and understanding of a series of statistical techniques that help benchmarkers better interpret the data. In this way, organizations can determine how they stack up against peers and world-class organizations and, more important, can determine the magnitude of any return they are likely to receive by closing these gaps. Usually these findings are summarized in some sort of report that goes to the board for review. We have seen a few sales benchmarkers who prefer to highlight areas of weakness and strength with graphical flourish. They draw big red circles around the sales metric results contributing disproportionably to failure and big green circles around those metrics where performance is well above the peer group, even occasionally above world-class. This latter indication identifies internal centers of competency that are every bit as important as determining where improvement must be made to exposed areas of weakness. Whatever the format or version of this report takes, it should clearly indicate the gaps by sales metric and summarize the financial opportunity for improvement.

TO REVIEW

- The four computations used in sales benchmarking typically include:

  1. Arithmetic Mean—the arithmetic average of data values.
  2. Median—the number in an ordered data set where there is an equal amount of numbers below and above it.
  3. Percentiles—a division of a set of data into two parts where certain percentages are below the given value.
  4. Standard Deviation—the most commonly used measure of variation, measuring how spread out the values in a data set are.

- The revenue or cost opportunity that exists if performance is improved to match your peer group should be quantified. To do this, measure your company's current revenue production at its current performance level and compare that to the peer group revenue production.
- Once data has been segmented it should be arranged by at least five computations—mean, median, twenty-fifth percentile, seventy-fifth percentile, and standard deviation.

CHAPTER 17

FOCUSED ACTION (STEP 4)

"After all is said and done, a lot more will have been said than done."

—AUTHOR UNKNOWN

"Talk doesn't cook rice."

—CHINESE PROVERB

cme's sales leader gives his team a big pat on the back. By coming this far, they have already accomplished something of which few sales organizations can boast. They have located a root cause of why its sales force is underperforming. They have answered, at least in part, the question, "Why did we miss the number?" The loudest voice in the room (the previous sales leader who was convinced that sales is only an art form that cannot be accurately measured) has been replaced with data-driven decisionmaking and fact-based analysis. Opinion has been displaced by science.

Acme has persevered through some difficult tasks—selecting the strategic sales metrics, collecting internal data, compiling that internal data with the input definitions, determining a relevant peer group, acquiring the necessary data from this peer group, comparing all the data using statistical techniques, and finally determining the magnitude of the opportunity presented to close the gap in sales performance. What Acme needs now is to actually close the gap, not just talk about it. To do that will require them to complete Step 4–Focused Action, the subject of this chapter.

DOCTOR'S VISIT–AN EXERCISE IN SALES BENCHMARKING?

You have chest pain and decide to pay a call to your doctor. She informs you that your arteries are baldy clogged and, in all likelihood, you are in danger of having a heart attack—soon. What would you do next? Probably get started immediately on some behavior modification! In other words, having knowledge is important, but does not by itself solve any problems. To move from diagnosis to solution, the doctor would first "benchmark" the results of the various tests she put you through compared to your personal medical history as well as patient data found in a number of medical studies and journals at her disposal (Steps 2 and 3).

From these findings, she would then put you on a customized program to improve your health. The program, based on years of trial-and-error testing on many patients before you, would focus on the areas likely to produce the biggest impact on your overall health. If followed, this would prevent the heart attack and remove the danger, possibly altogether, from your health status. This, the creation of a remediation plan, is exactly what is accomplished in Step 4.

Last, your doctor would likely recommend regular check-ups over several years' time to measure your progress, repeat various testing regimens, compare the resulting data to new peer groups of similar patients, and make minor changes to your program to reflect these updated findings. This ongoing support is equivalent to Sustained Improvement (Step 5), which we discuss in the next chapter.

Actors, as they say, must act. And so does Acme.

THE WRONG WAY TO ACT

In its initial benchmarking report, Acme drew big red circles around the sales metrics it identified as the ones in most need of action. The company is confident that, when addressed, the results will be impressive. However, if attempts to close the gap fail, Acme will face the fact that not only has the sales-benchmarking initiative not created lasting value, but also has made matters worse by showing the areas of opportunity but not providing the means to fill them. For this reason Acme's sales-benchmarking team needs to be as committed to applying the remedies to sales challenges as it is to accomplishing its data-driven diagnosis. It is in the realization of a solution to a sales problem that value is created, not in the illumination achieved through peer group and world-class comparisons.

That is why the quickest way to destroy the political capital built up around the sales-benchmarking process at this point would be for the Acme vice president of sales to prematurely rush to adopt sales programs advertised to "fix" areas of identified weakness without testing them first. Sales-improvement programs are often launched this way, and this invariably ensures their failure. Cutting to the chase in this fashion results in false starts, dashed expectations, and a frustrated sales force that loses its motivation for change. Focused action is the antidote for the typical sales leader urged to implement a major improvement program across the board as soon as possible without having ensured success through a well-designed pilot effort.

HYPOTHESIS TESTING

Focused action is based on the concept of hypothesis testing. Hypothesis testing provides managers with a structured analytical method for making decisions in such a way that the probability of error can be controlled or at least measured. Using a statistical approach to hypothesis testing does not eliminate uncertainty in managerial environments, but the techniques often allow managers to identify and control some of it.

SOLUTION SELECTION METHODOLOGY

Sales Benchmark Index recommends a seven–step methodology to help organizations identify, test, and select the most effective solutions to the business problems exposed by sales benchmarking. Figure 14 depicts this approach as a series of steps:

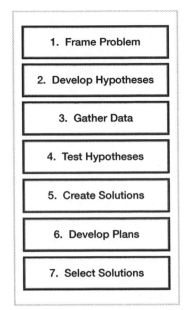

Figure 14: Sales Benchmark Index's Seven-Step Hypothesis Testing Approach

A brief description of each step in this approach is as follows:

1. *Frame the Problem:* Define the problem being addressed in specific terms.
2. *Develop Hypotheses:* List potential causes for the problem and key drivers that impact or influence each potential cause.
3. *Gather Data:* Gather relevant data, information, and background on the key drivers that will allow each potential cause to be proven or disproved.
4. *Test Hypotheses:* Analyze each potential cause to determine if the data supports the hypothesis as being the most likely cause of the problem.
5. *Create Solutions:* For those hypotheses that prove to be valid, identify possible solutions and examine each solution's feasibility for successful implementation.
6. *Develop Plans:* For those solution(s) determined to be viable, estimate all necessary tasks, investments, milestones, resources, metrics, and returns.
7. *Select Solutions:* Determine which solution(s) should be implemented using some form program approval criteria (e.g. hurdle rates for internal rate of return (IRR)).

ACME USES HYPOTHESIS TESTING

In order to see how this approach works when applied to real-world problems, let us return to the example of Acme Company. In Step 3 (Compare and Contrast), Acme identified its areas in most need of performance improvement. Now, in Step 4 (Focused Action), the company is ready to do something about it. The following explains how Acme can apply hypothesis testing to improve its performance in the metric sales deal size.

#1: FRAME THE PROBLEM

Acme's first step is to clearly identify the problem. One of the most common reasons a sales problem does not get resolved is that a complete and accurate problem description is not identified and defined up front. Acme Company's goal is to grow top-line revenue by 6 percent. The problem, whose solution will achieve this goal, is that Bronze customer deal size is 32 percent below the external benchmark of peers.

#2: DEVELOP HYPOTHESES

The second step is to identify the hypotheses that will be proven or disproven by completing the remainder of the steps in this approach. By identifying these up front, Acme will keep focused throughout its review, not careening from one idea to the next without addressing the causes and consequences of what has already been put on the table. The most important aspect of this step is to identify the key drivers of each hypothesis. There are many such factors, but we recommend including no more than two or three for each hypothesis. In fact, there is a danger in listing too many. Scientists and statisticians use a theorem called the *Square Law of Computation* to ensure that they do not construct a problem too difficult to solve. This theorem states that "for every additional variable, the complexity of the problem is equal to the square of the number of variables." For example, a problem with four variables is sixteen times ($4^2 = 16$) more complex to solve than a problem with a single variable. That is why we keep the key drivers to a manageable few. To more clearly communicate the results of this step, some choose to display each hypothesis and key drivers pictorially in an "issue tree" diagram. Figure 15 shows the issue tree diagram for Acme's hypothesis and key drivers. It will serve as a problem-solving map moving forward into the rest of the hypothesis-testing efforts.

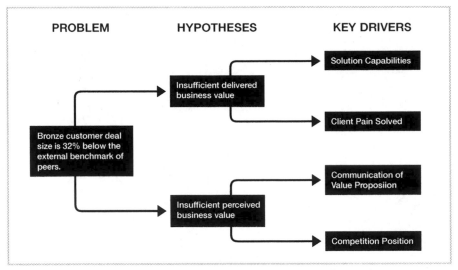

Figure 15: Acme's Issue Tree Diagram for the Sales Deal Size Improvement Effort

#3: GATHER DATA

The third step is for Acme to gather facts that support or refute each hypothesis. Facts are the building blocks of the solution. For those extremely close to a problem, it is difficult to separate facts from opinion. This is one justification some use to engage a third party to provide a more objective perspective. In either case, relying on gut instinct may be the reason a sales leader finds him in a difficult situation so it is no substitute for an objective perspective. This step often reveals areas where intuition or corporate wisdom is flatly contradicted by fact. For those sales leaders new to a situation, facts compensate for the lack of institutional memory.

That challenge Acme faces is in the actual finding of fact. Often, data gathered from different data sources will appear to conflict with each another. This is not a reason to doubt the veracity of either, but instead represents an opportunity to learn. When this occurs, further investigation typically reveals one fact is more grounded in verifiable data and the other closer to opinion or even speculation, although both may contain elements of truth. Also, when analyzing more deeply such apparently counterpoised facts, additional mitigating factors can be uncovered. Such factors warrant further consideration so as to better understand their causality. Such follow-up investigation may require the need to return to *Step #2: Develop Hypotheses* to explore these factors further. The bottom line is that when facts conflict, dig deeper. The fact-finding phase must be collectively exhaustive.

Acme, for example, gathered its facts from the following sources: internal interviews, customer surveys, observations, documentation review, and market research.

#4: TEST HYPOTHESES

The fourth step is to test each hypothesis using the facts collected in Step 3. A hypothesis can be accepted when no facts refute it. Be prudent; be cautious. When testing a hypothesis Acme will be looking for the one or two factors that contribute most to the problem. To help in identifying these, answer the following questions:[1]

- Is this the most likely cause of the problem based on what has been learned to date?
- Have all the issues be thought through?
- Have all the key drivers been identified?
- Is this a cause or an effect?
- Is this hypothesis relevant based on how the problem is defined?

Acme used these qualifying criteria questions to evaluate its two hypotheses as follows:

HYPOTHESIS #1: INSUFFICIENT DELIVERED BUSINESS VALUE

Summary of Findings:

- Per market research, customers are more satisfied with Acme's solution than the competition's.
- Acme's solution has all key capabilities as competition and some additional features.
- Acme's solution addresses the same key customer pains as competition including many "nice to haves."

Decision: Hypothesis #1 is REJECTED as not valid.

HYPOTHESIS #2: INSUFFICIENT PERCEIVED BUSINESS VALUE

Summary of Findings:

- Customers see Acme's solution as the low-cost alternative.
- Most sales are for the core offering and rarely include add-ons.
- Acme's sales force does not use consistent pricing standards.
- Acme does not use return on investment tools to justify its sale or value proposition.
- Acme has been targeting customers only minimally impacted by pain.
- The Acme message resonates loudest with financial service and health care firms, but most sales are to retail companies.

Decision: Hypothesis #2 is ACCEPTED.

#5: CREATE SOLUTIONS

Acme's fifth step is to develop tactical solutions to its problem. They should resist the urge to 'reinvent the wheel; many solutions to almost all common sales-related problems already exist elsewhere. The solution to almost any sales-related challenge can be modeled after one that has already been tested and deployed by another organization. Such solutions should contain enough detail to identify all the key tasks that need to be completed and be executable by all those who are expected to participate. Once the solution or solutions are identified, Acme must then test them to decide which is the most worthy of implementation. Such testing can be done in two basic ways. The first is a less-expensive but less-accurate approach of conducting a rigorous thought exercise. The second is the more time-consuming, expensive, but fundamentally more effective approach of conducting a pilot. The latter route is typically the best because it comes much closer to simulating the real challenges that will face the real implementation—systems issues, cultural resistance, training needs, skills deficiencies, and so on.

Acme developed a list of proposed solution to *Hypothesis #2: Insufficient perceived business value* based on a series of solutions originally proffered by the sales-benchmarking core team. The elements of the proposed solution are as follows:

- Alter commission schedule to better reward larger deals.
- Bundle more products together for total solution.

- Focus on selling add-ons.
- Develop cost-justification tools.
- Target different customers (financial service and health care groups are willing to pay most for the solution).

#6: DEVELOP PLANS

At this point the entire sales-benchmarking core team has the opportunity to review the plan and sign off on it. By this time, all the hard work to get to this point in the process will be apparent. Typically, this thoroughness of due diligence will convince the management team to sign off on the program. Acme looked at the division of responsibility between sales and marketing and divided up the core responsibilities as follows:

- Sales/Sales Operations
  - Modify commission schedule to better reward deals above $12.5 thousand.
  - Develop cost-justification tools.

- Marketing
  - Create bundled offerings of products for small customers.
  - Create common add-on packages for small customers.
  - Develop lead lists targeting small financial service and health care customers.

The rest of this step encompasses developing the actual plan with attendant tasks, milestones, dependencies, critical path, dates, roles, and so forth. These items are all typically encapsulated in a formal remediation plan.

#7: SELECT SOLUTION(S)

The last step is for Acme to select the desired solution and implement it. This step cannot be taken lightly as most problem-solving initiatives break down in their execution. Appointing a strong, proven leader to manage the project and see it through to completion is a must. Based on the plans developed in the previous step, Acme selected a solution that promised the following in terms of investment and expected return:

- Expected Costs:
  - 160 indirect hours
  - $100,000 in increased commissions paid

- Projected Results:
  - Within thirty days, develop and roll out solutions.
  - Within sixty days, increase deal size by 10 percent in target customers.
  - Within ninety days, increase deal size by 15 percent in target customers.

Having methodically analyzed small customer sales and determined the most significant ways to achieve the goal of increasing sales to these customers by at least 10 percent, Acme starts to see results that make all the effort worthwhile. Within three months of beginning the benchmarking exercise, sales to these customers is up 29 percent, far exceeding the 10 percent objective.

Acme's Actual Results:

- Within thirty days, all solutions were developed and rolled out.
- Within sixty days, deal size was up 16 percent in target customers.
- Within ninety days, deal size was up 29 percent in target customers and is nearly at the external benchmark level.

In summary, Focused Action (Step 4) calls for the identification of possible explanations for a problem, the collection of facts to prove or disprove these hypotheses, and the development and selection of solutions to address them. This chapter also described a seven-step methodology for solution selection as a tool for decision makers.

In Step 5, Sustained Improvement, we will see how Acme ensures that the recent improvements it has attained are not short-lived.

TO REVIEW

- Knowledge of defect is an important first step, but it doesn't solve the problem.
- The quickest way to destroy the political capital you have built up around the sales-benchmarking process is to prematurely rush into sales programs advertised to "fix" areas of identified weakness without testing them first.
- Hypothesis testing provides managers with a structured analytical method for making decisions. Statistical hypothesis testing does not eliminate all

uncertainty in managerial environments, but often allows managers to identify and control the *level* of uncertainty.

- Once you know high-return areas to focus on, you need to put a remediation plan in place and test it over time to measure its effectiveness, constantly tweaking it to get the results you're looking for.
- The best way to accomplish the this phase of sales benchmarking is to follow a seven-step methodology that recommends framing the problem, developing hypotheses, gathering data, testing hypotheses, creating solutions, developing plans, and selecting solutions.
- Most unsuccessful problem-solving initiatives break down in their execution. When implementing a solution to a sales problem unearthed by benchmarking, appoint a strong, proven leader to manage the project and see it through to completion.

CHAPTER 18

SUSTAINED IMPROVEMENT (STEP 5)

"All this improvement is great, but all that does is get us in the game
to play for improvements that we need in the future, so that we can
be aggressive in the marketplace."

—RICK WAGONER, CEO OF GENERAL MOTORS

A fter completing Step 4 (Focused Action), the value proposition illustrated
in Acme's business case has come to life. The senior leadership team is encouraged and wants to continue. The front-line salespeople will see that
the information being generated is relevant and that somebody is actually
doing something with it; they will begin to buy in. Time-wasting, nonvalue-adding exercises issued weekly by panicky managers have stopped, and salespeople
finally have time to go see customers and locate new opportunities.

Although Acme has come a long way, its sales leader should resist the temptation to declare all-out victory. Sales benchmarking is a program, not an event.
It should be built for the long term and ingrained in the culture of the company
so that the techniques, talents, and behaviors are not lost. Claiming permanent
victory at this point—where all that is known is the magnitude of the opportunity and some initially positive results—would be premature. Those who tout
success at this point run the risk of having sales benchmarking labeled as the latest program du jour—nice, but essentially insignificant in the long term. What
Acme wants and the sales leader needs is sustained competitive advantage, not

merely a momentary success. Completing Step 5—Sustained Improvement will ensure sustainability for the benchmarking program.

Is such sustainability even possible? Does not every program, every attempt at corporate betterment eventually diminish and stop impacting overall performance? Much research has been done surrounding the tendency for corporate performance to revert to the mean[1]. Although the details are somewhat arcane, the conclusions they reach lend powerful support to the notion that benchmarking, as a form of modeling, can improve an organization's chances of staying continuously above the norm in performance. This research has shown that persistence does exist; in other words, some companies generate persistently good economic returns, and the existence of ongoing business modeling appears to be an explanatory factor. So, for those who do not want to expend much effort and resources in conducting a benchmarking-improvement effort only to have its positive results dissipated over time as the company slouches back to the mean, this chapter is for you.

At this point, Acme's sales-benchmarking process has produced notable results and is becoming well understood. Though the amount of work put into this project has been extensive, the results have been proportional, even greater than hoped. Sustained competitive advantage is the goal, and it will only be obtained if this program moves from being a one-time event to being one that is thoroughly embedded in the company's operating procedures.

SALES BENCHMARKING AS A STANDARD OPERATING PROCEDURE

Sales benchmarking can to become standard operating procedure at Acme without replicating the heavy lifting of Steps 1 through 4. The benchmarking process can be administered by a small number of staff members and continue to bring value. The approach we recommend when an organization is ready to move the benchmarking process into the mainstream of their sales operations system is to implement an established form of quality improvement. Such programs provide techniques for monitoring and repairing existing processes that have started to get out of control. This is important to sales-benchmarking organizations because, once they have launched an improvement initiative, they need to continue to achieve its goals, maintain momentum, and not demonstrate any variations that would indicate problems with the chosen solution.

For those sales leaders who thought they had seen the last of analytics in terms understanding the complete 5-step process will have to wait for their satisfaction. There are several quality management concepts that need to be explained and understood so that sales benchmarking can be woven into the fabric of the organization.

STATISTICAL PROCESS CONTROL (SPC)

SPC is a philosophy popularized by W. Edwards Deming and others in the mid-twentieth century to help provide a rigorous model around which ongoing improvements could be made to discrete internal processes. SPC later matured into Total Quality Management (TQM), a management strategy aimed at embedding awareness of quality in all organizational processes. One SPC technique—measuring process variation—is relevant to sales benchmarking. SPC provides guidance on how to use control charts to monitor quality of conformance and level of variation.[2]

There are two types of variation in a process—special cause variation and common cause variation.

SPECIAL CAUSE VARIATION VERSUS COMMON CAUSE VARIATION

Special cause variation, which is sometimes called assignable cause variation, deals with abnormal conditions where something out of the ordinary has occurred. Since this type of variation can be traced back to a special event or sequence of events, it is the easiest type to eliminate. On the other hand, common cause variation, which is sometimes called stable and predictable variation, is inherent in any process. An example of this might be the tossing of a coin. Common cause variation would indicate that 50 percent of the time it would land on heads and 50 percent on tails. Special cause variation would result if you placed more weight on one side of the coin so that it was more likely to land there and, thus, impact the probability. Common cause variation is often very difficult to remove from a process without significantly altering the process itself, because it is inherent to the process. One way to help better analyze such variations is through the use of a control chart.

CONTROL CHARTS

Control charts monitor variations in data, highlighting trends that allow for correction before a process becomes out of control. They show when variation (or fluctuation) in data is due to a special cause not inherent to the process. They also help highlight problems that need to be corrected and identified by data outside the control limits or trend. A control chart provides a visual metaphor to help better understand the existence and magnitude of variation in a sales process.

There are several steps to plotting a control chart:

1. Take data samples over multiple subgroups of time.
2. Calculate the subgroup mean ($\bar{x}$).
3. Calculate the average of the subgroup means ($\bar{\bar{x}}$).
4. Plot the subgroup means as a line chart.
5. Calculate both the upper control limit (UCL) and lower control limit (LCL), which should be three standard deviations from the subgroup mean.

CHART FOR A PROCESS IN CONTROL

A process is said to be "in control" when points are randomly distributed around the center line and all points are within the control limits. Figure 16 is an example of a chart for a process that is in control. This process is in control because the variation around the mean is systematic and roughly predictable. There are no wide and anomalous swings in the data and the pattern is relatively consistent as opposed to a more random distribution.

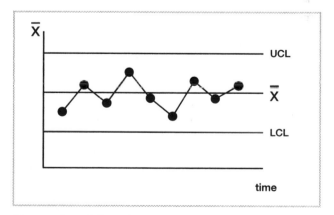

Figure 16: Control Chart of a Process in Control

CHART FOR A PROCESS OUT OF CONTROL

A process is said to be "out of control" if any of the following conditions are true:[3]

- One or more points outside control limits
- Nine or more points in a row on one side of the center line
- Six or more points moving in the same direction
- Fourteen or more points alternating above and below the center line

Figure 17 represents just such a process:

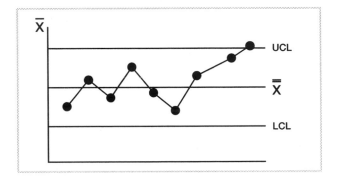

Figure 17: Control Chart of a Process Out of Control

When a process is determined to be out of control, the goal is to identify the special cause variation. Despite the seemingly perjorative connotation, an out of control process may actually be a good thing. For instance, special cause variation may be the result of sales-benchmarking enhancements implemented earlier in the process that are still playing out. In this case, the right course would be to continue monitoring the variation but take no action. However, if the special cause variation cannot be fully explained, additional analysis may be warranted to identify and eliminate its cause. This will improve your ability to specify design specifications (tolerances) and quantify the expected performance improvement.

THE ACTION PLAN

Implementing the techniques of statistical process control and applying them to the sales force will enable sales benchmarking to transition from a one-off project to a best practice inside a company. Some companies have whole departments dedicated to Six Sigma—a formal quality-improvement program first launched by General Electric that has helped many organizations govern and guide their continuous improvement efforts. A program of this magnitude is not warranted to support sales benchmarking. However, ignoring the need for variance measurement and cause analysis will doom many sales-improvement efforts, especially those that show initial promise, to eventual stagnation.

SUSTAINABLE ACTION PLANS

A formal action plan should be developed and deployed to maintain performance improvements. The first decision to make would be to appoint a sales-benchmarking project manager responsible for ongoing administration and oversight of the effort. This manager would control the plan itself, which would include, at a minimum, the following periodic activities:

- Internal review of company performance versus goals
- Attempts to do more granular sales process-specific benchmarks
- Monitoring of focused-action implementation, ensuring expected results are produced
- Data scrubbing and validation
- Monitoring of the benchmarks in the context of some formal quality improvement program

Members of a peer group will not stand still; their performance will improve as well. So, in addition to sheperding existing improvement initiatives, sales-benchmarking organizations should periodically revisit their peer group for follow-on comparison. As new areas of gap and opportunity are identified, they can be addressed through the existing program for sustained sales improvement.

ACME'S ATTEMPT TO IMPLEMENT CONTINUOUS IMPROVEMENT

Three months have passed since Acme completed Step 4 (Focused Action). In the interim, Acme sales operations staff members have been measuring and reviewing weekly the average sales deal size for new transactions to Bronze customers. The SPC chart has been used to plot performance to date.

The eighth-week performance results were the best to date with an improvement of 82 percent from the baseline prior to implementing changes. Management was delighted with the results of the project. Figure 18 depicts a control chart plot for the last nine weeks of sales deal size values:

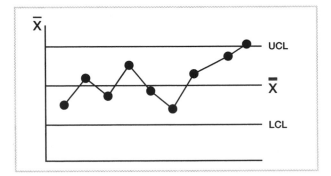

Figure 18: Acme Sales Deal Size Control Chart After Improvements Were Made

The ninth and final week saw another spike in performance that, when plotted, exceeded the upper control limit. This means that the expected value for sales deal size is now statistically out of control—the desired result. Although this is a favorable trend, it is not yet possible to determine if the lack of control stems from common cause or special cause variation. Acme decided to dive deep into the data to understand what drove the latest performance attainment. Was it an across-the-board contribution based on the new improvement effort's programs and guidance or was it due to a handful of individuals who, for unrelated reasons, had changed their behavior and reaped success? Further investigation by Acme revealed that the improvement was largely due to five Bronze sales reps in the Southeast who tripled their average deal size from the initial baseline.

ACME'S SUCCESS IN THE SOUTHEAST—A REPEATABLE PERFORMANCE?

After seeing that performance was being measured and how each region ranked against one another, the Southeast sales manager challenged his team with a competition. He hosted a best-practices sharing session during which the team reviewed the largest deals sold to Bronze customers. Together, they identified what contributed to these successes. Additionally, he announced a Sales Performance Incentive Fund (SPIF) that would reward the largest transaction over the next thirty days. Salespeople left the session with the tools they needed to be successful and were fully motivated to outperform their peers.

Upon speaking with the Southeast sales manager and his group, the sales operations team learned of the changes that had been made and summarized the best practices to be shared with the other regions. Within days of this discovery, the Southeast team was recognized by the sales leader on a nationwide teleconference and rewarded with bonuses for helping to raise the bar for the entire organization. Such sharing measurement and stack ranking of team information within an organization can spur innovation. This confirmes the organization's commitment to excellence through the recognition of star performance. The entire sales team now understands the value in providing feedback to senior sales leadership and trusts that the information provided will be put to productive use. Through this type of ongoing regular measurement and data analysis, future local innovations can be identified and shared more broadly across the organization.

At this point, Acme is on a run rate to exceed the external benchmark of Bronze deals by over 40 percent for the year. Focus on the strategic sales metric known as sales deal size has proven the concept to the firm, and Acme is now ready to repeat Step 4 for other customer categories. The power of benchmarking has been realized, the original business case expectations exceeded, and many in the organization are eager to fully adopt the methodology across the sales force.

WRAP-UP

Acme's example proves the power of benchmarking and demonstrates the results a step formal methodology can produce. In addition to understanding how organizations are performing internally as well as against their external peers, benchmarking provides a path to strategic relevance, even prominence, for any sales organization.

Acme was successful. It achieved a sustained competitive advantage. What once seemed a dream for them is now a reality.

What is stopping you now?

TO REVIEW

- Sustained competitive advantage can be obtained if sales benchmarking moves from being a one-time event to being embedded in the operating procedures of the company.
- The benchmarking process can be administered by a small number of staff members and continue to bring value.

- Implementation of process control charts and statistical process control inside the sales force allows sales benchmarking to migrate from a one-off project to a best practice inside a company.
- Your peers will not stand still. Sales benchmarking must become a standard operating procedure and part of your company's long-term strategy for success.
- In addition to understanding how the organization is performing internally as well as against its external peers, sharing the measurement and stack ranking of each teams' information within an organization spurs innovation.

SECTION IV

CALL TO ACTION

CHAPTER 19

OVERCOMING OBJECTIONS TO SALES BENCHMARKING

"Nothing will ever be attempted if all possible objections must be first overcome."

—SAMUEL JOHNSON, ENGLISH POET, CRITIC, AND WRITER

It would not be fair to spend an entire book discussing the merits of sales benchmarking, arm readers with a few examples to explain the concepts, and then consider our task complete. The real world is one where the battle of ideas is intense. Particularly in the sales discipline, where objection handling is a well-established discipline, we would be at fault if we did not provide a list of the most common objections to sales benchmarking, especially when these objections arise from sales leaders themselves.

Sales leaders have very strong personalities. They sometimes suffer from the "not invented here" syndrome, particularly with regard to any attempt to change sales processes, tactics, or strategies that did not originate from within their organization. It is for this reason that new ideas like sales benchmarking can find themselves quickly discounted.

Some of the gripes we have heard from sales leaders include:

- If benchmarking is widely deployed in corporate America, then surely it has been attempted before in sales.

- It must have been tried before and didn't work, otherwise we would have heard about it.
- At the end of the day, *sales is an art*. Relationships are what matter and they can't be measured mathematically.
- Sales benchmarking is nothing more than a fad that will soon pass with time.

Sound familiar? Accordingly, we have developed a list of the most common objections sales leaders express to sales benchmarking. The list may not be exhaustive, but it is still comprehensive enough to anticipate the approach most resisters will take. In addition, we have created a talk track of sorts to respond to these detractors in the hopes that any latent doubts can be overcome. We'll show you what lies behind each objection and some of the counterarguments that can be used to refute it.

COMMON OBJECTIONS TO SALES BENCHMARKING

OBJECTION #1: LUCK IS ENOUGH

Many below-average salespeople produce fantastic results. How does this happen? If sales really is a science and success or failure is determined by the systematic execution of a sales process backed up with irrefutable, factual evidence, how can you intelligently respond to the concept that "it is better to be lucky than good?" Flippantly, one might say that "lightning doesn't strike twice in the same place"; but that does not really address the observation that some mediocre salespeople overachieve while other top performers miss the mark.

OBJECTION #2: HARD WORK WINS IN THE END

Is it true that the harder your work, the luckier you get? Can outworking the next person deliver the results you want? Some very hard workers, both inside and outside the sales profession, fail. This is a sad situation. Everyone roots for the hard worker. Many sales managers, if given the choice, would choose an inexperienced salesperson with little track record who will run through walls to reach quota over an experienced salesperson with a pedigree who seems more concerned with the trappings of customer relationships and maintaining a favorable work/life balance than with achieving the number. Will beats longevity every day.

OBJECTION #3: CHARISMATIC SALESPEOPLE ARE THE BEST PERFORMERS

What is the role of charisma on sales results? Behavioral scientists believe that one of the reasons people succeed as leaders is not due to a set of practical skills they possess, but instead is based on a somewhat superficial impression people make on others through sometimes barely perceptible nonverbal signals.[1] Industrial psychologists have studied charisma and are still undecided as to its exact definition and cause. Many in today's sales organizations feel they know enough to spot who has charisma and who does not—they feel the same way Supreme Court Justice Potter Stewart felt about pornography: "I know it when I see it."

OBJECTION #4: INTERNAL NUMBERS TELL THE WHOLE STORY

Do the sales numbers tell the whole sales story? No, they don't. Some who first warm up to the idea of sales benchmarking do so because they think they can hide behind an artifice of statistics, driving out the need for managerial judgment and other critical sales skills. Admittedly, there are not many sales leaders who demonstrate this proclivity, but there are a few. Their objection to sales benchmarking is not so much that it is numbers-driven, but that it establishes accountability by comparing internal numbers to external ones. This is what unmasks those sales leaders who swim in numbers but hide behind them as well.

OBJECTION #5: WE DROPPED EVERYTHING TO TRY IT—AND IT DIDN'T WORK

Is sales benchmarking a lone silver bullet? If you deploy sales benchmarking and scrap everything else you're doing, are you likely to achieve success? Hardly. The sales profession is too complex, too extensive, and too dynamic to be reduced to the unitary solutions of one management discipline. Sales leaders looking for a get-rich-quick scheme will be disappointed if they put all their chips on sales benchmarking to the exclusion of all else.

OBJECTION #6: SALES BENCHMARKING IS A FAD

This objection has some teeth in that innovative concepts can boast of longevity only if they yield continual value for those who adopt them. Benchmarking as a management tool supporting other business functions has withstood the test of time and continues to extend its deployment across many disciplines.

Benchmarking as a business initiative has progressed from an interesting idea to a compelling program to an integral aspect of business. Benchmarking's applicability to the sales profession, however, is still undetermined. Initial forays have been made by early adopters, and this book constitutes one signpost on the way to industry acceptance; still, though, the chapter on the final success of sales benchmarking has yet to be written.

Certain sales fads will work for short periods of time. As Nassim Nicholas Taleb, in his ground-breaking book *Fooled by Randomness,* suggestd: An appropriate analogy can be found in investing techniques. We all know a person who has generated an excellent return on their capital over short periods. He claims to have figured out the market and tries to convince you that he has the secret sauce. But the real reason he has had success in the short run is that his specific investment style suited the macro conditions of that time period. For example, he may have deployed an approach that worked as long as interest rates stayed benign. However, as time goes by, we learn that this investment genius is out of the market after sustaining large losses. The reason is that he was never really skilled in the first place. He just happened to be in the market with the right approach at the right time. But once the environment changed, he suffered losses.[2]

Sales fads are very much the same. They come and go with the times. Many deliver short-term successes but can't produce these over longer time periods. Sales leaders who adopt these fads find themselves flashes in the pan. One day they are on stage receiving an award, and the next day they are on a performance-improvement plan and at the bottom of the stack. Then they change their story, switching back and forth between sales fads to fit recent reversals of fortune. Sales leaders know that this year's sales fad is the next quarter's flop. They avoid adopting "flavor of the month" sales programs until some critical mass has developed. Such is the thinking of a sales leader who has been burned once in the past by a sales-improvement initiative with no legs.

OBJECTION #7: LET'S JUST DIP OUR TOE IN THE WATER

Sales benchmarking is an interesting idea, but others in the organization are still not convinced. They suggest a "try before you buy" approach before committing. This is a common and understandable reaction. The concept as it is laid out in this book makes sense and after reading the book, you will be better able to leverage some of these ideas on your own.

There are two basic ways to gain experience with a new initiative prior to fully implementing it. The first is to read and speak with others who have already deployed a similar program. The other is to run a pilot or implement a simulation. This book attempts to address the first approach in that it contains case studies of sales-benchmarking implementations. But the reality for most sales leaders is that though they have a respect for other people's pasts, they are not inclined to learn from them in an academic fashion. Sales leaders seem temperamentally oriented towards experiential learning. They frequently make claims such as "these times are different" or "my [market, customer, sales model, competitive environment] is unique." Executing a pilot program allows these types of sales leaders to understand concepts through tangible experience. Then they embrace the idea as though it were their own. Psychologists call this the hindsight bias, or the "I knew it all along" effect.[3] Sales leaders prefer running a pilot to eliminate mistakes. This is built into the Focused Action (Step 4) part of the Sales Benchmark Index implementation methodology described earlier in this book.

OBJECTION #8: SALES BENCHMARKING ISN'T WORTH THE EMOTIONAL COST

Sales leaders have been burned in the past by "can't miss," improvement programs. From this perspective, they are predisposed to react negatively to sales benchmarking. One of the most common reasons sales leaders decide not to adopt sales benchmarking is due to the emotional residue from these failed initiatives. Psychologists estimate the negative effect from an average disappointment to be 2.5 times the magnitude of an average positive outcome.[4] The list of projects that have burned sales leaders is long, including sales training programs that did not bring a noticeable return on investment, expensive and eventually failed implementations of CRM or SFA software, and strategic sales initiatives sold to the boardroom but critically lacking in tactical viability. With this as a backdrop, even the most self-aware and dedicated sales leader has a difficult time controlling the degree to which these fears influence his decision making. Consequently, sales leader are less willing to commit to new programs like sales benchmarking.

OBJECTION #9: SALES BENCHMARKING WON'T REALLY WORK

This objection is usually not provided as a factual rebuttal but more as an observation that sales benchmarking violates some corporate norms or operating culture. Some might insist that the disciplines needed for sales benchmarking would be too disruptive to implement or too foreign to understand or too difficult to obtain. Since culture is central to how a company sees itself, this objection is not insubstantial. Although sales benchmarkers should take it seriously, this objection is offered to almost any initiative that promises change—especially change in behavior. Add the exposure of internal operating performance to an to outsider comparison, and it is easy to understand why sales leaders might believe that sales benchmarking might work "over there" but won't work "in here."

OBJECTION #10: BENCHMARKING IS GOOD IN THEORY, BUT NOT IN PRACTICE

Industrial theories suffer three basic fates:

- They are accepted and woven into the fabric of business.
- They are falsified by being proven wrong and therefore rejected.
- They are exposed to the hothouse of experience and, though not falsified, are not yet proven either.[4]

Since the jury is out on which category applies to sales benchmarking, the best course is to do nothing.

OBJECTON #11: THINGS ARE GOING WELL—WE DON'T NEED IT

How relevant is past performance when forecasting future performance? Is it reasonable to think that if an organization performed better than the market in the past, it will also do better in the future? This objection literally cries out for leading indicators, not lagging ones.

Many sales forces report fantastic numbers even though they break down according to the 80/20 (or Pareto) rule, which has the top 20 percent of salespeople producing 80 percent of the business. Is such an organization biased in its view by only claiming organizational sucess whom a minority of high performance is responsible? Is their view distorted? When their top 20 percent stumbles, what happens then? Panic and overreaction.

Many sales leaders become satisfied with narrowly defining their success. They consider they are doing great against immediate competitors only to see their success get wiped out by a new entrant to the market. Those who are blinded by past success have difficulty seeing their bias against new ideas.

OBJECTON #12: WE ALREADY DO THIS

Some or maybe many in your sales force may feel they already do sales bench-warming. They may already be participating in a data-oriented sales culture where internal measurement is constant. They may also have more data than they can reasonably manage. Thus, they question why they should add to an existing data-collection workload the new requirements of sales benchmarking.

OBJECTION #13: NOTHING BAD HAPPENS ON MY WATCH

Sales leaders tend to be defensive about the state of their organization, especially when they have been in charge for some time. They will often defend an improvement effort regardless of whether it is working or not. The introduction of sales benchmarking poses the threat that all was not well while the sales leader was accountable.

OVERCOMING THESE OBJECTIONS

OBJECTION #1: LUCK IS ENOUGH

Response: Not if You Want to Succeed in the Long Term

The fact is that, in the short term, some salespeople succeed not because of their own personal merit but because of favorable market conditions or being part of a company that is a clear market leader. The converse is true usually for top performers—they can get caught in a down market that severely punishes their company or value proposition. These conditions are only temporary, though. Poorly performing salespeople will eventually reveal themselves to be underequipped for the challenge and unable to consistently exceed quota. Top performers will, sooner rather than later, figure out how to succeed and then relentlessly work to attain their goals. Just as in the stock market, so too in sales: there can be short-term irrational exuberance but in the long run the quality companies emerge and deliver consistent returns.

Lady Fortuna is a powerful force—there is no question. Experience dictates that the vast majority of a sales professional's efforts will be met with rejection. If there is anyone in this world that deserves the occasional lucky break, it is salespeople.

However, that which came with the help of luck can be taken away by luck.

And oftentimes, the reversal of fortune that bad sales luck brings is rapid and unexpected. Salespeople risk their incomes on their ability to make things happen, many times without a safety net. If success has been obtained by luck in the past, what happens when the luck runs out? Does it matter how frequently something succeeds if the failure is too costly to bear? Banking on fortune alone is irresponsible. There are people in every salesperson's life counting on him to deliver; the cost of failure is high. Play the odds and bet on something predictable, dependable, and proven—sales benchmarking.

OBJECTION #2: HARD WORK WINS IN THE END.

Response: Without the Right Direction and Strategy, Hard Work Will Not Succeed

In sales, he who wants it more wins. But is work ethic enough? No. The hard workers, even those who are not outright grinds, will eventually lose focus and dissipate some of their intellectual acuity. High levels of energy and intensity cannot be sustained indefinitely. And what then? Sales campaigns are chess matches and having the right strategy is very important. The ability to think trumps the ability to work hard.

Because hard workers have a bias towards action, almost any action, they can spend precious time focusing on "noise"—pieces of information that do not mean anything or have no bearing on the outcome of a sale. Hard work and discipline do not by themselves lead to success with a high degree of probability; they are just not enough. That the old truism of "one has to work hard and work smart" is actually true. However, the accuracy of this statement is often distorted by those who use it to justify inactivity or a lack of accountability.

Sadly, these unproductive empty suits are almost as common as the hard-worker types spinning their wheels. Conversely, sales benchmarkers combine hard work with intelligence to produce outstanding results.

OBJECTION #3: CHARISMATIC SALESPEOPLE ARE THE BEST PERFORMERS

Response: Productivity Merits More Than Attractiveness—charisma Can Be Measured

Charismatic sales leaders have the advantage that the perceived cost of the alternative is too high. One doesn't judge performance in any field (sales, investments, medicine, etc.) by results, but rather by this opportunity cost—what is the price of my other options? When sales results are not scientifically analyzed, performance is not accurately analyzed. Sales benchmarking ends such inaccurate analysis, placing the charismatic sales leader in a compromising and uncomfortable position in the beginning of the process.

Let's assume that candidate A sells $100,000 and candidate B sells $75,000; from this information, one would conclude that candidate A is a better salesperson, correct? Therefore, candidate A should be given a better territory, a better compensation plan, or be promoted, right? Not necessarily. Data-driven decision making would get to the root cause of each candidates and performance. It might demonstrate, for example, that $75,000 out of candidate B's territory is a much greater accomplishment than $100,000 out of candidate A's territory. Maybe candidate B won all her business from new customers in a harshly competitive territory, while candidate A collected fax orders from existing customers doing repeat business. Or, maybe the skills deployed by candidate B in the sales campaigns had a much greater impact on results than did the contribution of candidate A.

Yet an executive making a critical human capital decision might be fooled by the impression that candidate A made during a performance assessment. Maybe he looked the part and had the numbers to back it up. Candidate B, on the other hand, may have been rough around the edges and her results, on paper, appeared inferior. So the sales executive promotes candidate A, thinking he is a sure bet. Candidate B resigns, takes a job with the competition, and goes on to eat candidate A's lunch in the marketplace.

This happens more than it should. Being able to demonstrate sales charisma is certainly an advantage, but it should not be determinative.

OBJECTION #4: INTERNAL NUMBERS TELL THE WHOLE STORY

Response: Internal Numbers Show The Facts, External Numbers Reveal the Truth

A mere grasp of computations and formulas and an orientation to sales numbers does not ensure success in sales benchmarking. It is true that sales benchmarking is a numbers game, but it is also a way of thinking. Numbers help *tell* the story; however, managerial judgment enables leaders to see inside the numbers to the root cause of the outcomes, especially when making a comparison to relevant peer groups. At that point there is no place to hide. So, in a sense, numbers do tell the story—but it is only when all the numbers are considered can the whole story be told.

OBJECTION #5: WE DROPPED EVERYTHING TO TRY IT—AND IT DIDN'T WORK

Response: Integrate Sales Benchmarking with the Other Programs

Sales benchmarking is both a tool and a thought process. It should become part of your collection of methodologies and business practices already in place. Successful benchmarkers avoid extremes as sales benchmarking works best when incorporated into the other key initiatives that may be part of in your organization's process—CRM, sales training, Six Sigma, etc. Look for ways to leverage ongoing programs—for quick wins, shared resources, and internal best practices on how to boost program adoption.

OBJECTION #6: SALES BENCHMARKING IS A FAD

Response: A Relatively New Improvement Approach to Sales—Yes, but a Fad—No; Ignore This Business Tsunami at Your Peril

Americans seem to be programmed to favor the new over the old, but there is value in not jumping on the latest bandwagon, at least not in its earliest stages. The opportunity cost of missing the "new" thing is small when compared to the damage done by having to experience all the bad business ideas in order to determine what has value and what does not.

It is possible that sales benchmarking may not survive in your organization, and if it does fail the reason may be less obscure than you might think. Realism can be punishing; the intelligence gathered through sales benchmarking can be difficult for some in leadership positions to accept, if not outright threatening. It takes guts to deploy sales benchmarking and weather its storm. Whether the courage to overcome such resistance exists in your organization or, for that matter in the sales profession as a whole, remains to be seen.

The ancient Greeks noted that "heroes are heroes because they are heroic in behavior, not because they won or lost."[5] Getting behind sales benchmarking and allowing your entire firm to understand the sales force's abilities with such clarity require heroic behavior. The outcome of the project, winning or losing, won't be determined until after the project is completed.

The difference between sales benchmarking and other sales fads lies in the duration of its success and the compounding size of its results. History reveals that many of the great scientific discoveries were initially shunned by those in positions of power and even those with specific subject matter-expertise. Those advocating radical new theories had to overcome groupthink and establish new paradigms.

From a "logical" perspective, sales force leaders should adopt sales benchmarking as a means of driving improvements in their business. However, when assessing the advisability of such "risky" ventures, *emotions* can affect our decisions. And fear, the most powerful of all negative emotions, can distort otherwise rational views to prevent sale benchmarking from gaining a foothold.

Ironically, here is where the opportunity lies for the early adopters. Just as the scientific groundbreakers persevered through adversity and reaped their rewards in terms of academic notoriety, so too can sales leaders realize a disproportionate results with sales benchmarking.

OBJECTION #7: LET'S JUST DIP OUR TOE IN THE WATER

Response: Don't Do a Pilot if You Are Not Convinced; Do a Pilot to Ensure Rollout Success

The first instinct to pilot something before committing all the funds and other corporate resources can be a good decision. Whether this approach is wise or not depends on the support of the pilot and the seriousness with which it is conducted. Piloting can be nothing more than a passive-aggressive corporate process for killing an initiative.

Sales leader expectations should be reasonably calibrated. A pilot cannot predict the future like some sales swami. It can only provide glimpses of the success that might be enjoyed and the opposition faced if it was implemented corporatewide.

However, if the purpose of the pilot is to increase the success rate of the production rollout, then a pilot can be a good use of time. Eventually, employees will have to be trained, and a pilot is a good way to get that accomplished ahead of a full rollout. This is the primary purpose of a pilot. Go forward with a pilot if it is meant to determine exactly how to deploy sales benchmarking, but do not do a pilot if the decision is whether to do sales benchmarking at all. If you aren't sure this is something you want to commit to, resist the temptation to "ry before you buy." It won't be much of a try and you will surely not buy. The effort will be a waste of time.

OBJECTION #8: SALES BENCHMARKING ISN'T WORTH THE EMOTIONAL COST

Response: Fear of Failure Is Not a Strategic Justification to Inaction

As it replaces the emotions, personal opinions, and the views of a few with facts, data, and objectivity, sales benchmarking represents an initiative truly worth the effort.

Sales benchmarking and its support of data-driven decision making offer the real possibility for breakthrough achievement. The key for future sales benchmarkers is to rebut factually the accusations that it is not worth the effort. We forget until we read history that great achievements are hardly ever accomplished without strife or the need to overcome resistance. It is the exception, not the rule, that peers acknowledge and support the need for bold change. The cacophonous noise of detractors, doubters, and delayers is the common refrain, so sales benchmarkers should expect it. Sales benchmarking is worth the time and trouble, and about as close as you are going to come to a "sure thing" in today's corporate climate.

OBJECTION #9: SALES BENCHMARKING WON'T REALLY WORK

Response: Value What Makes You Different, but Understand That You Are Similar Enough to Warrant Effective Comparison

Sales benchmarking delivers large, company-changing results. It is a "skewed bet" that presents a large payoff when allowed to succeed. The key question to ask when comparing sales benchmarking to other sales ideas is not how likely it is that it will work, but how much will be gained when it does work. It is the magnitude of the outcome that counts. It doesn't matter how often you are right or wrong. People do not take home a check linked to how often they were correct.[6] Today, thankfully for those who are about to embrace it, sales benchmarking is rarely deployed. Your competition is unlikely to have implemented it. This is why the payoff is bound to be big in the near future.

OBJECTION #10: BENCHMARKING IS GOOD IN THEORY, BUT IN PRACTICE

Response: The Theory Is Sound and Its Application Is Proven, and All That Is Wanting Are Sales Leaders up to the Challenge

Sales leaders have it easy—it was the CFOs and the chief operating officers of a generation ago who validated the concept of benchmarking. They are the ones who invested the sweat equity and took the risks. Benchmarking is firmly lodged in their business function, and the reservoir of external figure data for comparison grows yearly in depth and variety. The same holds true for the supply chain and technology disciplines. Thus, as a theory, benchmarking has also been proved out; it has been tested many times and been show to produce excellent results. It has been repeatedly exposed to the harsh light of corporate reality and not found wanting. It has left the early adopter phase and enter the corporate mainstream. Sales leaders can draft on this success and experience. The risk has largely been squeezed out of the concept. It is a foregone conclusion that sales benchmarking will one day enjoy its kissing cousins in the other business functions. Though experience is a stern taskmaster, she will provide the crucible through which the theory of sales benchmarking will pass the test of perpetual validity.

OBJECTION #11: THINGS ARE GOING WELL—WE DON'T NEED IT

Response: Look Ahead, Not Backward. You May Be Right That Today's Success Means Tomorrow's as Well. Wouldn't You Like to Know for Sure?

Sales benchmarking allows a company and sales leader to compare themselves against a large sample size. This raises the comparison bar to what is possible. It is a common occurrence for a sales leader to mine internal data and present it in such a way that makes senior leadership feel good about the results. But when the first quarterly target is missed, the sales executive is greeted with looks of astonishment on everyone's face. He asks himself, "How could this happen to me?" Objectivity and external measurement are musts.

OBJECTION #12: WE ALREADY DO THIS

Response: True, You Are Already Doing Some of This, But Probably Not the Most Important Part—Comparing Yourself to Others

Collecting data and applying sales analytics is not new. If you are doing it already, then that is a great first step. But what types of data are you collecting? What have you done with the data? What is an example of an action you took as a result of data analysis that had a material effect on the sales results? What external sample did you measure yourself against? Oftentimes, the answers to these questions are less than compelling—indicating that the existence of a data-collection capability and some capacity for sales analytics does not imply an active benchmarking program. Usually, data is being collected to inform the sales management team, but nothing of significance is accomplished by analyzing it. Not surprisingly, the information being collected is not benchmarked externally.[7] And without an objective external comparison, you are only measuring against yourself, which produces limited gain.

OBJECTION #13: NOTHING BAD HAPPENS ON MY WATCH.

Response: Maybe so, but wouldn't you like to expose future opportunities to secure the future of your watch?

Inventors develop new products largely by incorporating lessons derived from past mistakes. The key for them is to be comfortable with the habit of challenging assumptions and, more important, in admitting that prior efforts were not successful. So, too, sales leaders should be open to evaluating deficiencies that occurred under their management or serious improvement opportunities that they have not yet explored. Sales benchmarking would likely reveal such opportunities.

It is not uncommon for there to be a gap between a sales leader's self-assessment and his or her true performance. Still, the gap can be bridged and egos tucked away. One possible solution is to combine an existing initiative with certain aspects of sales benchmarking. In any case, the focus should be on the validity of the concept itself—not on who was the person responsible for claiming it as his or her own.

GETTING THE SALES LEADER TO BECOME AN EARLY ADOPTER

This chapter was devoted to the subject of handling objections, specifically from the sales leader. For sales benchmarking to be successful, the sales leader should embrace and adopt this discipline, going where the data takes you. It will open up whole new areas of opportunity currently hidden.

TO REVIEW

- There are thirteen common objections that sales leaders tend to present when faced with the question of whether to adopt sales benchmarking. These objections are:

    1. Luck is enough.
    2. Hard work wins in the end.
    3. Charismatic salespeople are the best performers.
    4. Internal numbers tell the whole story.
    5. We dropped everything to try it—and it didn't work.
    6. Sales benchmarking is a fad.
    7. Let's just dip our toe in the water.
    8. Sales benchmarking isn't worth the emotional cost.
    9. Sales benchmarking won't really work.
    10. Benchmarking is good in theory, but not in practice.
    11. Things are going well—we don't need it.
    12. We already do this.
    13. Nothing bad happens on my watch.

- Each objection can be overcome.
- Sales benchmarking is a relatively new technique. Early adopters are even now receiving much value from its implementation.
- Sales leaders who are confident enough to take the risk will be rewarded handsomely, but this requires courage.
- Be open to ideas not of your own making; objectively consider sales benchmarking on its specific merits.

CHAPTER 20

OVERCOMING IMPLEMENTATION OBSTACLES TO SALES BENCHMARKING

"The greater the obstacle, the more glory in overcoming it."

—MOLIÈRE, FRENCH ACTOR, PLAYWRIGHT, AND WRITER

At this point, we hope to have the attention and support of sales leaders who see the wisdom of adopting sales benchmarking to transform their sales forces. There will always be, however, those inside the corporation whose job it is to throw water on any proposed initiative. These professional idea vetters are good at what they do and, frankly, needed. Usually from the finance or operations area, these executives have saved many corporations from wasting investment capital on projects that posed little chance of success. They are the corporate watchdogs, fiduciary custodians, and fact checkers. Sales benchmarking, unlike many other strategic initiatives, welcomes such scrutiny.

Accordingly, as a helpful reference for a sales leader preparing to present a sales-benchmarking initiative for review, we have developed a list of the ten most likely implementation obstacles. Understanding the basis of these rollout hurdles and how to address them will assist in the course of discussion with internal project managers, executive sponsors, and others whose support will be needed to launch such an effort.

IMPLEMENTATION OBSTACLES

#1: IT TAKES TOO MUCH ORGANIZATIONAL SUPPORT

Sales benchmarking requires time, funding, leadership, and support from senior management—all of which are in short supply for today's sales leaders. Also, the strategic nature of a sales-benchmarking effort often places it in a zero-sum-gain competition with other corporate improvement efforts. The fight to acquire such precious support can starve a benchmarking effort before it gains sufficient traction.

#2: SALES LEADERSHIP IS NOT SKILLED IN STATISTICAL PROCESS CONTROL, A DISCIPLINE OF OPERATIONS MANAGEMENT

Sales benchmarking is a mission-critical process and needs to be managed accordingly, yet sales leaders invariably lack the experience in statistical process control, a discipline employed by operations management. Further, sales staff lack hands-on analytical skills so they are usually unprepared in how to support, collect, assess, and take action on rich data. Not only does operations management posses the people with a high comfort level in data manipulation, they also control the business processes that generate revenue and ultimately maximize shareholder wealth.

#3: STRATEGIC PLANNERS DO NOT SEEK INPUT FROM SALES LEADERSHIP

When companies fail to realize their strategic goals, it can usually be traced to a break down in planning, especially when the goals touch on the sales function. One key reason for this is that most executive conferences rooms lack a dedicated voice for the sales function. Thus, when strategic plans are developed, this important voice is missing. If the sales force is expected to execute corporate long-term strategy, they should be included in the strategic-planning process.

#4: SALES DEPARTMENTS LACK CHANGE-MANAGEMENT SKILLS

This discipline, which helps ensure that efforts aimed at organizational transformation succeed, has not been widely adopted by sales leaders. Accordingly, sales-related improvement efforts sometimes experience a destructive "start and stop" sequence. Sales leaders generally don't think through the feasibility of such change, the sequence of which process areas to improve and when, the need to modulate change, location issues, cultural concerns, and the effect on each major stakeholder. Their lack of expertise in organizational change management can doom a project to failure.

#5: SALES LEADERS DO NOT UNDERSTAND HOW TO ACCURATELY FORECAST

A good forecast must be credible to the decision maker and have utility for the decision-making process. It must serve as a guide for future action, use powerful analytical tools and valid data, and be quantifiable rather than qualitative. Yet often sales leaders lack the formal training and data-oriented aptitude to produce defensible, accurate, and consistent predictions of future business. They believe, sometimes rightly, that providing too much transparency to the pipeline can reveal less-than-favorable future results and endanger their tenure. One would think that the widespread adoption of CRM systems with their data-capture needs and basic reporting features might improve this deficiency. However, sales leaders have remained uniformly resistant to developing the skills necessary to excel in forecasting.

#6: COLLABORATION BETWEEN SALES AND MARKETING DEPARTMENTS IS POOR

Sales benchmarking requires a detailed understanding of customers, competitors, markets, partners, and the internal capabilities of the company itself. The function most appropriate for management of this information is the marketing department, which is responsible for product, price, position, place, and promotion. No other department is as closely linked to sales as is marketing. Yet this familiarity often breeds contempt as the two disciplines can find it difficult to cooperate, even to communicate. The first casualty of this conflict is the handling of leads, which are usually generated by marketing and passed along to sales for closing. The lack of collaboration between these two departments damages the organization's ability to grow top-line revenue, exploit marketing opportunities, outflank the competition, and conduct joint ventures such as a sales-benchmarking effort.

#7: THE HUMAN RESOURCES (HR) DEPARTMENT'S OVERRIDING COST FOCUS CONFLICTS WITH THE SALES DEPARTMENT'S REVENUE IMPROVEMENT FOCUS

HR is focused on lowering human capital investments rather than weighing the value each piece of human capital contributes to the bottom line. Conversely, sales benchmarking involves helping companies improve productivity by generating more revenue per employee. The benefit of sales benchmarking increases exponentially when its focus is on revenue growth versus merely cost containment. This runs counter to HR's typical mandate to control expenses. This conflict can limit the ability of the sales leader to follow through on improvement ideas that drive revenue.

#8: THE SALES AND INFORMATION TECHNOLOGY (IT) DEPARTMENTS DO NOT COLLABORATE WELL

Decision support systems (DSS) operated by IT departments are not leveraged adequately by many sales forces. Sales leaders are not comfortable committing scarce resources to the task of presenting, summarizing, and analyzing data. The very idea of creating and testing models to support sales-related decision making makes them uncomfortable. Yet IT has the capability to perform these tasks, and most corporations have already made a sizeable investment in DSS technology. Many sales leaders fear that implementing sales benchmarking is a manual process and are concerned by the time commitment required. However, collaboration with IT can automate many of the data collection and assessment tasks.

#9: IT IS DIFFICULT TO COST JUSTIFY THE INVESTMENT NECESSARY TO SUPPORT A SALES-BENCHMARKING PROGRAM

A benchmarking initiative requires funding. When trying to obtain this funding, the conversation between the sales leader and CEO often breaks down because the sales leader is focused on revenue as a *measure of value* and the CEO is focused on true value, which is measured as *revenue generated by customers less the costs associated with those customers*. Sales benchmarking uncovers the cost of all activities required to create and maintain customer relationships, which enables the sales leader to frame business-justification conversations in a context relevant to the CEO.

#10: RISK-AVERSE SALES LEADERS WILL NOT ADOPT SALES BENCHMARKING UNTIL IT BECOMES MAINSTREAM

Sales benchmarking is a relatively new technique and so carries with it a certain degree of risk. As with any new program, early adopters receive the most value; latecomers will realize improvement, but to a lesser degree. Eventually, sales benchmarking will be adopted by the majority of sales leaders, but by that time its strategic competitive advantage will be diminished. Those who have the confidence to take the risk early will be rewarded handsomely, but this requires organizational courage. Luckily, many sales leaders have grown accustomed to such risk-taking in their careers and will warm to the challenge.

OVERCOMING THE OBSTACLES

You may be tempted to think that these obstacles pose too stiff a challenge. Maybe you are beginning to believe that deployment of sales benchmarking would be too difficult and time-consuming. Nothing could be further from the truth! Overcoming these challenges appears daunting and putting forth the effort seems perilous, but for those who leave their comfort zone to adopt benchmarking, the results will be dynamic—competitors will be eclipsed and businesses transformed. Despite the obstacles, sales benchmarking can be deployed with success. Let's overcome each of the obstacles one by one.

OBSTACLE #1: IT TAKES TOO MUCH ORGANIZATIONAL SUPPORT

Response: Sell Inside the Organization—That Is Your Skill Set Anyway!

It is true that sales benchmarking will only work if senior leadership is behind the effort. You will need money, time, and support from the other functions as well. So how do you get it? Sell! This is a sales campaign just like any other. You need to understand the customer's problem, suggest a solution, and calculate the return it will generate for all stakeholders involved.

In this particular case, this should be relatively easy to do. The problem is a lack of revenue growth and high selling expenses. The solution to the problem is to apply benchmarking to the sales department. This can be validated by pointing to examples of benchmarking in other parts of your company and the results it has generated. If you are not sure what departments have conducted their own benchmarks, ask finance, manufacturing, human resources, distribution, even information technology. The likelihood that one or more of these functional areas have leveraged benchmarking is high. They can serve as built-in references. Calculate a return by running a net-present-value (NPV) analysis on the project. Do your homework, go meet the decision maker, and pitch your case.

OBSTACLE #2: SALES LEADERSHIP HAS NOT BEEN TRAINED IN OPERATIONS MANAGEMENT

Response: Get the Education You Need to Be Effective; No Formal Statistics Training Program Is Required

This project is going to require expertise in SPC analysis, the basics of which can be taught to the sales force without much trouble. Sales leaders, on the other hand, must be capable of *interpreting* the data after the number crunching has been done. They need to understand what the information is telling them and *in what direction that information is pointing them.* While they don't have to be experts in the area of business statistics, they will need some analysts on the team.

Here's how to get this done. Visit the head of operations and ask if he has any employees who might like an opportunity to help grow sales. In all likelihood, the head of operations will greet such a partnering opportunity positively and respond by offering a resource or two on a full- or part-time basis. If not, the second approach would be tothat doesn't work engage some third-party statisticians early in their careers who are looking for an opportunity to apply their skills to the sales arena. These jobs are cost-effective and generate a great return.

OBSTACLE #3: STRATEGIC PLANNING DOES NOT SEEK INPUT FROM SALES LEADERSHIP

Response: Show How Sales Is The Lynchpin of Corporate Strategic Execution Success

Strategic plans have a much better chance of being executed if the people responsible for the execution of the plans are involved in their creation. Despite this basic planning requirement, sales leaders are often omitted from the crucial strategy development process. For those few CEOs still resistant to the idea that the sales leader should be a key participant to strategy creation, a mountain of literature agures to the contrary. The key to this discussion is making sure the CEO understands that the sales organization is crucial to strategic plan execution. This justifies a sales seat at the table.

OBSTACLE #4: SALES DEPARTMENTS LACK CHANGE-MANAGEMENT SKILLS

Response: Physician, Heal Thyself. To Gain Credibility with the Executives, Demonstrate That Your Sales Force Embraces Organizational Change and Can Handle the Shock from the Changes Sales Benchmarking Will Bring.

The lack of change-management expertise has prevented successful implementation of more than one strategic program (such as CRM deployments or Six Sigma quality improvement initiatives). The irony is, of course, that many salespeople gain footholds in their customer accounts exactly because of such organizational change—in that it often creates sales opportunities where none previously existed. Part of this type of opposition stems from the observation that sales professionals tend to be highly skeptical—possibly even more so than their counterparts in other departments. Many projects focused on sales force improvement have fallen well short of their goals, and even those that achieved some initial success have had a difficult time maintaining their gains. Any effort to deploy benchmarking to sales must, from its inception, anticipate and overcome sales bias against or lack of comfort with organizational change.

Sales leaders must master the discipline of change management and ensure their own sales forces do not derail an otherwise well-constructed benchmarking-improvement program. Developing staff behaviors conducive to change management will be the best approach to achieving sustainable success with sales benchmarking.

OBSTACLE #5: SALES LEADERS DO NOT UNDERSTAND HOW TO ACCURATELY FORECAST.

Response: Admit This Is a Deficiency but Demonstrate That Your Team Has the Wherewithal to Adapt to the Rigors of Forecasting Discipline.

Forecasting the gain derived from sales benchmarking is a credible exercise. But in order to earn buy in, the best method is to demonstrate the facts— demonstrate *how* the data-driven decision making process will reduce selling expenses and grow sales. Outline the specific action items you will take, be sure the data you use in the forecast is validated and the analytical tools used to collect it are well understood. Adopt a forecasting methodology that enjoys broad industry acceptance to support your conclusions; home-brewed forecasting systems often do as much to undermine benchmarking as they do to establish and support data-driven decision making. Quantify, quantify, quantify!

OBSTACLE #6: COLLABORATION BETWEEN SALES AND MARKETING DEPARTMENTS IS POOR.

Response: Take the First Step and Show Marketing That Interdepartmental Cooperation Is Achievable. Benchmarking Is the Perfect Tool to Support Such Collaboration.

Recall that sales benchmarking cannot be successful without the help of marketing. Marketing maintains the data on customers, competitors, markets, partners, and other critical aspects of the sales environment. Sales benchmarking is a data-intensive process and marketing, as a rich source of information, is central to its success.

The best way to approach this issue is to offer marketing a compelling partnership proposition from the outset. Show how benchmarking will allow the sales force to better execute the efforts of the marketing department. In most organizations, marketing is frustrated with sales because they feel sales is where the growth strategy breaks down. Marketers ensure the organization is focused on the "4 Ps of Marketing"—being in the right markets with the best mix of *products*, most advantageous *promotion*, correct *pricing*, and delivered in the proper *place*. Place mostly concerns how products and services are distributed, the one element marketing cannot control, but sales can. By offering marketing an opportunity to exert some control over distribution through collaborative benchmarking, sales can help bridge this divide.

OBSTACLE #7: THE HUMAN RESOURCES (HR) DEPARTMENT'S OVERRIDING COST FOCUS CONFLICTS WITH THE SALES DEPARTMENT'S REVENUE-IMPROVEMENT FOCUS.

Response: Solve the Turnover Problem First, Then Demonstrate to HR That It Should Assist in Investing in the Productivity Side of Your Sales Force Staff.

HR departments have been taught that the majority of cost to their business walks in the door every morning. They are encouraged to view sales staff as loaded cost burdens, not revenue-generating assets. CEOs frequently ask their HR executives to evaluate the possibility of outsourcing as many functions possible—all to reduce labor expense since variable labor expenses are a more productive focus than fixed ones.

The quickest way to win over the HR executive is to show how much mis-hires cost the organization and the relationship between these mis-hires and the overall turnover rate in sales. The amount of money wasted due to high sales force turnover is staggering. By adopting benchmarking, organizations can realize a larger contribution from their sales force, which will raise overall productivity per employee, reduce the need for new hires, and reduce losses associated with high turnover.

OBSTACLE #8: THE SALES AND INFORMATION TECHNOLOGY (IT) DEPARTMENTS DO NOT COLLABORATE WELL.

Response: Cios Are Waiting to Work Closely with the Executives They Support. Make It a Point to Engage More Closely to Improve Technology Support.

Sales benchmarking will not require a large investment in technology—the investment has already been made. Most companies have invested in decision support tools and these systems are generally underutilized! Chief information officers are trying to demonstrate how their department can help generate revenue rather than be considered solely a cost center. Sales benchmarking gives them that opportunity—make it a common cause with the CIO. He or she will welcome it with open arms.

OBSTACLE #9: IT IS DIFFICULT TO JUSTIFY THE INVESTMENT COSTS NECESSARY TO SUPPORT A SALES-BENCHMARKING PROGRAM.

Response: Run the Numbers and Show Them the NPV (or Whatever Approval Metric Your Company Uses).

This may be the easiest-cost justification proposal you have ever made. Calculate the cost of the project as you would any other (i.e., labor, time, facilities, systems, fees). Forecast the expected increase in cash flow due to the growth in revenue and the reduction in costs benchmarking will deliver. Use the cost of capital established by the company as the discount rate. Run an NPV analysis over a three-year period. Table 20 shows a summary of an NPV calculation for a sales-benchmarking project for a member of Sales Benchmark Index. They used a 15 percent discount rate to derive a $9.2 million payback on a $2 million investment.

Table 20: Sample NPV Justification for a Sales-Benchmarking Effort				
	Year 0 ($M)	Year 1 ($M)	Year 2 ($M)	Year 3 ($M)
Benchmarking Project Cash Flow	$0	$5.0	$6.0	$7.0
Benchmarking Project Costs	$2.0	$1.0	$1.0	$1.0
Net Benchmarking Project Cash Flow	-$2.0	$4.0	$5.0	$6.0
Discounted Benchmarking Project Cash Flow	-$2.0	$3.5	$3.8	$3.9
NPV	$9.2			

OBSTACLE #10: RISK-AVERSE SALES LEADERS WILL NOT ADOPT SALES BENCHMARKING UNTIL IT BECOMES "MAINSTREAM."

Response: Wait Too Long and You Lose the Punch. Adopt Now and Win.

Do you have the organizational fortitude to introduce sales benchmarking? It is true that embracing sales benchmarking can be risky, and there are few sales leaders currently embracing it. By definition, then, benchmarking for sales is not yet a best practice, despite its widespread adoption by other departments. Many will doubt the worth of sales benchmarking and you will face some dogged resistance. But persevere, address the obstacles discussed earlier in this section, and the results will be dramatic.

TO REVIEW

- There are ten common implementation obstacles to sales benchmarking that are often raised by those within a corporation whose role it is to ensure that unsuccessful projects are not launched. These obstacles are:

  1. It takes too much organizational support.
  2. Sales leadership is not skilled in statistical process control, a discipline of operations management.
  3. Strategic planners do not seek input from sales leadership.
  4. Sales departments lack change-management skills.
  5. Sales leaders do not understand how to accurately forecast.
  6. Collaboration between sales and marketing departments is poor.

7. The human resources (HR) department's overriding cost focus conflicts with the sales department's revenue-improvement focus.
8. The sales and information technology (IT) departments do not collaborate well.
9. It is difficult to cost justify the investment necessary to support a sales-benchmarking program.
10. Risk-averse sales leaders will not adopt sales benchmarking until it becomes "mainstream."

- Each obstacle can be addressed and overcome.
- The success of your sales benchmarking project is in your hands.

CONCLUSION

"Jumping to conclusions is not half as good an exercise as digging for facts."

—Anonymous

"Not to draw a conclusion, in some cases, is as much a breach of correct reasoning as it would be to draw a mistaken conclusion."

—Anonymous

NOW WHAT?

The quotes that begin this concluding chapter attempt to capture the essence of doubt that may still linger about the need to inject the discipline of benchmarking into sales decision making. The first quote is directed at those in sales, of which there are many, who survive by professional intuition and hunch. We have argued that the time of data-driven decision making is rapidly approaching. Those who reach quick conclusions based on gut instinct will begin to see that the accuracy of this approach pales in comparison to a deliberate search for the facts. Sales benchmarking is the key to breaking the bad habits and practices of the past. The second quote is directed to those who are not averse to data but seem unable to make a decision. They are overwhelmed by a blizzard of figures, reports, formulas, and graphs; nothing seems easy or clear. The focuesd discipline of sales benchmarking is the key to unlocking this confusion and tendency to inaction.

DO NOT DELAY

If you have made it this far into the book, we hope you have developed a strong desire to benchmark your sales force. Congratulations on your desire to be the best and your courage to try something different! Our advice is, don't wait. Start your adoption effort now! Why be in a rush? Because once sales benchmarking becomes an accepted and common practice—and it will—you will have missed the opportunity to capture the competitive advantage it can bring. Think about your CRM system now. Does it differentiate you from the competition? Maybe at one time it did, but no longer. It has become table stakes, something you need just to keep going. Today, the likelihood is that your competition is either unaware of sales benchmarking or too timid to do something about it.

For those who fear that their sales forces will refuse to accept external comparisons, prevent any improvements, and block change, we offer the following observation from Regis McKenna, one of the great marketing gurus of the twentieth century:

> companies often welcome new sales tools because increased sales means increased profits. While sales and marketing functions constantly adapt to modernization, old techniques are not always abandoned. Selling has thrived because it has diversified along with the markets it serves. As technology has created a vast array of products and options, global markets, and niche markets, it has also fragmented and expanded the sales person's role. In the mid 1980's, sales people began to adopt personal computing software as another tool in their problem solving package. A computer program might help a sales person track and analyze customer's buying patterns, allowing him to get a jump on the most appropriate products and services to offer.[1]

Such trends are virtually unstoppable. Sales force automation systems were one of them. Sales benchmarking is the latest.

In closing, we have a few suggestions on how to put your sales-benchmarking plan into action.

THE TIME IS NOW—A CALL TO ACTION

It is a best practice to develop "A" player skills required for your next position in business prior to needing them. This allows you to hit the ground running when you find yourself in a new leadership position and need to deliver great results quickly. Nothing builds momentum like quick, visible victories. Therefore, don't wait to learn how to use benchmarking in sales. This will be a *must-have* job requirement for every chief sales officer within a few short years. The hiring manager, in this case the CEO, simply has too much to lose by making the wrong decision. He will not bet the farm on someone he can't communicate with and who won't be able to supply the board with objective comparisons of relevent sales facts. As discussed in previous chapters, he can no longer consistently differentiate on just products or price. He will have to rely on the sales force as the means of creating a unique customer experience to establish a sustained competitive advantage. Would he hire a CFO who didn't understand how to analyze potential acquisitions? No! And he soon won't hire a CSO who can't scientifically assess a sales force, either.

THE FIRST COURAGEOUS STEP—ASSESS YOUR MATURITY

Your very first move should be to assess your sales force board on the Sales Force Maturity Model, shown in Figure 19.

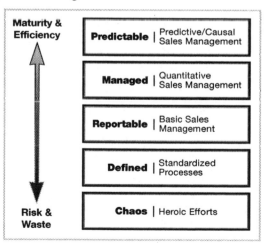

Figure 19: Sales Force Maturity Model Scale

This will tell you where to start the benchmarking process and help you build a project plan. If you skip this step and move right to metric identification, you run the risk of the sales team's rebelling because they are likely already measured on a slew of metrics and consider that adding more is of little value. By the same token, if you assume without proof your operation would rate highly on the maturity scale, your benchmarking effort will fail. Lack of necessary support infrastructure will result in much work with little gain. Start by understanding your current state of organizational maturity.

THE FORMULA

Once you determine your sales force maturity, install the Sales Benchmark Index Formula for Sales Success as shown in Figure 29.

This will allow you to organize your analytic information into a format that enables you to make sense of the data. The result will be a clear understanding of how you are doing internally and will highlight risks in hitting the sales objective.

GET YOUR EXTERNAL DATA SOURCE SAMPLE

Compare yourself to the outside world. This is the most important element of the program and will require you to either build your own statistical sample or contract with someone to do this for you. The outcome of this exercise will be a detailed understanding on how you are doing on a relative basis and a priority list of what needs to be fixed—your "low hanging fruit".

LAUNCH THE BEST PRACTICES IMPROVEMENT PROGRAM

With the improvement opportunities this indentified, next apply an appropriate problem solving methodology. Be careful to capture before and after data points so that you can measure your progress and hold key stakeholders accountable. Whether your program involves sales training, adoption of new tools, a standardized hiring process, or something else, be prepared to be objective about its effectiveness. Resist the temptation to raise the victory flag before your realize tangible results. By engaging in sustained improvement (Step 5), you will see clearly whether or not the program is working.

INSTALL SALES BENCHMARKING IN YOUR PERMANENT PLAYBOOK

Sales leaders should treat this book as a key part of their sales playbook. Sales benchmarking is the special teams part of the sales game plan. It may seem unfamiliar and uncomfortable at first, but with time it will become the best weapon in your arsonal. Sales leaders must prepare their organizations for this reality. Companies will need to develop new tools and internal systems to work effectively in this data-rich environment. Capabilities to analyze data, install collection infrastructure, and leverage standardized measure will become the bread and butter of successful sales forces. Is your organization ready for sales benchmarking and the world-class performance that will result?

The penalty for failure to adopt benchmarking will be obsolescence. McKenna said this about salespeople becoming obsolete:

> As the automobile and telephone radically changed the sales function, so will telecommunications and the new computing environment. The salesperson as a "convincer" or "closer" of orders will go the way of the slide rule and instead become synonymous with "service." The sales person will carry information, education, training, detailed design, quality, and reliability information. He or she will be the link between product design and factory and customer. Today, we are still in the primitive stages of automating the sales function.[2]

In other words McKenna says, "Salesmen are dead, long live salesmen!"[3] Those who think the sales profession is not going to change significantly have an insufficient grasp of history. Those who think that the sales profession is going away, replaced by a hyped-up marketing department and Internet virtual sales capability, are equally deluded. McKenna has it right—sales is changing and how. Better yet, the change has just begun.

Why do people go "out on a limb"? Because that is where the fruit is. So go for it!

EPILOGUE

THE PATH FORWARD

"In a time of drastic change it is the learners who inherit the future. The learned usually find themselves equipped to live in a world that no longer exists."

—ERIC HOFFER, AMERICAN WRITER

Sales leaders are like most successful business people in that they want to be first. Adopting a new approach ahead of the curve can be a source of personal accomplishment. Sales leaders are driven to achieve and want an edge. If you are a person who wants to jump past of even the top sales leaders of today, continue reading.

The relentless pace of corporate change, increasing globalization, and ongoing competitive pressures are forcing sales management to consider new business models and improvement approaches. So, even though this book addresses the need for organizations to adopt a cutting-edge discipline—sales benchmarking—it is by no means the last word on emerging trends of relevance to a sales leader.

There is, in fact, a trend close on the heels of sales benchmarking. This trend, known as *peering,* is an emerging new approach for acquiring innovative best practices. We believe that peering will revolutionize the sales-improvement industry in the coming years. Standing at the intersection of information technology, social networking, and the business world, this emerging trend will impact benchmarking as well, even before benchmarking becomes firmly rooted in sales forces. We give it the name "peering," but the trend is still too new to have a universally accepted label. It has been brewing under a variety of labels—peer production, collective insight, syndicated research, bottom-up belonging, democratic business solutions, global brainstorming, business-oriented social networking, decentralized peer-to-peer networks, open-sourced idea sharing, and even sales "mashups." The common thread that unites all these terms is that they describe the process of peers collaborating together to form professional affinity groups that share content, communicate, and build value in an interactive, Web-enabled fashion.

DEFICIENCIES IN SALES PROBLEM SOLVING

Sales leaders, when trying to solve a problem, usually first try a do-it-yourself approach, looking inside the organization for help. The individuals they lean on are usually overworked, understaffed, underresourced, and time starved. If they had the answer to the problem at hand, they probably would have surfaced already. Due to such conflicting priorities and burdensome responsibilities, these folk are not likely to produce creative thinking, breakthrough solutions, or implementation expertise. Instead, the usual result is low-quality answers delivered within a slow turnaround time.

Another approach is fee-based consultants. The value of their solutions is derived from their personal experiences and their client roster. They may have superior knowledge to those inside the organization, but there are limits to even this resevoir of expertise. The solutions this group will produce are of higher quality, but at much higher cost, too and still will take significant time to implement. Consultants make money by selling time, and it is in their best interest to move at a slow and steady pace. Sales leaders do not have time nor sometimes the budget. Thus, neither of these standard approaches to sales problem solving is attractive in today's environment,

A THIRD APPROACH—PEERING

Peering entails a community of sales leaders openly sharing best practices with each other for the "common good." Technology enables this new breed of advice. Tools make it possible to easily find relevant answers, automate research requests, distribute explanations through live virtual events, aggregate benchmarking data, establish a platform for collaboration, host-member driven topic-specific learning sessions, and communicate via Internet, distributed text, audio, and video. Never before has it been possible to learn from one's peers with such ease. Lessons from those walking in your shoes are the best lessons of all. This new approach has the following substantial advantages over the do-it-yourself model and fee-based consultants:

- It attracts the best ideas from the most people in the shortest amount of time.
- It leverages a virtual army of galvanized sales leaders.
- It delivers relevant solutions quickly.
- It creates a community of interested members that provides perpetual help in solving pressing issues.
- It is a low-cost method to extract ideas and share them across the syndicated group.

INDUSTRY-SPECIFIC EXAMPLES OF PEERING

Evidence of this new type of peer-produced best practices can be found in many industries. Don Tapscott and Anthony Williams, in their ground-breaking work, *Wikinomics,*[1] introduced the concept of *versions of collective intelligence.*

Faced with changing consumer needs, rising research and development costs, and a diminishing supply of scientists to solve problems, this industry created the organization known as Innocentive.

Innocentive pools ninety thousand off-payroll scientists into a community solving problems for companies such as Proctor & Gamble. Tapscott and Williams highlight several innovative peering organizations, one of which originated in the consumer products industry. Another example is in the financial-services industry, where fund managers created Marketocracy to find ideas to beat the S&P 500 Index. Marketocracy is an organization of some seventy thousand investment advisers who pool investment advice. A third example is the pharmaceutical industry which created the Alliance for Cellular Signaling to confront the challenges of a very slow drug-development process. This group aggregates genetic information into a shared database and has reduced the development process for personalized medicine by 50 percent. These are just a few examples of successful peer business networks; the list grows daily.

SALES BENCHMARKING AND PEERING

Sales benchmarking requires its practitioners to proactively seek best practices, which, when adapted and implemented, drive superior results. Chief sales officers of benchmarked companies are the source of these benchmarking best practices. By accelerating the process of sales benchmarking through the effective use of technology, adoption of best practices will increase. Another means to enable the benchmarking process is through proprietary peer-to-peer networks of committed sales benchmarkers; these groups can remove or avoid the friction often encountered when attempting to leverage for this purpose existing personal networks or corporate networks, neither of which have a benchmarking focus. Peering technology decreases communication and coordination inefficiencies that are latent in other techniques of collaboration, enabling chief sales officers to engage directly with each other, allowing for real-time idea exchange.

OLD AND INEFFECTIVE PEERING

Some might argue that there have been peering groups in existence for some time. For instance, there are many legacy "networking" organizations available to sales leaders. Some of these deliver, in part, on the promise of enhanced access, face-to-face peer contact, and improved professional opportunities. Most do not. The inability of legacy networking groups to meet the increased demands for depth, speed, and accuracy can be attributed to at least several causes:

1. They rely on live events and in-person sessions. Chief sales officers' calendars are too fluid, filled, and frenetic to allow for such a sustained on-site commitment. Sales executives need to consume relevant sales material when and where it is convenient for them, not at the time and place of an event organizer's choosing.
2. They typically do not require significant membership fees. As a result, they attract job seekers versus "A" players. Ultimately, the value of these networks derives from the quality of its constituent members; therefore, free and open networking groups are filled with lower-quality executives who produce lower-little in the way of useful content.
3. They are often managed by nonprofit organizations with limited resources and capabilities. Problem-solving capacity of interest to the CSO, however, requires more robust capabilities. Top-quality researchers,

advanced technology, and disparate data sources are all prerequisites to achieving high-quality content solutions. None of these is free of charge.

4 They do not build a wall between practitioners and vendors. Service providers tend to flock to these groups, hoping to sell their wares. A natural conflict of interest develops when a chief sales officer has to choose between the best solution generated by his peers and the solution being pushed on him because a major sponsor has asked for it.

CHARACTERISTICS OF A SUCCESSFUL SALES PEERING GROUP

We have just described some of the deficiencies of the legacy networking groups and have provided several examples of successful peering groups in various industries. In order to assist sales leaders in discerning whether a new sales peering group will deliver the value described above, we have provided five key guidelines:[2]

1. *Tightly define the focus.* Free-form brainstorming is vague and unproductive. Don't confuse being open-minded with being poorly organized. A crisply defined problem is a must. For instance, the peering membership should support grassroots experiments around principles that give them the best chance to succeed.

2. *Increase the range of participants.* It is not enough to have lots of people offering ideas if there is a limited variety in the group. Successful peering depends on many different kinds of people offering ideas. The membership works if the number and variety of the participants are constantly expanding. A sales peering group should boast of many different kinds of sales leaders, all looking at the same problems; this will generate the most penetrating insights.

3. *Keep it fun.* Sales leaders should come together to tap their collective brainpower and contribute to the better good of the membership, but not at the expense of their sense of joy. A sales-peering group should be interesting, energetic, and dramatic for it to be of use and survive. It is the job of service providers to make sure participation is engaging.

4, *Demonstrate the proper motivation.* Sales leaders are not motivated simply with traditional incentives, such as money or recognition. They seek an opportunity to push themselves, develop their skills, and interact with the best people in their field. It is the job a peering-service provider to be grassroots innovators, allowing participants to learn from the most innovative of their fellow sales leaders, and to let the world see the best of their innovations.

5. *Educate this new form of leadership.* Bottom-up leadership does not diminish the need for executive leadership. It increases it. The peering membership should challenge its sales leaders to ask of themselves: Do other smart people want to work with me? Can I conduct myself openly and with transparency as a participant of a project? Do I have the strength to demonstrate intellectual humility?

PEERING AND THE FUTURE OF SALES LEADERSHIP

The top-down method of innovation is less effective in a participatory environment. The world is teaming with smart, skilled, and passionate sales professionals who are eager to offer their insights and willing to invest time if they can benefit from others. By working together within a network—a decentralized peer-to-peer group where everyone has an equal stake—sales professionals can obtain fast, relevant answers at an affordable cost. The benefits of such a model are recaptured calendar control, proven techniques, speed of implementation, and a reduction in fees paid to nonvalue-adding third parties.

Sales peering networks will develop where sales challenges need to be solved. Sales leaders will tap the collective brain power of many to master their day-to-day challenges. Peering networks deliver unmatched best practices, a field of research driven exclusively by the membership, unmetered help, and no conflict of interest.

Sales leaders are risk takers; they want to be in the vanguard. It is just such adventurous sales leaders who will redefine the profession, as McKenna said:

sales people of the new century will not recognize their forebears of the 20th century. The sales person of the future will have to be as adept at information technology as the design engineer of today. In the twenty first century I believe the sales person will be held in the same esteem as the science and engineering professions of today.[3]

SALES PEERING AT ITS BEST—SHORTCUTT

Sales Benchmark Index has created just such a network—Shortcutt—whose members constitute a real-world sales-benchmarking community of interest. Shortcutt boasts advisory services, quarterly sales-benchmarking comparisons, and a wide variety of proprietary peering opportunities. If you are interested in this approach to sales benchmarking, please visit http://www.salebenchmark index.com to explore further.

SECTION IV

CASE STUDIES

We are focused on providing its customers with verified benchmarking services. We have spent the time thus far explaining how firms may use our methodologies if they are interested in benchmarking. However, we want to offer more than just our view. Therefore we have included a series of case studies from some of the world's leading companies, all of whom used benchmarking to help drive improvements in their sales organizations. In providing these real-world examples of sales benchmarking, we encourage readers to compare their organization to those in the case studies. Look for points of similarity and difference, and gain inspiration from these fellow sales leaders who did not let the novelty of the sales-benchmarking concept prevent them from applying it to their business. In addition to inspiration, we recommend that readers see in these case studies examples worthy of emulation—like-minded sales leaders who deployed sales benchmarking as a strategic initiative that yielded extraordinary results.

CASE STUDY #1

NETSUITE, INC.

DEAN MANSFIELD, PRESIDENT, WORLDWIDE SALES AND DISTRIBUTION

Founded in 1998, NetSuite Inc. is the leading provider of on-demand enterprise-resource planning (ERP) and customer relationship management (CRM) application software for small and midsized businesses. NetSuite's goal is to enable companies to make better, faster decisions in a fiercely competitive market. NetSuite products combine complete CRM, ERP, and Ecommerce capabilities in a single powerful application. Using NetSuite, companies can unite departments and automate processes, beginning with sales leads and ending with customer invoices. Delivered via the Internet, NetSuite can be implemented all at once or modularly, depending on the company's needs. With thousands of customers globally, NetSuite is the largest provider of integrated, on-demand business application software.

In working with Dean Mansfield, president, worldwide sales and distribution, Sales Benchmark Index identified a world-class sales organization. On

each variable, NetSuite's results are outstanding, earning them world-class sales status.

ACTIVITIES

NetSuite sells a complex enterprise software application with transaction values ranging from thousands of dollars to millions—and they do this entirely *over the phone.*

The company has roughly 140 Web-enabled salespeople spread across the world, averaging an estimated 36 sales calls per workday. This equals 5,040 sales calls per workday, 109,000 per month, and more than 1.3 million per year.

This level of activity per rep involving such a complex sale is rare in the software industry and certainly in the broader technology industry. Sales Benchmark Index has witnessed technology companies with very large call center operations with similar activity levels. However, these groups are typically customer service centers, with salespeople selling low-cost, add-on products or, in some extreme cases, telemarketing outfits focused on booking appointments, not closing business. It is important to note that this is NetSuite's only sales force and an estimated 85 percent or more of its revenue stream comes from this group.

A distinguishing aspect of NetSuite's activity levels is the role marketing plays. Jay O'Connor, chief marketing officer, and his team provide 90 percent of the leads for the direct sales force. Providing leads to support the 1.3 million annual sales call volume is no easy feat, but it frees up the sales force to *sell.* Salespeople are no longer burdened with the task of finding people to call. Instead, they are empowered to sell. The partnership between sales and marketing at NetSuite is the most productive Sales Benchmark Index has seen.

The NetSuite level of activity would not be possible by deploying an outside direct sales force like the ones used by most enterprise-software companies. The benchmark for outbound call activity in enterprise software is 20 calls per week per salesperson. NetSuite is doing 180 per week per rep, making them 9 times more productive. Sales Benchmark Index believes NetSuite is a glimpse into the future. They have proven that the model works and when one considers the productivity rate and investment return of this model, it will soon be difficult to compete selling any other way.

CONVERSIONS

Typically, when Sales Benchmark Index benchmarks a company and finds excellence in the activities category, performance is below average in conversions. Or, if a company has superior conversion rates, they have below-average activity. Very rarely does a company excel at both. NetSuite is unique.

For example, a NetSuite salesperson who makes thirty-six sales call per day converts an estimated one of them, or 2.8 percent, to demos. The success rate for call center activity is typically below 1 percent. NetSuite's measure of quality, i.e., conversions, is estimated to be three times better than the mean. When combining an activity rate nine times better than the average, with a conversion rate three times better than the average, the growth is explosive. A superior conversion rate is indicative of many things, but two of the most obvious observations for NetSuite is that they have a very skilled sales force selling over the telephone and marketing is producing an enormous quantity of high quality leads.

The sales force's time management is also maximized by allowing salespeople to have a system sales engineer drive the formal demo portion of the sale. Sales reps often do their own brief online demonstration to stimulate interest, using WebEx technology for the demo. Once the sales rep does a *needs assessment* of the prospect, a more formal, complete online demo is prepared and presented to the prospect, showing how the product meets the company's requirements. The sales force is freed from preparing and driving these more time-consuming demos, allowing them to focus on closing the sale and making more calls. In this model, an engineer can easily handle four complete, tailored demos per week—and can perform more when needed on any given week. This is an impressive level of productivity. With the required travel, set up, and scheduling, an enterprise-software company deploying geographically dispersed engineers might get only one to three demos a week.

TRANSACTIONS

Transactions are measured on a GAAP basis, typically the twelve-month value of a contract. Dean applies this measurement system to two different sales teams—one for new business and the other for existing customers. The new business sales reps have an extraordinarily high call rate, which corresponds to a much greater number of product demonstrations than their industry peer group. Further, these reps are able to convert at rates greater than industry averages—even for software firms. This, combined with the fact that the NetSuite new business reps enjoy a shorter sales cycle than the benchmark median for technology providers, results in a dedicated, high-octane sales capability. As for the reps to the existing customer base, Dean measures their performance by customer renewal rates and incremental revenues generated per customer. By focusing on farming activities and leveraging detailed product usage data on all customers—what CEO Zach Nelson calls the "gold mine"—a sales rep in this group closes over twenty times more deals than a typical new business rep. This program has been so successful that they are doubling headcount for these "farmers."

TALENT

Between 2005 and 2007, NetSuite nearly tripled revenue with a small increase in sales headcount. The company has perfected its hiring model and focuses intensely on making newly hired salespeople successful very quickly. NetSuite has achieved the most hiring success by choosing new reps with the right balance and type of experience. New reps who sell to small and midsize companies generally have four to six years of sales experience, and most have prior experience selling over the phone. These reps have enough experience to have solid skills but are still eager to learn and take direction. Reps who sell to larger companies tend to have more experience. First-year turnover of sales reps at NetSuite is now a low 10 percent to 15 percent, far below the standard software industry annual turnover rate of 36 percent. NetSuite attributes its low attrition to hiring with the right level of experience, providing ramp-up quotas, a buddy system, training, one-on-one coaching, real-time performance metrics, a positive work environment, and a strong product to sell. NetSuite deploys a compensation plan with a 50 percent base and 50 percent variable compensation, which is in line with industry norms. As you can see, using the Sales Benchmark Index Formula for Sales Success as a basis, NetSuite is a world-class sales organization in every dimension.

SOLUTIONS AND RECOMMENDATIONS

Sales Benchmark Index is focused on helping companies build sustained competitive advantages through sales force execution. The Sales Force Management Maturity Model (SM3) was used as the basis for this analysis. Please see the model below:

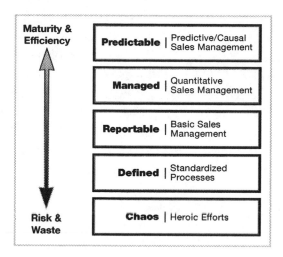

NetSuite will soon be faced with the challenge of sustaining its torrid growth rate. The technology industry has a long history of hot young companies that appeared one day only to be forgotten the next. Can NetSuite sustain the competitive advantage it has built with its sales force? Dean Mansfield states his top three priorities moving forward as:

1. Growing the sales force (hiring, onboarding, and ramping new sales talent)
2. Expanding into new geographic markets
3. Sustaining growth numbers

Sales Benchmark Index has benchmarked NetSuite as a Level 5 sales organization. Evidence is visible that they have defined processes. There is strong sales management earning a high level of compliance with these processes. The organization has turned the acquisition of customers into a science and measures everything with hard numbers. They leverage data to make key decisions and understand the causality between each distinct part of the process. Many of the leaders of the company have years of experience in the enterprise software industry and bring external perspective to everything they do. They have demonstrated this by implementing a radically different sales model, which has produced outstanding results over a sustained period of time.

NetSuite and Sales Benchmark Index share the curiosity surrounding sustainability. Can they remain at Level 5?

In his book *The Tipping Point,* Malcolm Gladwell wrote about the "rule of 150." This rule states that "as human beings we can only handle so much information at once. Once we pass a certain boundary, we become overwhelmed." As it relates to groups and their performance, the magic number is 150 people. Dean currently has 140 people in his sales group. He has them laser focused on the sales process and their level of productivity is world-class. The company has grown very quickly and as such new and different tasks must be completed.

For example, Dean and his team were once measured exclusively on signing up new customers and growing revenue from the existing customer base. Recently, the measurement system changed to one based on contribution margin. Contribution margin is simply variable margin divided by revenue. Companies switch to this mode of measurement when the focus becomes less on revenue and more on profitability. This new focal area will require the sales management team to focus on issues outside of growing revenue. Sales Benchmark Index has witnessed this shift in the past and in some cases it has resulted in a dip in productivity. Doing more with less is a must have in today's global economy. It is easy to understand the motive behind this. However, NetSuite must be cautious to strike the right balance when proceeding in this area.

It is very difficult to make a recommendation to a Level 5 sales force. They are among the most elite in the world. In fact, less than 7 percent of sales forces in the business-to-business environment ever obtain this distinction.

However, if Sales Benchmark Index was asked to look into its crystal ball and offer some objective guidance to NetSuite, it would offer the following:

The sales and marketing function at NetSuite obtained greatness by throwing out conventional wisdom and traditional approaches. They heard from everyone that enterprise software could not be sold virtually and that it would never work. They demonstrated courage and conviction by pushing forward with their model and should celebrate proving everyone wrong. However, the company is coming up on its tenth anniversary and it may be time for a new twist on the model. It may be wise to take a step back and look out five years from today. The world will have adopted this new sales model and the one time source of competitive advantage is now commonplace. What will be the new bleeding edge model at that time? As the world races to copy what NetSuite has accomplished, the company will have raised the bar to an even higher level, preserving its competitive advantage.

CASE STUDY #2

DISCOVER FINANCIAL SERVICES

GERRY WAGNER, VICE PRESIDENT OF SALES

Discover Financial Services markets, supports, and processes a full range of credit, debit, and stored-value programs/cards, including Discover Card, which has been ranked #1 in overall customer loyalty and has more than fifty million card members. Discover also operates the Discover Network, one of the most trusted and secure full-service payment networks in the United States, and PULSE ATM/debit network. The Discover Network, which connects to more than four million merchant and cash access locations, provides customer-centric tools designed to help issuers and merchants drive loyalty, increase revenue, and run their business more effectively and efficiently. The PULSE ATM/debit network serves more than 4,400 financial institutions and includes nearly 260,000 ATMs and approximately 3.4 million POS terminals.

ACTIVITIES

Gerry Wagner, vice president of sales, has been with Discover Financial for twenty-two years. In an effort to increase acceptance of Discover Network–issued cards and grow its transaction volume, Gerry and his team have conducted extensive analysis identifying areas for improvement. In addition, they have exhaustively studied their accounts to determine levels of transaction volume.

These metrics, along with several submetrics, are the key drivers of their success. For example, when Gerry and his team identify a gap in acceptance, they gather external data from sources such as the Nielsen Report to identify partners that can perform the activities necessary to close the gap. This partner selection process is cut by both industry penetration rates as well as geography. So, when the company recently needed a channel partner to increase coverage in the Western half of the United States, it researched the options and focused on Wells Fargo to help bring Discover into this market. The result of this due diligence is a recently launched partnership that delivered immediate success.

CONVERSIONS

Discover brings innovative offerings to market in an effort to convert more of the available market to Discover transactions. Each product's effectiveness is measured in conversion rates. For example, each new program has a volume goal, which is then projected on a percentage basis to a group of merchants.

Gerry gathers real-time data comparing actual results to goal results and determines variance. Armed with this level of granularity, Gerry can speak to his team members responsible for the program and the merchant, and make midcourse corrections in order to drive volume.

Another example of a best practice at Discover Financial is the conversion measurement system for the small-business segment. Gerry has outsourced this sales function to a network of independent sales reps. These organizations are measured on the percentage of small-business owners in a specific geography and in a specific industry that accept Discover Network cards as a payment option for their customers.

TRANSACTIONS

The business model for card issuers is one based on millions of transactions each day, each earning Discover Financial a small fee. Therefore, measuring transactions is not done on a per-transaction basis, but on the sum total within a set of parameters.

Gerry has separated his organization into two groups: the third-party acquisition group and the client relations group. The key metrics measured for third-party acquisitions are how many merchants are accepting competitor cards versus Discover Network cards, and what percentage of total-transaction-processing volume Discover has in a marketplace.

The key metrics measured for the client relations group are the percentage of a corporation's total sales that are made through Discover, and what discount to the transaction fee was extended. This proves that it is possible to leverage metric analysis inside a transactional variable for companies that process millions of transactions each year.

TALENT

Nine years ago, Gerry had approximately 700 people in his sales and service force. Today, he has around 150. The key difference between then and now is that Gerry now outsources the acquisition of small-business owners to an independent network of sales professionals who work on a commission basis. This has dramatically lowered his customer acquisition costs, while significantly and rapidly expanding acceptance points for Discover.

The problem Gerry had was that small merchants could not produce enough volume to generate the profit dollars required to pay a direct sales rep. This channel is now productive because Gerry has set them up to earn money based on volume and profit, which serves as a significant incentive for them to promote Discover products.

This successful blend of direct and indirect selling channels is somewhat unique. In fact, Sales Benchmark Index often finds conflict between these two functions, as they vie for limited corporate resources, typically have separate and parallel management structures, sometimes compete over the same leads, and even have conflicting compensation plans. It is the rare sales organization that is able to deploy both direct and indirect sales channels simultaneously and without any friction. One reason Discover has avoided strife between the two is its culture. Turnover is less than 10 percent and over half of the sales force has been with the company for more than ten years. Salespeople are well tenured, are very loyal, and love the company. This should serve as an example for companies that are struggling with high turnover rates.

SOLUTIONS AND RECOMMENDATIONS

Sales Benchmark Index used the Sales Force Management Maturity Model (SM3), shown in Figure 21, as the basis for analyzing the building of sustained competitive advantage through sales force execution.

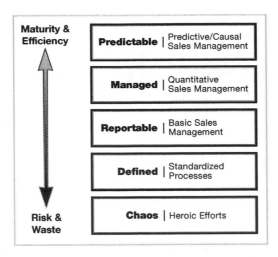

Figure 21: Sales Force Management Maturity Model (SM3)

There is evidence that Discover Financial Services has invested in the proper infrastructure to sustain its level of performance. The company has streamlined its processes, allowing for few people to produce high levels of productivity. The resources deployed are laser focused and the organization's priorities are clear to all. The compensation plan clearly aligns the rewards for the individual with the company's goals. There is a standard process in place to de-prioritize initiatives as well, which is distinctive at Discover. Sales Benchmark Index often finds companies rolling out the "flavor of the month" program, putting a strain on the infrastructure, which often cracks under this pressure. Gerry has his team focus on the designated top three items each year and does an excellent job of shielding the force from the many distractions.

The infrastructure in place extends beyond the company's walls as well. Discover is constantly benchmarking itself against competing networks such as Visa and MasterCard with objective and quantitative numbers. This element of transparency has crept throughout the entire company and has encapsulated customers as well. For example, each quarter, the client-relations salespeople meet with their customers to make sure, on a relative basis, that they are fulfilling their original objectives and that the client is satisfied. This is more than a customer scorecard. It is a customer satisfaction rating as compared to their competitors. As this external data is combined with internal metric data, a rich understanding of performance is achieved.

After examining Discover Financial Services on the five levels of sales force maturity, it is apparent that the company has moved beyond the heroic contributions of the few, has installed standardized processes that are adopted by all, and has standardized the sales management process. The quantitative analysis is done consistently and is both internal and external. And last, the organization understands the causal relationship between each of the metrics and as such is enabled to make data-driven decisions.

CASE STUDY #3

FRANKLINCOVEY

DAVID M.R. COVEY, SENIOR VICE PRESIDENT OF U.S. SALES

FranklinCovey is the global leader in effectiveness training, productivity tools, and assessment services for organizations, teams, and individuals. FranklinCovey helps companies succeed by unleashing the power of their workforce to focus on and execute top business priorities. Clients include 90 percent of the Fortune 100, more than 75 percent of the Fortune 500, thousands of small and medium-sized businesses, as well as numerous government entities and educational institutions. FranklinCovey has nearly 1,500 associates providing professional services and products in 37 offices serving more than 100 countries.

ACTIVITIES

The FranklinCovey sales management team measures activity from three primary lead-generation sources using the above formula. First, they hold more than 1,300 yearly public events with over 80,000 attendees in total. Second, the company participates in physical or virtual marketing events which are hosted either by them or by a partner and draw significant attendance. Third, they generate leads from people who have read *The 7 Habits of Highly Successful People* by Steven Covey and then contact FranklinCovey themselves to learn more about the principles in the book.

CONVERSION

David M. R. Covey, senior vice president of U.S. sales, and his team rigorously study analytical information to uncover conversion trends from marketing activities. A few years ago, over 40 percent of the attendees at a public event evaluated FranklinCovey for enterprisewide training rollout. Last year, the percentage of this type of participants was around 10 percent. The findings revealed that more individuals are attending public events for their own self-development, rather than on behalf of their employer. In response to this trend, FranklinCovey is developing offerings that will turn self-development individuals into future buyers of additional FranklinCovey products.

With eighty thousand attendees at public events and a 10 percent attendee-to-lead conversion rate, FranklinCovey is producing over eight thousand highly qualified leads per year. By further dissecting these leads, the company has found that 50 percent are existing customers and 50 percent are new prospects. This detailed understanding of leads, accomplished by studying movements in conversion rates, has allowed the company to offer better targeted content resulting in accelerated sales growth.

In addition to tracking leads, David and his team measure face-to-face appointments weekly. The company is very selective about who they have face-to-face visits with, requiring the customer to demonstrate a certain level of commitment to warrant the additional investment of a one- or two-hour appointment. Additionally, they require reps to sell high in the organization and focus on individuals with budget responsibilities. The company has found that selling outside of HR helps insulate the business from market downturns that result in cutbacks in HR spending. The result is an appointment-to-close rate of over 50 percent. The discipline in FranklinCovey's appointment setting places them in the top 1 percent of sales forces when compared to similar companies.

TRANSACTION

Transaction size is a significant contributor to FranklinCovey's success, and there are two ways in which the company can improve in this area. They can either hold more public events each year or increase the revenue production of each event. After careful study, David determined that the increased cost and logistical complexity of adding more events to the calendar were not worth the investment. A better approach was to benchmark the revenue production per event, which was determined to be about $5,000.

However, in performing this analysis, FranklinCovey found that some event facilitators produce in excess of $50,000 per event. The company learned after studying this variance that there are transferable aspects of sales rep performance that greatly affect event revenue production.

TALENT

David has determined that FranklinCovey could generate an additional $6.5 million in annual business each year if the per-event yield increased from $5,000 to $10,000. When first hearing this, it would appear that doubling event yield would be a difficult goal to obtain. However, since some facilitators are producing ten times the average, FranklinCovey already has in house the best practices that are proven to work. The company has deployed a team to study and document the process these successful individuals are using with plans to share this insight across the organization. This internal talent benchmark will save thousands of dollars in sales training costs and will likely produce a better training experience for the team overall.

Internal sales management techniques such as the one described above is one of the reasons FranklinCovey enjoys one of the industry's lowest turnover rates—5 percent. In addition, the company has developed a level of commitment from its employees who believe in the product they offer. The company has created a great working environment where people are fairly treated and those who are successful are given the opportunity to share what they have learned.

SOLUTIONS AND RECOMMENDATIONS

Sales Benchmark Index is focused on helping companies build sustained competitive advantages through sales force execution. The Sales Force Management Maturity Model (shown in Figure 22) was used as the basis for this analysis.

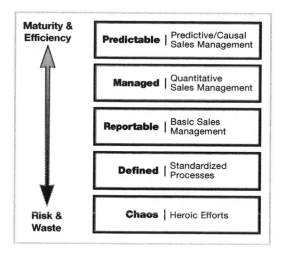

Figure 22: Sales Force Management Maturity Model

Sustained competitive advantage is all about putting repeatable processes in place and investing in infrastructure to enable these processes. FranklinCovey's sales organization has much of this in place already, which is why it is a Level 4 on the maturity scale. This is largely because of the company's outstanding performance and investment in the future, which have placed it among the elite in the levels of maturity. Recommendations to move the organization from Level 4 to Level 5 are primarily in the areas of applying a more thorough quantitative analysis in determining when to add salespeople and in addressing the 80/20 rule that plagues so many of today's sales forces—of which FranklinCovey is no exception.

Today, David and his team use Hoover's data to analyze market penetration. Their target customer is one with over one hundred employees. In analyzing geographical trends, they have on average penetrated about 4 percent of the available market. Deciding where to place salespeople is primarily based on market penetration rate. If a territory is under the 4 percent penetration, salespeople are added.

This approach is better than what most companies use and has worked well for FranklinCovey so far. However, advanced companies apply even more thoroughness to this decision and *automate* it. For example, they use psycho-graphic analysis to proactively monitor the market for behaviors that indicate the propensity to purchase their products and services. This predictive, causal element is one of the elusive last steps organizations take to become Level 5.

CASE STUDY #4

COVAD COMMUNICATIONS GROUP

DAVID MCMORROW, EXECUTIVE VICE PRESIDENT OF WORLDWIDE SALES

As the first company to commercially deploy DSL in the United States, Covad's heritage is broadband innovation. Covad owns and operates the largest national broadband network, and is the only national facilities-based provider of data, voice, and wireless telecommunications solutions for small and medium-size businesses. As a wholesaler, Covad is also a key supplier of high-bandwidth access for telecommunications services providers such as EarthLink, AOL, Verizon, and AT&T. Covad broadband and Voice-over-Internet Protocol (VoIP) services are currently available in 44 states and 235 major markets and can be purchased by more than 57 million homes and businesses.

ACTIVITIES

In the role of distributing Covad's branded services to small businesses directly, Covad's leads are generated primarily from three sources: marketing, customer referrals, and old-fashioned cold calling. In the past year, David McMorrow, executive vice president of worldwide sales, and his team performed a lead-generation benchmark where closed sales were tracked back to the originating activity with effectiveness being measured in terms of *closed business per dollar spent generating the lead.*

For the first time, Covad could clearly rank lead-generating activities in terms of the returns they produced. The findings revealed that the traditional investments they were making in radio and print were largely ineffective. After deploying a pilot, Covad rolled-out a new program focused on *search engine optimization*. The result was a 30 percent improvement in yield in the first year, *measured as a dollar earned compared to a dollar spent.*

CONVERSION

Covad's inbound call center had a close rate of about 13 percent on leads received. Their outbound call center close rate was around 2.5 percent and that was after a prospect was deemed a "PosQual," a proprietary term used by Covad to describe a lead that meets a certain set of criteria. By measuring the difference in close rates, Covad determined that generating additional inbound activity needed to be a top priority. The company decided to hire a chief marketing officer and place a greater emphasis on generating quality inbound leads.

Through studying and tracking its sales-cycle length of business-class VoIP, Covad determined that its 120–day sales cycle was largely the result of carrying the burden of educating the marketplace on this "leading edge" service. It was also the result of unfocused targeting of the SMB sector. To address this problem, the Covad team consciously began targeting accounts that had a specific propensity to buy the Covad solution instead of using a shotgun approach. Also, Covad simplified its sales process and the prospect education requirements. This allowed Covad to begin hiring salespeople with less experience at 35 percent less cost. The less-experienced team required more training up front and a more structure relationship with the sales manager. David and team created "success in a box" as a way to ramp and retain their newer and less-experienced salespeople with a more measurable process. The result was a sales cycle of 65 days, down from 120 days a year earlier, at 35 percent less cost. The improvement is one of the most drastic reductions in sales-cycle length the Sales Benchmark Index has ever seen and speaks volumes to the quality plan Covad put in place to achieve it.

TRANSACTION

Covad measures several metrics including customer churn, deal size, revenue per sales rep, channel yield, rate of up-sell/renewal, and post-sale cancellation. Most recently, the company has invested heavily in addressing the issue of customer churn and has developed a software-aided program, "Event Triggered Marketing," that analyzes, tracks, and helps manage the customer life cycles.

This program revealed that the primary events leading to customer "fallout" (or churn) were typically a rough implementation, an outage (or chronic service issues), or renewal time. This may seem obvious, but when a company is managing over five hundred thousand active accounts, it is not a trivial task to compile data that will reveal patterns in customer attrition. It is even more difficult to respond in real time to change a customer's experience from a negative one to a positive one. In Covad's case, an automated solution enabled this to take place.

Today, in the case of a fallout event categorized as a "rough ride" (a poor installation experience), Covad proactively apologizes, offers the customer a Starbucks gift card, or simply makes more frequent contact so the customer feels valued and important. Covad takes a similar tact to address customers' "chronic" service problems. In addition to being proactive in reducing churn, Covad has also implemented a "save desk" for challenging accounts.

Though Covad has cut its churn in half with these programs, at 2.3 percent, it is still almost a percentage point above the industry benchmark. Customer churn and fallout, the two items that have the largest impact on companywide profitability, will continue to be an area of focus.

TALENT

Covad has a unique approach to managing telesales talent that can serve as a model for many companies. The company has outsourced some 80 percent of its sales force, but continues to keep 20 percent in house. The in-house sales force sets the benchmark against which external partners are measured. Though this carries an additional expense to the company, it has been very effective in providing a compelling way to manage vendors. New products are launched through the company's in-house sales force first to refine the sales process before handing them over to the outsourced sales forces to sell.

Through these outsourcing practices, Covad Communications was able to reduce SG&A expenses from 36 percent of revenue to 25 percent of revenue while still growing the top line by 24 percent. Through having a well-developed and well-executed plan, a $20 million cost savings was realized.

SOLUTIONS AND RECOMMENDATIONS

Sales Benchmark Index is focused on helping companies build sustained competitive advantages through sales force execution. The Sales Force Management Maturity Model (SM3), shown in Figure 23 was used as the basis for this analysis.

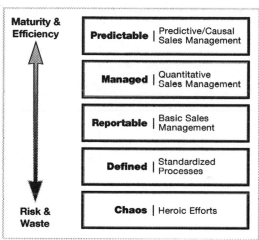

Figure 23: Sales Force Management Maturity Model (SM3)

Covad Communications was rated between a Level 3 and Level 4. Processes surrounding legacy product offerings like Access are at Level 4, while the processes associated with new offerings such as hosted VoIP are still evolving and are at Level 3. Evidence of a high level of maturity can be found in programs such as "success in a box," which systematically ramps new hires to productivity in a repeatable way.

The use of a chat room inside its CRM system, which spreads real-time information on products and services, has consistently raised awareness in the company's system engineering ranks. Covad is an avid user of its CRM system with salespeople constantly being drilled to keep information useful and up-to-date. The result is a system that has unusually relevant and clean data. The use of video has also considerably improved the company's training program. Top performers are videotaped and the content is made available online for salespeople to view. These are both examples of infrastructural enhancements made to create and sustain a high level of sales performance.

Covad recently restructured its sales force as the result of a profitability study. Rather than continue to invest in expanding an inefficient sales model, the company decided to optimize first, then expand. This level of discipline is rarely found in sales organizations today and Covad deserves credit for being smart in its proactive approach to sales.

Covad Communications operates in a very competitive industry with a rate of innovation that frequently shakes business models at their foundations. This makes it extremely challenging for the company to be predictive and causal in the sales force, the two primary requirements to reach world-class and Level 5 status. Sales Benchmark Index believes Covad is doing an excellent job. However, in order to reach world-class status, the company should inject external benchmarking practices into its sales force performance-measurement system on a monthly basis. This would enable Covad to keep ahead of the industry pace and proactively meet new demands.

The power of external benchmarking is evident in the work that has been done to reduce customer churn. After reducing churn by 50 percent, the company could have stopped and celebrated its success. But because the external benchmark is still 35 percent lower than what Covad is experiencing, there is continuing work to be done.

The improvements Covad has made, though impressive, have been to a large degree reactive. The numbers reported in the areas of churn, fallout, and selling expenses could still stand to improve, though many of these areas may have been reduced had more consistent benchmarking been deployed.

CASE STUDY #5

SMART MODULAR TECHNOLOGIES

WAYNE EISENBERG, VICE PRESIDENT OF WORLDWIDE SALES

SMART Modular Technologies is a leading independent designer, manufacturer, and supplier of value-added subsystems to original equipment manufacturers (OEMs). SMART Modular Technologies subsystem products include memory modules, embedded computing subsystems, and thin film transistor–iquid crystal display (TFT–LCD). Success is derived from a customer-focused approach characterized by a commitment to quality, advanced technical expertise, fast time-to-market, build-to-order flexibility, and high-quality customer service.

ACTIVITIES

Wayne Eisenberg, vice president of worldwide sales for SMART Modular Technologies, and his team believe in tracking leading indicators to enable future success. They have a very long sales cycle that dictates the need to manufacture a design plan for a client and receive orders only when the client starts shipping the finished product.

Due to this business model, the importance of measuring metrics other than the billing report is very high. For example, SMART Modular Technologies recognized that there were many potential customers in the marketplace that were small companies today but could become larger businesses tomorrow. The ability to prospect this base requires a high volume of activities since there are many,

many companies that need to solicited through marketing efforts. This is very different than the current customers who are small in number but large in revenue contribution.

Therefore, Wayne launched a telesales group just over two years ago. The group uses a call management software tool that tracks time on the phone, prospects' progress, and weekly pipeline. These are example of leading indicators. The analysis shows a direct correlation between prospect sales-cycle movement and pipeline movement. The number of accounts identified as possible customers is also positively correlated to size of pipeline. By tracking leading indicators in these categories, Wayne has opened an entirely new market for his company's products.

CONVERSIONS

Wayne and his team have invested heavily in understanding the difference between quality and quantity. For example, certain segments of their available market need their products more than others. Examples of demand concentration can be found in the server, telecom, and storage industry segments.

In some cases, these companies are existing clients of SMART Modular Technologies, and Wayne wants to leverage this relationship and introduce new products to this group. As the company plans its product road map, Wayne is at the decision-making table with his peers, explaining how he can leverage his sales force to generate more revenue with existing customers by selling add-on products.

This is a best practice that many companies would benefit from if deployed. Too often, the sales leader is not involved in the product decisions. As new products enter the market, Wayne is measuring the "qualification to production order rate," which is an indication of which new products are selling and which are not.

TRANSACTIONS

Wayne and his team measure transactions in unit volumes and gross profit performance. These are the leading indicators for his business. When it comes to defining a transaction, most companies typically measure revenue or average deal size. Wayne realized this would not work for his company due to the commodity price fluctuations of his raw materials. Revenue and deal size were outside of his control and therefore a waste of time to measure with regards to sales force effectiveness. The only way to maintain revenue with a falling average selling price was to increase volume.

Each customer has a defined total available market for SMART Modular Technologies and Wayne measures transaction effectiveness on the percentage of the market he captures. This is an example of proactively using metrics to get senior sales executives better information to manage the force.

TALENT

Wayne Eisenberg is a breath of fresh air when it comes to talent management. In an environment plagued by poor employee relations inside the sales functions and very high turnover rates, Wayne sticks out like a sore thumb.

His turnover rate is approaching low single digits. He sets quotas quarterly with the goal of giving his team a realistic target. He wants his salespeople to make a lot of money and pays them with a smile on his face. He backs them up with overlay business-development specialists who have expertise in a market, product, or technology.

Many sales leaders deploy the same techniques, so what is unique about Wayne? He does all of this with SG&A expenses at just 9 percent. The benchmark in his industry is 33 percent. This saves the company millions of dollars per year and allows it to be profitable.

Wayne has achieved the balance sought by most, which is to do what is right for the company and what is right for the employee. For example, Wayne's sales reps do not get paid until a sale is made and the product is shipped. This is a company-focused approach to pay about which many salespeople would complain. However, this is offset by setting equitable quotas, providing great sales resources, and being focused on the individual's success. The result is a win-win. Sales Benchmark Index has not been witness to a better talent management process in the sales function to date.

SOLUTIONS AND RECOMMENDATIONS

Sales Benchmark Index is focused on helping companies build sustained competitive advantages through sales force execution. The Sales Force Management Maturity Model (SM3), shown in Figure 24, was used as the basis for this analysis.

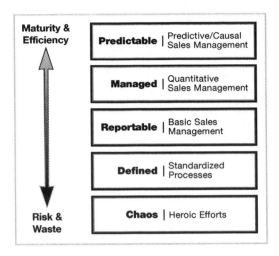

Figure 24: Sales Force Management Maturity Model (SM3)

The exceptional performance at SMART Modular Technologies is inspiring. But is it sustainable? There are many factors outside of Wayne's control that could prevent perpetual success. The technology industry, especially the embedded technology segment, is very volatile and competitive. Managing a dynamic random access memory (DRAM) portfolio in many ways is harder than managing a portfolio of stocks. SMART Modular Technologies is not a commodity speculator and cannot bank on everyone valuing the commodity the same way it does. The company must stay consistent and manage for the long run.

The manufacturing of these products has moved offshore. Will the design do so as well? Globalization is constantly reshaping the business world, and it will no doubt affect SMART Modular Technologies' success in moving forward. That is why SMART Modular Technologies now supports design services in China and Korea and has a manufacturing footprint with six manufacturing sites outside of the United States. Smart has jumped on the globalization bandwagon, making it likely their success will continue.

There is strong evidence to support that sustained sales force excellence is possible. The sales force is built on information and knowledge. The company objectively measures sales metrics in a quantitative way. It is not dependent on the effort of a few superstars and has embraced standardized processes with very high adoption rates. It has modified sales best practices to meet its business needs. The company uses leading indicators and has begun to understand the causal relationships between activities and outcomes. Last, it has invested in the infrastructure needed to support these initiatives.

The analysts only see one potential problem on the horizon. SMART Modular Technologies does not use external benchmarking to objectively compare itself to a set of peers. The company does not do this because it feels it would not be practical. For example, the two leading companies in their marketplace, SanDisk and Micron Technology, have very different business models. These two companies own silicon fabrication plants and have more control over the commodity pricing. SMART Modular Technologies is an independent service OEM. This makes for a tough comparison.

Other companies may be used for peer comparisons, such as Simple Tech (STEC), whose sales model has only recently shifted to the OEM model, again making it hard to do a comparison. STEC is also mainly in the flash-memory business, which doesn't make it the best peer to analyze. External sales benchmarking may be valuable to Wayne and his team to the extent that differences can be distilled. However, at the corporate level, benchmarking is used to maintain a watch on Simple Tech, White Electronics, Radisys Corporation, Mercury Computer Systems, and other companies in the embedded-memory-system (EMS) industry.

This is a common issue with external benchmarking. Companies often feel the exercise is not for them if they cannot find a dead-on match of peer companies. It is the view of Sales Benchmark Index that this is a mistake. Benchmarking, as discussed in earlier chapters, has been deployed in almost every other function in the company. If corporations required the comparisons to be 100 percent accurate, then the benefits this tool has delivered to executives in finance, information technology, operations, human resources, and several others would never had been realized. The key is not to seek perfection, but to be directionally correct. This level of accuracy will deliver results in far excess of the level of effort.

APPENDICES

APPENDIX A

BONUS MATERIAL

In many ways, we have only skimmed the surface of the topic of sales benchmarking.

There are techniques, examples, formulas, and aids that make the implementation of sales benchmarking much easier. Plus, many people like to know where they stand relative to their peer group or world-class, even before they get started.

To help with the continuing-education aspect of the sales-benchmarking discipline, we have made some tools available exclusively to our readers on our book Web site—www.makingthenumber.com. These reader-only tools include

- a detailed how to guide on performing in-depth break-even analysis using sales-benchmarking techniques
- a quarterly report known as the world class 100, which showcases the top performing sales forces
- a benchmarking white paper on lead-source evaluation
- a method to generate a benchmark for your company against a relevant peer group
- world-class status for the crucial metric of return on sales and many other metrics

To access this material, enter the address www.makingthenumber.com/readers in your browser. When you receive the prompt, type in the code word "benchmarking." This will unlock the exclusive reader-only tools. Over time we will make available other tools and techniques on this reader-only section of our Web site, so please check back to see what is there for the taking.

Once again, good luck in your sales-benchmarking efforts!!

APPENDIX B

SALES BENCHMARKING REPOSITORY

Sales Benchmark Index, with assistance from the students at the Georgia Institute of Technology, assembled a breakthrough resource from the sales data of over 10,900 organizations, over 11 years of history, across 19 industries, and compiled into over 250 metrics. Figure 25 depicts the sources and flow into this repository.

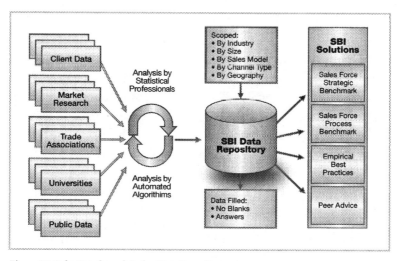

Figure 25: Sales Benchmark Index Data Repository

Rather than rely on a single source of data—a single supplier or survey—Sales Benchmark Index has relationships with and uses data sources falling into the following categories in creating an unmatched information repository:

- Client Engagements
- Market research firms
- Public information
- Trade associations
- Universities

Data from these sources is analyzed using rigorous statistical analysis processes by highly trained, industry-experienced professionals with a focus on removing biases from any single provider while ensuring quality, accuracy, timeliness, and integrity of the data. Data from these multiple sources undergoes a proprietary and rigorous research process that includes:

- Constant refinement
- Correlation
- Deductive reasoning
- Inductive reasoning
- Pattern and trend recognition
- Predictive analysis
- Regression analysis
- Verification

The strengths of this research include its reliance on multiple data sources combined with the rigorous statistical analysis methodology. Having eleven years of data further solidifies the findings and trends in world-class sales performance over time. The modeling methodology quantifies the effective correlation of the metric on sales force excellence, its impact on best-in-class status, and its contribution to business outcomes. The Sales Benchmarking Index model is self-weighting to maximize the explanation of best-in-class status on business outcomes.

The Sales Benchmark Index data repository contains empirical data on each of its sales metrics. Each metric possesses a very specific and well-defined taxonomy. Clients that conduct sales benchmarking typically select a healthy subset of the total metric population against which to compare their performance as compared to a relevant peer group. Table 21 is an excerpt of this formal taxonomy, showing the metric name and a plan language description of its calculation. The complete taxonomy represents valuable intellectual property for sales benchmarking.

Table 21: Sales Metrics Taxonomy Excerpt		
Metric	**Definition**	**Calculation**
Total Available Income	Average total available income a sales professional will receive at plan	(Sales Force Available Income) / (Quota-Bearing Sales Force Size)
Breakeven Point	Minimum sales revenue required to cover selling expenses	(Sales Expense) / ((Operating Income) + (Sales Expense)) * (Revenue)
Close Rate	Percentage of sales transactions closed out of the total number of forecasted sales deals (usually over the course of a year)	(Sales Transactions Closed) / (Pipeline Transactions)
Cost of Sales	Percentage of company revenue spent on sales	(Sales Expense) / (Revenue)
Cost per Sales Rep	Total cost for each sales professional	(Sales Expense) / (Quota-Bearing Sales Force Size)
Customer Acquisition Cost	Total cost to acquire a new customer	(Sales Expense) / (New Customers)
Customer Churn Rate	Percentage of customers a company loses	(Customers Lost) / ((New Customers) + (Existing Customers))
Customer Lifetime Value	Total value of a customer's long-term relationship	(Revenue) / (Customers Lost)
Customer Share	Percentage that one organization provides of an average customer's demand for the relevant products/services across all marketplace suppliers	(Revenue) / ((New Customers) + (Existing Customers)) / (Customer Spend)
Customers per Sales Rep	Average number of customers assigned to each sales professional	(Customers) / (Quota-Bearing Sales Force Size)

APPENDIX C

ABOUT SALES BENCHMARK INDEX

Sales Benchmark Index (SBI) is a strategic advisory firm that helps executive leadership understand how well they are performing relative to a peer group and world-class levels. Sales Benchmark Index is differentiated through its use of empirical data housed in the repository described in Appendix B. Using SBI's sales-benchmarking services, a company can deploy comparative data sets to identify the improvement opportunities available through leveraging best practices of world-class sales forces, as shown in Figure 26.

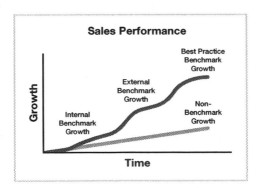

Figure 26: Sales Performance Improvement Through Benchmarking

By leveraging a network of sales leaders where sales benchmarking pinpoints challenges that are solved by tapping the collective intelligence of the membership, Sales Benchmark Index delivers the most relevant answers to sales problems in the shortest period of time for the lowest cost. Through strategic advisory services that pioneer the management discipline of benchmarking in the sales function, organizations learn how to implement data-driven decision making to achieve growth, transitioning away from the old mentality of sales as an art to the new paradigm of sales as a science.

Sales Benchmark Index, arguably the only sales-benchmarking strategic advisory company, offers all of the following:

- Centuries of operating experience—Sales Benchmark Index's sales membership taps the collective intelligence to solve shared challenges.
- Day-to-day realities—Sales Benchmark Index members use a new style of thinking everyday to improve personal and corporate performance.
- Originality of ideas—The Sales Benchmark Index syndicated cost model unleashes membership brainpower to champion relevant, quality solutions, separating it from the noise resulting from the quantity of ideas in the consulting industry.
- Field of research—Sales Benchmark Index's exclusive focus on the sales function results in original blueprints for success.
- Sales-benchmarking database—Sales Benchmark Index possesses one of the largest and most comprehensive sales-benchmarking databases in the world.
- Sales management studies—Sales Benchmark Index undertakes the world's most in-depth ongoing study of sales management innovation and benchmarking.
- In-the-trenches experience—Every day, Sales Benchmark Index works with sales managers who enable the constant validation of data and approach in the real world.

Sales Benchmark Index was founded on the belief that:

- A top-down model of innovation cannot compete with global brainstorming. Growth companies have the best ideas. Sales Benchmark Index's task is to invite smart, skilled, and passionate sales leaders of these companies into the membership to offer their insights. Sales Benchmark Index extracts these ideas and makes them easily available to share throughout the membership for everyone's collective benefit.
- In partnership with its members, Sales Benchmark Index seeks to be a nettlesome strategic challenger to the sales improvement model and a metaphor for innovation itself. By contributing ideas that range from

small collections of thoughts to killer new approaches, Sales Benchmark Index has an equal stake in making sales improvement content that is most useful to its members.

Through these beliefs and service offerings, Sales Benchmark Index has the data, expertise, and tools to move organizations quickly from diagnosis to implementation and results.

In its role as the leader in the sales improvement industry, Sales Benchmark Index helps many roles within an organization including:

- Boards of directors
- Chief executive officers
- Chief financial officers
- Chief legal officers
- Chief marketing officers
- Chief operating officers
- Chief sales officers
- Field marketing
- Front-line sales managers
- Human resources
- Sales and customer support
- Sales operations
- Sales reps
- Training and development
- Vice presidents of sales

For more information on Sales Benchmark Index, visit www.salesbench markindex.com.

ACKNOWLEDGMENTS

Writing a book is hard work. Without all of the wonderful people who helped make this book a reality, we never would have completed it. First and foremost, thanks to the team at Sales Benchmark Index for their tireless efforts.

Thanks goes to the Sales Benchmark Index membership—this select group of organizations has enabled us to bring increasing value to the marketplace. Without customers, there is no business, and without you, we would not be here. Thank you.

A special acknowledgment goes to each of the five distinguished sales leaders who contributed case studies to this book. Thank you to Dean Mansfield and NetSuite, Gerry Wagner and Discover Financial Services, David M.R. Covey and FranklinCovey, David McMorrow and Covad Communications Group, and Wayne Eisenberg and SMART Modular Technologies for sharing benchmarking experiences and keys to superior sales performance.

Thank you also to the faculty of Georgia Tech for transitioning Greg from a sales leader to an entrepreneur. Without your passion, Greg would have not reached his dream. Thank you to Team 4 (Jason Howard, Dan Carter, Greg Alexander, and Aaron Bartels) who exemplified the power of teamwork and collective knowledge.

Last, we would like to thank all those who told us we could never write a book. At first, there were many of you. We found that sustaining the effort to simultaneously launch a business and to write a book tests even the most optimistic of people. Sources of motivation are precious; we are truly grateful for the doubters. You got us through the tough days.

FROM GREG

To my fabulous wife, Brooke—the greatest sales accomplishment of my life was convincing you to marry me.

To the great twentieth-century philosopher and my father, Rennie Alexander. The thousands of hours you invested in my "Street IQ" is the reason for the success I have obtained. You were right again when you told me, "It's only you kid."

I am grateful to EMC Corporation for hiring me, some fifteen years ago, and giving me a solid foundation for success in sales leadership. While at EMC, I worked with some of the best sales professionals in the entire world. Thanks to all of you for setting the benchmark of excellence that stays with me today. A special thanks goes to Roger Marino, who convinced EMC to hire a kid who was short on experience but long on potential.

FROM AARON

To my entrepreneurial parents, Robert and Diana Bartels, thank you for all the love and support over the years. You showed me that anything is within reach with hard work and dedication. And to my brothers, Doug and Ross, thank you for constantly pushing me to overachieve.

I am thankful for all the residents of Colfax, Illinios, and the faculty at Ridgeview High School for instilling in me the values of small-town USA that drive me today. Thanks also to the University of Notre Dame for recognizing my potential and giving me the opportunity to earn a world-class education. After schooling, CGI/AMS helped me translate my years of education into an approach that produces outstanding business results that exceed client expectations in the real world.

FROM MIKE

To my loving, supportive, and underappreciated wife, Mary—thank you for twenty years of joyful married life. To our seven children (Nicholas, Jonathan, Daniel, Marie, Anna, Christina, and Amy)—my hope for you is that you reach your human potential and stay faithful in the process. To my parents, sister, friends, and old shipmates—thank you for helping me learn, grow, and succeed.

I am profoundly appreciative for a lifetime of challenging and eclectic professional opportunities. The eleven years I spent as an officer in the United States Navy, four at the Naval Nuclear Propulsion Program and three onboard USS *Nicholson* (DD 982), prepared me for life in a way no other set of experiences ever could. Ditto the three years as management consultant for CSI where I learned the inestimable value of ethical business conduct, two years at TRADEX where I saw the dotcom bubble from the inside, five years of professional formation with EMC in the sales cauldron, and last, several more years running a consulting business.

NOTES

INTRODUCTION

1. T. Boone Pickens, *The Luckiest Guy in the World* (New York: Beard Book, 2001).
2. Michael Lewis, *Moneyball: The Art of Winning an Unfair Game* (New York: W. W. Norton & Co., 2003).
3. Ibid. Paul Deposta had reduced success and failure of a baseball season down to a calculation. The team needed to win 95 games to make the playoffs, and he worked backward from there. He figured the team needed to score 135 more runs than they gave up to accomplish 95 wins and, therefore, the playoffs. Throughout the book we use the same logic. Start out with the end goal in mind and work backward to achieve it.
4. Sales Benchmark Index Repository of Sales Metrics Data, 2008. These are many other references to metrics, and statistics embedded in this book are derived from this repository. More details on this information resource can be found in Appendix B: Sales-Benchmarking Repository.
5. Regis McKenna, *Relationship Marketing: Successful Strategies for the Age of the Customer* (New York: Basic Books, 1993), p. 39.

CHAPTER 1: SOURCES OF COMPETITIVE ADVANTAGE

1. Thomas L. Friedman, *The World Is Flat: A Brief History of the Twenty-first Century,* 1st ed., (New York: Farrar, Straus and Giroux, 2005).
2. Michael E. Porter, *Competitive Strategy:Techniques for Analyzing Industries and Competitors* (New York: Free Press, 1998), pp. 35–40. Porter's initially discusses the three dominant means of establishing competitive advantage. The remainder of Porter's book is, in fact, and exploration of how these strategies can be analyzed, improved, combated, and combined.

3. "10 Best Supply Chains of 2004," *Logistics Today,* (December 2004). This magazine reported the best supply chains year after year until 2004.

CHAPTER 2: THE CUSTOMER EXPERIENCE

1. Ben McConnell, and Jackie Huba, *Citizen Marketers: When People Are the Message* (New York: Kaplan Business. 2006). This is the preeminent treatment of social media and the marketing profession. Most books of the Web 2.0 trend tend to cover it from the consumerist or blogger perspective. McConnell and Huba bring their marketing expertise to provide insight from the professional's view, one whose discipline has been rocked by recent technological and societal changes.

2. Jonathan M. Tisch, *Chocolates on the Pillow Aren't Enough: Reinventing the Customer Experience* (Hoboken, NJ.: John Wiley & Sons, 2006). Although this book is less academic than many would like, containing a series of stories rather than a bevy of statistics, it helps in explaining how successful the customer experience approach can be. The book reflects a series of observations from the CEO of Loews Hotels on those customer-centric flourishes that worked and those that didn't. Other, nonhospitality-related industry, companies can still benefit from the insights and approaches advocated by Tisch. There are a number of books, most written very recently that address this topic of customer experience from several angles. We provide them below for those who wish to delve more deeply into this rich topic.

   - Daniel Altman, *24 Hours in the Global Economy* (New York: Farrar, Straus and Giroux, 2007).
   - Hamid Bouchikhi and John Kimberly, *The Soul of the Corporation: How to manage the identity of your company* (Upper Saddle River, NJ: Wharton School Publishing, 2007).
   - Ram Charan, *What the Customer Wants You to Know: How Everybody Needs to Think Differently About Sales* (New York: Portfolio, 2007).
   - Jeremy Haft, *All the Tea in China: How to Buy, Sell, and Make Money on the Mainland* (New York: Portfolio, 2007).
   - Chip Heath and Dan Heath, *Made to Stick: Why Some Ideas Survive and Others Die* (New York: Random House, 2007).
   - Sasha Issenberg, *The Sushi Economy: Globalization and the Making of a Modern Delicacy* (New York: Gotham, 2007).
   - Steve Kaplan, *Beg the Elephant: Build a Bigger, Better Business* (New York: Workman Publishing Company, 2007).
   - Robyn Meredith, *The Elephant and the Dragon: The Rise of India and China and What It Means for All of Us* (New York: W. W. Norton, 2007).
   - B. Joseph Pine and James H. Gilmore, *The Experience Economy: Work Is Theater & Every Business a Stage* (Boston: Harvard Business School Press, 1999).
   - Antoine van Agtmael, *The Emerging Markets Century: How a New Breed of World-Class Companies Is Overtaking the World* (New York: Free Press, 2007).

3. Pine and Gilmore, *The Experience Economy*. The authors argue that even services are becoming commoditized. Their target audience, like Huba and McConnell, is fellow

marketing professionals, but their insights into the future of service differentiation are valid for all of us. If they are right, any industry and any product can topple quickly with a compelling and sustainable customer experience.

4. Regis McKenna, *Relationship Marketing: Successful Strategies for the Age of the Customer* (New York: Perseus Books, 1991), p. 49.

CHAPTER 3: ARE OUR SALES FORCES READY?

1. Nassim Nicholas Taleb, *Fooled by Randomness: The Hidden Role of Chance in Life and in the Markets*, 2d ed. New York: Texere, 2004). p. 19. Taleb discusses how an increase in a person's performance triggers an increase of serotonin, a chemical in the brain, which boosts confidence. This chemical reaction, and the subsequent behavior it causes, is often mistaken for a leadership ability of some kind, when in fact, the root cause could have been quite different. With such newfound confidence, a person's credibility increases as if he deserves it.

2. John Curtis, *Operation Charisma: How to Get Charisma and Wind Up at the Top* (Los Angeles: Discobolos Press. 1999). Curtis examines all the high-level intangibles necessary to demonstrate "good charisma." He convincingly demonstrates both its positive and negative attributes but focuses on how the average (read "uncharismatic") leader can develop into a dynamic, emotionally oriented influencer.

3. Taleb, *Fooled by Randomness*, pp. 59–60) Taleb speaks about the amount of garbage a person has to shift through to get to a piece of information that is valuable. He suggests the opportunity cost is too high. According ot Taleb, a better approach is to be a laggard, and if an idea is truly worthy, it will stand the test of time and find its way to you.

4. Bradford Smart and Greg Alexander, *Topgrading for Sales: World-Class Methods to Interview, Hire, and Coach Top Sales Representatives* (New York: Portfolio, 2008). This book has a wealth of tools and techniques on how to use hard data to find the sales talent best for your organization.

5. Sam Walker, "Why the NFL Is Drafting Benchwarmers," *Wall Street Journal*, Friday, April 28, 2006.

CHAPTER 4: WHAT'S IN IT FOR THE SALES EXECUTIVE?

1. Jim Collins, *Good to Great: Why Some Companies Make the Leap . . . and Others Don't* (New York: HarperCollins Publishers, Inc., 2004). Collins's work is similar to that in a research-based sales-benchmarking project. The case for Level 5 leadership with regard to long-term stock appreciation is compelling. Ibid., pp. 18–19. However, Collin begins a conversation about the resolve of leaders to do what is needed. Ibid., p. 30. Modern CEO behavior with regards to managing the sales function would suggest resolve is in short supply.

2. Jeffrey E. Christian, *The Headhunter's Edge* (New York: Random House, Inc., 2002)., p. 125. Christian speaks about his favorite trick questions. This is yet another example of the lack of relevance to qualitative information when dealing with issues related to sales. Why would an interviewer want to trick anybody? Data-driven decision making is

after the truth, no tricks. Yet the realities of the marketplace are that the majority of chief sales officers are placed by executive recruiters. Thus, their importance on the labor market cannot be dismissed.

CHAPTER 5: WHAT'S IN IT FOR THE SALES REPRESENTATIVE?

1. *Selling Power Magazine* (October 2006). Statistics were obtained from the Selling Power 500 CD.
2. U.S. Department of Labor, Bureau of Labor Statistics, 2007. To obtain a copy, call 540–752–7000.
3. Roger McNamee, and David Diamond. *The New Normal: Great Opportunities in a Time of Great Risk* (New York: Penguin Group, 2004), p. 58. ("The Impact of a Single Individual"). McNamee first started commenting on the diminishing importance of the corporation in March 2000 during the technology market correction.

CHAPTER 6: WHAT IS BUSINESS BENCHMARKING?

1. The list of Web sites, articles, magazines, forums, affinity groups, and discussion groups that pertain to the topic of industry-specific benchmarking is extensive indeed. Provided below is a list of resources (printed and online) that are specific to the topic of benchmarking within an industry. There are also commercial, for-profit firms that focus on benchmarking as a service or deliverable. In addition to Sales Benchmark Index, examples of such firms include Best Practices, LLC; Strassmann; Ravenworks; The Booth Company; and Thacker and Associates. Other organizations include:
   - Consortium for Higher Education Benchmarking Analysis—cheba.com
   - eBenchmarking newsletter—ebenchmarking.com. This site contains an exhaustive list of industry-specific benchmarking Web sites
   - The Benchmarking Network—benchmarkingnetwork.com. This site, mentioned earlier in our book, is really a collection of sites, each of which covers benchmarking from a specific industry.
2. Jon Anton and David Gustin, *Call Center Benchmarking (Deciding If Good Is Good Enough)*. (W. Lafayette, IN: Purdue University Press, 2000), p. 57. Call centers are at different stages of maturity, and evolutionary stage mapping can be a powerful tool.
3. Dotun Adebanjo and Robin Mann, "Benchmarking" (white paper), Vol. 4, No. 5. This was published on www.BPIR.com and was produced in coordination with the Centre for Organisational Excellence Research (www.coer.org.nz).
4. Bjorn Andersen and Per-Gaute Pettersen, *Benchmarking Handbook* (London: Chapman & Hall, 1996). p. 13 ("The Benchmarking Wheel").

CHAPTER 7: FIRST GLIMPSE INTO SALES BENCHMARKING

1. Munir Ahmad and Roger Benson, *Benchmarking in the Process Industries* (Rugby, Warwickshire, England: Institute of Chemical Engineers, 1999). Plant-to-plant benchmarking has delivered outstanding results for the process industry for many years. The

concept of comparing ones performance to world-class performance, versus a comparison to a mean statistic, was pioneered in the process industry. There is a wide and deep selection of books in the general benchmarking category that would be useful to consult for those who wish to learn this discipline more intimately. This book does not provide a rigorous, academic treatment of the topic, given that it audience is those in the sales profession and other executives, who have little stomach for the time and attention such an approach would require. We suggest that, for those who want to drink deeply at the well of benchmarking in all its facets, consult the following additional sources:

- M. Armstrong, "*Benchmarking goes to school,*" *Quality Progress,* Vol. 40, No. 5 (2007), p. 54.
- Robert C. Camp, *Business Process Benchmarking* (Milwaukee, WI: ASQC, 1995).
- Robert C. Camp, *Global Cases in Benchmarking: Best Practices from Organizations Around the World* (Milwaukee, WI: ASQC, 1995).
- Sylvia Codling, *Benchmarking* (Brookfield, Vermont: Gower Publishing Ltd., 1998).
- Robert Damelio, *The Basics of Benchmarking* (Florence, KY: Productivity Press, 1995).
- James Harrington, *High Performance Benchmarking: 20 Steps to Success* (New York: McGraw Hill, 1996).
- James Harrington, *The Complete Benchmarking Implementation Guide: Total Benchmarking Management* (New York: McGraw-Hill, 1996).
- William M. Lankford, "Benchmarking: Understanding the Basics," *Coastal Business Journal,* Vol. 1, No. 1 (Spring 2002).
- Michael Mard, Robert Dunne, Edi Osborne, and James Rigby, *Driving Your Company's Value: Strategic Benchmarking for Value* (New York: John Wiley & Sons, 2004).
- Carol McNair and Kathleen Leibfried, *Benchmarking: A Tool for Continuous Improvement* (New York: John Wiley & Sons, 1995).
- Jim Patterson, *Benchmarking Basics: Looking for a Better Way* (Canada: Crisp Publications, 1996).
- Rob Reider, *Benchmarking Strategies: A Tool for Profit Improvement* (New York: John Wiley & Sons, 2000).
- Anthony Tardugno, Thomas DiPasquale, and Robert Matthews, *IT Services: Costs, Metrics, Benchmarking and Marketing* (Indianapolis, IN: Prentice Hall PTR, 2000).
- Mohamed Zairi, *Effective Management of Benchmarking Projects* (Oxford, England: Butterworth-Heinemann, 1998).
- Joe Zhu, *Quantitative Models for Performance Evaluation and Benchmarking: Data Envelopment Analysis with Spreadsheets and DEA Excel Solver* (New York: Sciences & Busiess Media, Inc., 2002).

2. Sales Benchmark Index Repository of Sales Metrics Data, 2008.
3. John Davis, *Magic Numbers for Sales Management: Key Measures to Evaluate Sales Success* (New York: John Wiley & Sons, 2007), pp. 77–83 (Davis Magic Number 12 titled "Workload Approach").

4. Charles Hill and Gareth R. Jones, *Strategic Management Theory: An Integrated Approach* (Boston, MA: Houghton Mifflin Company, 2006). Hill and Jones, ibid, p. 54, discuss the critical role of distribution channels and sales force effectiveness while conducting a study on industry life cycle analysis. Many companies keep the same sales strategy and cost structure as the life cycle changes. This eventually leads to a sales force plan being out of alignment with the strategic corporate direction. For example, how one goes to market during the embryonic stage is very different than during the mature cycle of industry shakeout.

5. James Harrington, *The Complete Benchmarking Implementation Guide: Total Benchmarking Management* (New York: McGraw Hill, 1996). Ernst and Young has been benchmarking quality for global clients for years. Many of the methodologies they use have not been applied to the sales function but, nonetheless, are applicable. For example, the twenty activities recommended in this work, with modest alteration, could be useful when benchmarking a sales force.

6. Guy Kawasaki, *The Art of the Start: The Time-Tested, Battle-Hardened Guide for Anyone Starting Anything* (New York: Penguin Group, 2004), pp. 81–82. Kawasaki makes a strong case for bottoms-up forecasting. He provides an example of the inaccuracy of tops-down forecasting when trying to sell Internet access to 1.3 billion Chinese. The discussion about what percentages to use is irrelevant. The key point is that bottoms-up forecast is much more realistic than top-down marketing plans. We disagree on some details but concur in general. For example, what constitutes a "call" in Kawasaki's formula? Is it a face-to-face meeting, a dial, a telephone conversation, or an e-mail? The medium has an affect on the outcome.

7. Christopher Bogan and Michael English, *Benchmarking for Best Practices: Winning Through Innovative Adaptation* (New York: McGraw-Hill, 1994). Identifying best practices and implementing them are very different tasks. Best-practices benchmarking represents the most significant opportunity for growth, as compared to internal and external benchmarking. However, it has an added dimension of complexity due to the need for adoption of best practices.

CHAPTER 8: WHAT SALES BENCHMARKING IS NOT

1. Regis McKenna, *Relationship Marketing: Successful Strategies for the Age of the Customer* (New York: Perseus Books, 1991), p. 151.

CHAPTER 9: PROCESS SALES BENCHMARKING

1. Michael Hammer and James Champy, *Reengineering the Corporation: A Manifesto for Business Revolution* (New York: Harper Collins, 2003). This book, originally published in 1993, launched a revolution in corporate thinking and action. It set off a whole new consulting discipline and kick started innumerable reengineering projects that all sought to capture the bottled lightning of competitive advantage that Hammer and Champy described in their seminal work. So many of these projects failed, though, that Champy came out with a follow-up book in 1995, *Reengineering Management*, which

placed the blame for these failed initiatives at the feet of executives who wanted the benefit that process reengineering promises, without making the investment or commitment.

2. Henry J. Johansson et al, *Business Process Reengineering: Breakpoint Strategies for Market Dominance* (New York: John Wiley & Sons, 1993).

3. Christopher Bogan and Michael English, *Benchmarking for Best Practices: Winning Through Innovative Adaptation* (New York: McGraw-Hill, 1994), p. 7, which has a succinct discussion of process benchmarking, although no mention of the sales function.

CHAPTER 10: STRATEGIC SALES BENCHMARKING

1. Dotun Adebanjo and Robin Mann, "Benchmarking" (white paper), Vol. 4, No. 5. See www.BPIR.com.

2. Christopher Bogan and Michael English, *Benchmarking for Best Practices: Winning Through Innovative Adaptation* (New York: McGraw-Hill, 1994), pp. 8–9 which have a succinct discussion of strategic benchmarking.

3. Gregory Watson, *Strategic Benchmarking: How to Rate Your Company's Performance against the World's Best* (New York: John Wiley & Sons, 1993). This opus provides true one-stop shopping for those interested in strategic benchmarking from a general business perspective. It is dated though and not at all related to sales.

4. Ibid.

CHAPTER 11: BENCHMARKING AND BEST PRACTICES

1. In addition to the Bogan and English book (see note 2 in Chapter 10), there are many more that cover this issue from all possible angles. There are also fecund overlaps between best practices benchmarking and competitive intelligence, process reengineering, and quality standards–based improvement. We list below many sources in this field, both from magazines and books. This topic increases yearly in depth and scope.

- K. Anderson and K. McAdam, "A Critique of Benchmarking and Performance Management," *Benchmarking: An International Journal*, Vol. 11, No. 5. (2004), pp. 465–83.
- Robert C. Camp, *Benchmarking: The Search for Industry Best Practices That Lead to Superior Performance* (Portland, OR: Productivity, Inc., 2006).
- Sylvia Codling, *Best Practice Benchmarking: A Management Guide*, 2nd ed., (Brookfield, VT: Gower Publishing, Ltd., 1998).
- R. Cooper, S. Eggett and E. Kleinschmidt. "Benchmarking Best NPD Practices," *Research Technology Management*, Vol. 47, No. 1 (2004), p. 31.
- T. Dolan, "Best Practices in Process Improvement," *Quality Progress*, Vol. 36, No. 8, (2003), p. 23.
- L. Lapide, "Benchmarking Best Practices," *Journal of Business Forecasting*, Vol. 22, No. 4 (2005–2006), p. 29.
- L. Lewis, "Best Practice Begins with Sharing Best Practice," *Benchmarking Review* (January/February, 2000).

- J. Marie, V. Bronet, and M. Pillet, "A Typology of 'Best Practices' for a Benchmarking Process," *Benchmarking: An International Journal,* Vol. 12, No. 1 (2005), pp. 45–60.
- R. McAdam and M. Kelly, "A Business Excellence Approach to Generic Benchmarking in SMEs," *Benchmarking: An International Journal,* Vol. 9, No. 1 (2002), pp. 7–27.
- Gregory Watson, *Strategic Benchmarking Reloaded with Six Sigma: Improving Your Company's Performance Using Global Best Practice* (New York: John Wiley & Sons, 2007)..
- M. Zairi and M. Al-Mashri, "The Role of Benchmarking in Best Practice Management and Knowledge Sharing," *Journal of Computer Information Systems,* Vol. 45, No. 4 (2005), pp. 14.

2. Christopher Bogan and Michael English, *Benchmarking for Best Practices: Winning Through Innovative Adaptation.* See pages 124–151 which cover each of these seven levels in more depth.

3. Ibid., 129.

4. Ibid., 131.

5. There are many books that cover this interesting topic. Several of the best are listed below.

- Larry Kahaner, *Competitive Intelligence: How to Gather, Analyze, and Use Information to Move Your Business to the Top,* (New York: Touchstone, 1998).
- Craig S. Fleisher and Babette E. Bensoussan, *Business and Competitive Analysis: Effective Application of New and Classic Methods,* (New York: FT Press, 2007).
- Leonard Fuld, *The Secret Language of Competitive Intelligence: How to See Through and Stay Ahead of Business Disruptions, Distortions, Rumors, and Smoke Screens,* (New York: Crown Business, 2006).
- Kirk W. M. Tyson, *The Complete Guide to Competitive Intelligence,* 4th ed. (New York: Leading Edge Publications, 2006).

6. "What Is a Best Practice," Business Performance Improvement Resource, www.bpir.com/.

7. Ibid.

8. Robert C. Camp, *Benchmarking: The Search for Industry Best Practices That Lead to Superior Performance* (Portland, OR: Productivity Press, 2006).

CHAPTER 12: THE IMPORTANCE OF BEING WORLD-CLASS

1. Noel Tichy and Stratford Sherman, *Control Your Destiny or Someone Else Will* (New York: Doubleday, 1993). See ibid. Chapter 5, which especially captures how Welch was more consumed with how ideas, like his focus on being #1 or #2, would drive shareholder wealth. This idea, arguably his most important, set GE on a path unique among the global conglomerates.

2. Seth Godin, *Unleashing the Ideavirus.* (New York: Simon & Schuster, 2002).

3. The full definition for this sales metric is as follows: *Average number of months between the new hire start date of a quota-bearing sales professional and the point at which that*

sales professional reaches sales "full productivity," which is determined as 100% of their monthly sales goal. Count as 12 months the time for each sales professionals who never reaches "full productivity." The source for this definition is the formal taxonomy of the Sales Benchmark Index Repository, 2007.

CHAPTER 13: THE SELF-AWARE SALES FORCE

1. Philip Kotler, *A Framework for* Marketing Management, 2nd ed. (New Jersey: Prentice Hall, 2002), p. 333. The type of sales force a company deploys depends on many factors, such as how to recruit, select, train, supervise, motivate, and evaluate.
2. Lee Copeland, The Maturity Maturity Model September 22, 2003, *available at* www. stickyminds.com/sitewide.asp?Function=edetail&ObjectType=COL&ObjectId=6653.
3. Mardi Coers, et al. *Benchmarking: A Guide for Your Journey to Best-Practice Processes* (Texas: American Productivity & Quality Center, 2001). Part of APQC's "Passport to Success Series," this book was focused principally on process benchmarking and identifying best practices.

CHAPTER 17: FOCUSED ACTION (STEP 4)

1. Ethan Rasiel, *The McKinsey Way* (New York: McGraw-Hill, 1999), pp. 1–29. McKinsey's approach to problem solving has three steps: gather the facts; rigidly structure the study; and use hypothesis testing.

CHAPTER 18: SUSTAINED IMPROVEMENT (STEP 5)

1. Michael Mauboussin, "Death, Taxes, and Reversion to the Mean," December 18, 2007, *available at* seekingalpha.com/article/57615-death-taxes-and-reversion-to-the-mean.
2. David Groebner et al., *Business Statistics: A Decision-Making Approach,* 7th ed. (New Jersey: Prentice Hall, 2003). For those who have never studied business statistics, this text, written by the professors from Boise State University, is used in business schools across the world and is an adequate tutorial.
3. Lee Krajewski, Larry P. Ritzman, and Manoj K. Malhotra, *Operations Management: Processes and Value Chains,* 8th ed. (New Jersey: Prentice Hall, 2006). For those who have never studied operations management, this text written by professors from Notre Dame and Boston College, is a tutorial on value chains, process workflow, and the front and back office process areas.

CHAPTER 19: OVERCOMING OBJECTIONS TO SALES BENCHMARKING

1. Nassim Nicholas Taleb, *Fooled by Randomness: The Hidden Role of Chance in Life and in the Markets,* 2nd ed. (New York: Texere 2004), p. 193. Taleb discusses how people are susceptible to being impressed by something that has changed or is new. He does so by describing the Wall Street trader maxim "life is incremental," which states that net worth does not excite the trader but the change in net worth does, more so if it is negative.

Charisma in sales leaders is very similar. When a CEO has been disappointed in his sales leadership and meets a charismatic sales leader, he is susceptible to a false impression. The new candidate is different and represents a change, even though it may be a negative one.

2. Ibid.
3. Ibid., p. 56.
4. Ibid., p. 151.
5. Roger Lowenstein, *When Genius Failed: The Rise and Fall of Long-Term Capital Management* (New York: Random House Trade Paperbacks, 2000), p. 151. Lowenstein discusses how new ideas, known as fads, come and go, but enduring ideas are worth paying attention to. When someone says, "this time it is different," know they are not students of history and are making mistakes.
6. Taleb, *Fooled by Randomness,* p. 34.
7. Ibid., 222.
8. Secrets of Winning Sales Organizations, Miller Heiman's 2007 Sales Best Practices Study.

CONCLUSION

1. Regis McKenna, *Relationship Marketing: Successful Strategies for the Age of the Customer* (New York: Persues Books, 1991) p. 217.
2. Ibid., 51.
3. This is a modern-day equivalent of the ancient British expression of monarchial succession: "The King is dead, long live the king!"
4. Don Tapscott and Anthony Williams, *Wikinomics: How Mass Collaboration Changes Everything* (New York: Penguin Group, 2006).
5. Ibid., 286–89.

EPILOGUE

1. Regis McKenna, *Relationship Marketing: Successful Strategies for the Age of the Customer* (New York: Perseus Books, 1991), p. 219.

CASE STUDIES

1. Malcolm Gladwell, *The Tipping Point: How Little Things Can Make a Big Difference* (Boston: Little, Brown and Company, 2000), p. 169.

INDEX

[Index 10 pages TK]

ABOUT THE AUTHORS

GREG ALEXANDER

Greg Alexander serves as CEO of Sales Benchmark Index. He also serves as president of the Atlanta chapter of Sales & Marketing Executives International (SMEI), the premier international organization dedicated to providing a forum for knowledge, growth, leadership, and connections for the community of sales and marketing professionals. Founded in 1935 and with over ten thousand members around the world, SMEI is recognized as the standard for sales and marketing excellence.

Alexander has been featured in the media for his breakthrough benchmarking process. He was named *Sales and Marketing Magazine*'s "Sales Manager of the Year." Alexander was featured as a case study in *Topgrading: How Leading Companies Win by Hiring, Coaching and Keeping the Best People*, a global best seller by Dr. Brad Smart. He also coauthored with Dr. Brad Smart to write *Topgrading for Sales: World-Class Methods to Interview, Hire, and Coach Top Sales Representatives*. Alexander was profiled in the *Wall Street Journal* in 2008. Alexander has also been featured in periodicals such as *Selling Power, Sales and Marketing Magazine, Catalyst Magazine, Bestatselling.com, The Insurance Record*, and *The Dallas Business Chronicle*.

Prior to founding Sales Benchmark Index, Alexander served as the vice president of sales and marketing for Recall, where he was responsible for creating and implementing the sales leadership and management strategy across the United States, Canada, and Mexico. Alexander also served as a vice president of sales at EMC Corporation where he moved across the United States, turning around underperforming sales forces and restoring them to market leadership positions. His reputation as a sales force transformation specialist who can identify opportunities and create executable action plans that deliver measurable results has led to Sales Benchmark Index becoming a successful sales-benchmarking organization.

Alexander has an MBA from Georgia Institute of Technology and an undergraduate degree from the University of Massachusetts. He has previously served on the board of advisers to the Metro Atlanta Chamber of Commerce and as a member of the Southern Institute for Business and Professional Ethics, the Technology Association of Georgia, and the Atlanta Technology Angels.

AARON BARTELS

Aaron Bartels serves as executive vice president of Sales Benchmark Index. In his role with Sales Benchmark Index, Bartels is responsible for benchmarking and extracting best practices from organizations that help sales leaders across the globe better understand performance and implement improvements successfully.

Prior to joining Sales Benchmark Index, Bartels served as the director of sales operations for Recall, where he was responsible for improving sales force productivity across the United States, Canada, and Mexico. Bartels also served in numerous consulting leadership roles with CGI, where he implemented for clients process and system improvements that greatly increased revenues while reducing costs. His reputation as one who can turn executive strategy into measurable and tangible results has led to Sales Benchmark Index becoming a successful sales-benchmarking organization that embraces the latest process and technology solutions.

Bartels has an MBA from Georgia Institute of Technology and an undergraduate degree in computer science from the University of Notre Dame.

MIKE DRAPEAU

Mike Drapeau serves as executive vice president of Sales Benchmark Index. In his role with Sales Benchmark Index, Drapeau designed, built, and launched the membership portal that supports sales benchmarking and peering. Drapeau is responsible for delivering best-practices solutions around sales process improvement, organizational change behavior, and sales operations analysis.

Over the last fifteen years, Drapeau has repeatedly hired top-flight execution teams capable of carrying out strategic directives and driving home transformation within existing corporate cultures. Prior to joining Sales Benchmark Index, Drapeau for over fifteen years delivered product management and marketing expertise, using his insight into developing new markets, competitive intelligence, and technical prowess to develop product positioning and exposure techniques to aid sales teams. Drapeau's experience includes repackaging vendor software portfolios to exploit customer pain points, rolling out go-to-market programs that acknowledge deficiencies in vendor product lines, and repositioning entire sales lines to leverage competitive advantages.

Drapeau spent eleven years as a joint combat warfare officer and naval logistics tactician throughout multiple international conflict events and engagements. Having traveled to over fifty countries and speaking several languages, Drapeau provides a degree of international expertise of interest to Sales Benchmark Index's American members.

Drapeau has a bachelor's degree from the University of Virginia and an associate's degree from the University of Cambridge, Fitzwilliam College in Cambridge, England. He is the author of many articles published in various trade magazines.